*A Mythic Journey*

Bhavani-Trimurti-Mother

# *A Mythic Journey*

## *Günter Grass's Tin Drum*

Edward Diller

The University Press
of Kentucky

*for Lois &*
*the three little drummers,*
*Amie, Kevin & Steve*

The drum is beaten—for each family
has its own drum—and attempts are made
to incarnate the spirits. . . .
Mircea Eliade, *Shamanism*

Frontispiece from Niklas Müller, *Glauben, Wissen und Kunst der alten Hindus* (Mainz, 1922).

ISBN: 0-8131-1308-3

Library of Congress Catalog Card Number: 73–86402



A statewide cooperative scholarly publishing agency serving Berea College, Centre College of Kentucky, Eastern Kentucky University, Georgetown College, Kentucky Historical Society, Kentucky State University, Morehead State University, Murray State University, Northern Kentucky State College, Transylvania University, University of Kentucky, University of Louisville, and Western Kentucky University.

*Editorial and Sales Offices:* Lexington, Kentucky 40506

# *Contents*

# *Preface*

In the best and worst tradition of scholarly writing, what began as a short classroom lecture continued as running conversations in hallways, as plans for an article, as a seminar on "Elements of Mythology in *Die Blechtrommel,*" and emerged finally, several years later, as a manuscript of more than 300 pages. In retrospect it all seems logical and inevitable enough, but the path had more bumps and difficulties than I care to remember now. Years of preliminary curiosity centered on a suspicion that there was an underlying unity in this novel somewhere below its surface confusion of people, locales, styles, and events. A peripheral interest in religion and mythology led me subsequently to interpret several chapters in terms of ritual and archetypes, but always with a wariness of the dangers of finding mythology under every stone. A survey of the secondary literature on *The Tin Drum* reinforced scepticism, for although a few critics mentioned the possibility of mythic elements in the novel, only one spent more than a few pages dealing with it.

Eventually, however, a pattern of epic-mythic evidence established and confirmed itself undeniably in the triadic structure of the novel, in its supernatural events, its solemn and sacrificial rites and rituals, and in the stature of the dwarf-deity and his mission. Thus, the apparent anomalies of the novel fell into the framework of a single aesthetically pleasing and artistically conceptualized mythology, embellished with all the humor, drama, satire, distortions, and wisdom of traditional mythologies. I did not begin this study by searching for an overriding mythology in *The Tin Drum,* and at one point I consciously resisted the temptation to work exclusively, or even predominantly, with the attractive and easy generalizations of Jungian psychology. Rather, I chose to align myself more with the traditional practices of literary criticism; learning, borrowing, and applying the tools of classical criticism and finally deciding to conclude this total study from the perspective of classical authority and criticism.

Many mythological parallels and allusions were difficult to pin down in the vast arena of classical studies, and for help in that direction I am indebted to Cecil B. Pascal, professor of classics at the University of Oregon, whose constant flow of suggestions, references, corrections, and bibliography contributed so much to the progress and completion of this study. My thanks also to Professor Wolfgang A. Leppmann of the Department of German and Russian for several useful suggestions in the initial organization of this material and for his evaluation of the final manuscript. Most fortunate for me was the discovery, as I began my study, that Professor Jean M. Woods, also of the Department of German and Russian at the University of Oregon, was in the process of compiling a bibliography on Günter Grass, to be published in the *West Coast Review* in 1971. As her work progressed, she was generous in providing me with source material as needed; and indeed I must be doubly beholden to her for her careful reading of the semifinal manuscript and her suggestions for improvement.

Part of my research began while on a Fulbright grant in Germany in 1967-1968, and I am most grateful to the Fulbright Commission for its assistance. I also want to acknowledge the support I received from the Office of Scientific and Scholarly Research of the University of Oregon in the form of two summer research awards and several smaller grants for materials and the preparation of the manuscript.

Although I have worked primarily with the German version of the novel and have made my own translations, I have occasionally compared and evaluated passages of the English edition of *The Tin Drum* (tr. Ralph Manheim, Pantheon Books, 1963), pointing out at times where the literal meaning has been altered for the sake of readability. The page citations in the text of this study refer the scholarly critic to the German version of *Die Blechtrommel* (Luchterhand Verlag, 1968), but for those who have little or no knowledge of German and wish help in locating passages in the English translations, I have included in the appendix a German-English concordance of chapter titles and page numbers.

# ONE *The Mythology of The Tin Drum*

*If I deal in falsehood, let it be such as may persuade the ears of the reader.*
Pindar

The hero of the classical epic is distinguished at birth by the gods, educated in trial and ritual, and eventually singled out for a special mission of sacred importance. With time he travels over vast stretches of land or water and into the distant reaches of the cosmos, to Olympus or Hades, heaven or hell. After having passed through a number of trials and adventures in which he has proven his superiority over common men and uncommon monsters, he completes his special mission or quest (knowingly or unknowingly), gains stature as a result, and perhaps loses favor with the gods. (His memory is cherished in any case by members of the community and often a cult is founded on his behalf.) Frequently the hero relates his own story of deeds in battle, cunning exploits, and encounters with strange people in foreign places; but always on a larger tableau of epic unity the supernatural powers participate in his fate at their pleasure and by design. From beginning to end the gods themselves or their divine machinations prepare, encourage, and guide the hero in his travels along some predetermined path.[1]

Each and every one of these epic conventions is present in *The Tin Drum* but in large measure it is the last element, a unique and persuasive mythology, that gives this novel its essential character. Without a convincing mythology to motivate the hero and arrange his fate, his status would indeed be reduced from hero-deity to that of a mindless picaro (as some critics claim), a buffoon-like Simplizissimus or an Eulenspiegel.[2] But the dividing line between mythic hero and picaro is frequently a cloudy one, as critics of myth versus legend tell us: "In picaresque tales, in carnivals and revels, in magic rites of healing, in man's religious fears and exaltations, this phantom of the trickster haunts the mythology of all ages, sometimes in quite unmistakable form, sometimes in strangely modulated guise."[3] Oskar Matzerath is, of course, a trickster at times and consciously plays the Simplex role at others; but his farcical actions and satirical aspect are really of secondary importance in comparison to his purposes as a shamanistic drummer fulfilling a mission manifested at birth and prepared for throughout his childhood. Hermes, Heracles, Odysseus, Loki, and others were also picaros and tricksters of sorts, mythological heroes whose destiny required exploration of surreal realms as well as superhuman achievements within a more normal cultural context. Social absurdity and the grandeur of human existence also belong to the epics of history, and their presence here contributes in large measure to the fullness and international success of this great postwar novel; but it is nevertheless the underlying mythology of this novel that lifts the work from a possibly limited scope to a higher order of significance.

Although the gods may be mixtures of mortal and symbolic abstractions in this novel, knowledge of their divine presence is confirmed again and again by the symbolic pattern of their lives and by the way the hero translates his confidence in them into overt action. The protagonist lives his life responding to the gods in a calculated fashion, always careful to read their sacred messages in the conscious nature of all things. Yet surprisingly few critics have dared to pursue the subject of myth and magic in *The Tin Drum* as a main avenue to understanding.[4] From the very beginning Oskar focuses squarely on the mythic nature of people and things in the fashion of a true mythopoet, quickly perceiving the innate power and animism of each manifestation of existence. In every episode, as well as in the style of narration, the presence and participation of Oskar's gods—Anna and Jan Bronski, Susi Kater, Luzie Rennwand, Herbert Truczinski, Bebra, and the others—make themselves known.[5]

Most critics, however, have chosen an alternate reading of the evidence and insisted that if *The Tin Drum* is an epic at all, then it is a mock epic with the parodied hero a hunch-backed dwarf of a story that deals in empty conceits and political protestations, "full of sound and fury, signifying nothing."[6] They argue further that the abundance of mythic elements is mere elaboration and unnecessary in an already too lengthy, amorphous novel.[7] Such arguments, it would seem, are either partial interpretations or serve the needs of subjective reaction rather than objective evaluation. Oskar's adventures in *The Tin Drum* are no more disjointed or incoherent than those in Homer's or Virgil's epics. But contrary to classical mythopoets it is only natural that Günter Grass, who has to some extent been affected by Alfred Döblin, James Joyce, and T. S. Eliot as well as the entire apocalyptic tenor of his age, should create an earthbound hero belonging more to the deluge and chthonic cycle than to some transcendent solar theogony.

Not only in major questions but in minor conventions as well *The Tin Drum* conforms conclusively to the epic tradition. To begin with, Oskar literally states that he is the hero of his own narrative, just as Odysseus did in relating his own story at the court of Alcinous (Book 7); and then, like Milton in *Paradise Lost,* Oskar the author inaugurates the narrative proper with an invocation to the Muse followed by the traditional epic question regarding unknowable, sacred origins. With that the story begins, in medias res, at a critical point in the creation of the world, a point that becomes the central revealed mystery of a subsequent mythology. Thus, in the very first episode, the sweep of the novel transcends history and returns the reader to a sacred moment beyond time, to sacred history that can best be preserved and transmitted through myths. This is in fact part of the ritual function of art and myth: "It releases us from the flux of temporality, arresting change in the timeless, the permanent, the ever-recurrent conceived as 'sacred repetition.' Hence the mythic is the polar opposite of what we mean by the historical, which stands for process, inexorable change, incessant permutation and innovation. Myth is reassuring in its stability, whereas history is that powerhouse of change which destroys custom and tradition in producing the future. . . . "[8] Every myth takes place within a given culture, at some point in history, but then, as in a literary work such as *The Tin Drum*, myth is posited as an attempt to transcend history by shifting focus from measurable time and specific events to paradigmatic ritualized forms of a timeless order. It is precisely here, in the conjunction and pressure of mythogenesis colliding with secular reality, that the author of *The Tin Drum* most fully exercises his genius. The historical context of *The Tin Drum* is of course obvious and should not be ignored, for that is *the* significant moment of time which is to be transcended by sacred repetition and purpose. But our concern here is with the embracing sweep of the novel, the attempt to reconceive and experience myth as divine history and witness its triumphs and failures in relationship to profane history, to the "powerhouse of change."

A last question now of whether or not one accepts the supernatural beings as real or as fancy is surely among the most important; for depending on how it is answered, the novel becomes either an amusing fantasy or an earnest series of episodes for the reader. Were the novel not within the mythic realm, then how would one interpret Oskar's conversations with Jesus and with Satan, Oskar's miracles, his supernatural aids, his effective rituals? Are they merely to be considered parody? Burlesque? Satire? And if so, of what? Of a defeated Germany? Of national guilt? Of heroism? Of Oskar himself? Hardly. No compelling answer has yielded itself to such questions as yet. There might be some basis for the opinion that these adventures of Oskar's are all imagined, all psychological excrescences parading as reality through the mind and the pen of a madman. That might also be an observation that applies to many authors in at least a general way. As for the claim that Oskar is mad and nothing more, one may turn to the psychological-mythic defense of visions by Mann's devil in *Doctor Faustus:* "You see me; therefore I exist for you. Is it worthwhile asking if I really exist? Isn't that which acts something real? Isn't truth that which is felt and experienced?"

Ultimately, then, if seen from the vantage of mythic conceptualization, all aspects of the novel (style, structure, logic, patterns of narration, visual imagery, and symbolic development) identify this work as an epic with an intractable mythology, a carefully "composed story telling of origins and destinies: the explanations of . . . why the world is and why we do as we do, its pedagogic images of the nature and destiny of man."[9] The epic myth also deals with definitions and relationships as part of a totally anthropomorphized universe in which nothing can be discarded as insignificant. Nothing is mere delusion if it affects the visible world of man and the final measure of nature's truth. In fact the epic myth sets nothing less than the panorama of cosmic and human creation as its uncharted territory ready to be explored and formulated by the mythopoeic faculties of men.

Chapter 2 of this study of *The Tin Drum* deals with precisely that, the question of origins and destinies in a universe that "is as it is" because it is dominated entirely by the relentless powers of the Great Earth Mother who guides life from birth to the grave and back again. In chapter 3 we shall begin specifically with the mythic birth of Oskar Matzerath and his early emergence as a young demi-deity that must come to terms with his supernatural aids and with the world around him. The subsequent chapters chronicle those mythic adventures common to epic heroes and to Oskar–violent battles, initiation rituals and rites of passage, religious concerns and encounters, priestly functions, service to members of the community, and finally a kind of death and transfiguration. In this, the central part of our investigation, a good deal of support has been taken from Joseph Campbell's general concept of the *monomyth* with its three major stages of the hero's *departure, initiation,* and *return.*[10] Chapter 10, "Epilegomena to a Drumming Dwarf," returns us from Oskar's mythic world to that of scholarship again, where we consider the hero and his pantheon in accordance with some established categories and definitions used in classical studies and in the field of comparative religion.

Only the question of modus operandi remains now, the question of procedure in tracking down and identifying mythic elements. The answer must be dealt with on two levels, one observational and the other inductive and open only to confirmation by association. First of all, Günter Grass mentions literally a dozen or so well-known mythic situations and characters in the novel that in turn lend identity and significance to a given situation, although admittedly, in a negative fashion at times. (Grass often prefers to point out obvious mythological overtones by denying them: compare Vittlar's denial that he is a serpent and Oskar's denial that he is Odysseus.) Moreover, Grass's habit of punning and concocting significant names provides useful etymologies that often render the nature of its possessor more lucid. In more complex situations, the author provides the reader with so profuse a configuration of mythic symbols that it becomes impossible not to recognize the original source of the event (e.g., Vittlar as the serpent of Eden). Our second and more abstract gathering of evidence, by induction and association, will center on the author's (perhaps unconscious) use of psycho-mythic archetypes[11] and on the even more abstract level of mythopoeic symbolizing, an art in which Grass is impressively gifted.[12] Here two general divisions—"mythopoetic," properly referring to the creation of new mythic perception, and "mythological," implying the literary use and borrowing of known mythic forms—will be pointed out as occurring in Grass's writing. One can at times clearly observe playful, conscious, parodistic use of mythogyms in *The Tin Drum,* but more convincing is the author's creation of a private pantheon of gods and goddesses, episodes of sacrifice of demigods in Danzig and in the West, the salvation of Viktor Weluhn by the ghostly Polish cavalry, Oskar's messianic mission, and other mythic patterns.

If these observations on myth and literature, historical forms, and technical procedures seem unduly elusive or complicated, then perhaps the author himself, Günter Grass, can help focus them more succinctly in one of his rare statements on the nature of his novel: "*The Tin Drum* is first and foremost a realistic novel. The satire, the legend, the parable, the ghost story, in short, everything that is stupidly and simplistically stamped as surrealism nowadays, serve and belong to this realism."[13] Surrealism, therefore, fact and fantasy, blends into realism for Grass, just as for Ernst Cassirer who has said of mythmakers in the past: "The mythopoeic mind does not regard myth merely as a symbolic expression or representation of some independent reality."[14] Ultimately, for Grass, even when formulating his wildest inventions, "there are no abstract denotations; every word is immediately transformed into a concrete mythical figure, a god or a daemon."[15] Mythic imagery and creation are therefore basic and not mere literary elaboration or decor; they are the essential perception and ontological framework for a dynamic Weltanschauung that unites separate experiences into a cohesive artistic totality. And whoever can read the works of Günter Grass in this mode of experiencing reality as a form of progressive epiphany will not fail to grasp the fully unique essence of his artistry. His particular gift as an author, as his statement implies, is not in the rearranging or imitating of objects and events of an external order but rather in the dynamic re-creation and animation of being.[16] Thus, Grass's great contribution emerges somewhat in the manner and style of Hölderlin, Joyce, Döblin, Hermann Broch, or even Rilke at times, who occasionally spoke of "making visible the being that hides within the forms." With such magic—and as a literary tour de force—*The Tin Drum* can without reservation be placed alongside the most innovative and powerful works of fiction of these other authors. *The Tin Drum* clearly belongs to the great novels of world literature; and that statement, once made, enables us now to proceed directly to the heart of the novel, to a world of supernatural beings, bizarre adventures, complex rituals, and mythic configurations.

# TWO *The Masquerade of the Great Earth Mother*

In spite of its apparent diversity, disconnectedness, and shifting focus, *The Tin Drum* is guided in its conception by a single, encompassing unity. It reflects in its totality what Ernst Cassirer calls "the unity of a specific structural form of the spirit"[1] that with fluid dispatch combines the objective world and individual fantasy in one mythic narrative. But the myth does not tell only of heroic exploits, history, culture, or religion: it offers a composite of these and additional elements in one universe of its own making. And it is at this point that our real investigation begins, on the day of such a creation, far from civilization "in the heart of Kashubia."

### *Anna Bronski: The Demeter of the North*

After rejecting as statistics the sociological perspective of masses of a faceless people and insisting that he, Oskar Matzerath, is an individual hero of a classical dimension, Oskar introduces the central curiosity of this story, his grandmother and her four potato colored skirts. They fluttered about her in the four winds when she walked, bulged like a mountain when she stood; but when she sat upon the earth she gathered her skirts closely around her so that she and they appeared to converge and be fastened to one point on the ground (p. 13). And still they flared, bell-shaped and commodious enough to enclose below the fabric a sacred haven which dominated Oskar's fantasies from beginning to end.

The four wide skirts of Oskar's grandmother quickly grow in significance to represent the four sheaths of terrestrial space, the four corners of the earth, the points of the compass, the four basic elements, and therefore the whole sweep of the earthly realm and its embracing framework of creation. Below those skirts all life is born, contained, and sustained (frontispiece). As Anna Bronski sits in front of the fire on the barren field, blowing ashes and earth from the potatoes, we come to recognize her as a nourishing mother of nature. She carefully gathers potatoes, piles them to her left and to her right, tends the fire, is caressed by the winds and touched by the heavens with rain. But suddenly a maze of action invades this timeless scene as darting figures chase one another sporadically between distant telegraph poles, back and forth across the horizon, and around the brick factory. The chase is bizarre and chaotic, painted in stark, vivid lines of black and white, threatening and eerie; but all the while that the victim of the chase, Joseph Koljaiczek, is trying to elude his pursuers, Anna Bronski remains placid and tranquil in front of her fire spearing potatoes. And when Koljaiczek crawls up to her, panting, sweating, scared, "peering up at her like a squat little animal" seeking protection, Anna merely lifts her skirts without a word and allows him to enter. Under her skirts this pursued man-beast experiences a transformation; he loses his particular qualities and becomes a kind of universal man with an expansive nature: "He, short and wide could disappear entirely under them . . . then did not look like an animal anymore," and "vanished with his fear under the skirt, he did not slap himself upon the knee; he was no longer small or wide but occupied his place nevertheless; he forgot his coughing, shaking, and his hands on his knee: it was quiet as on the first day of creation or on the last" (p. 17). Order has been restored; the ritual reenactment of the hero's escape from the forces of dissolution are complete, and now, like Perseus after his flight from the Gorgons or Jason from King Aeëtes, Koljaiczek may take pleasure in his newly found protection.

After the danger has passed, evening arrives and the rain begins to fertilize the earth while Koljaiczek, still beneath the skirts, simultaneously fertilizes Anna Bronski. The parallel action of falling rain and procreation taking place on the earth under Anna's skirts is more than a literary contrivance. Rain in cosmogonic cycles of myth is regarded as a unifying or copulating phenomenon that unites heaven and earth in sexual union. The correspondence here is obvious: with the coming of rain and night, the fire and Koljaiczek's passions are extinguished, he buttons his trousers, Anna nourishes him with three potatoes (see the three nourishing breasts, frontispiece), and Koljaiczek follows her docilely off into the black woods where the town Goldkrug (the "golden pitcher") lies and beyond which is the city of Brenntau ("burning dew or water," the fire-water paradox of Joseph Koljaiczek himself). As in most chthonic journeys of fairy tale and of myth, the dark woods here constitute only a temporary darkness through which Koljaiczek must pass in order to reach a new quality of life and even special appointment, or as one critic states: "The hero who has come under the protection of the Cosmic Mother cannot be harmed. . . . What such a figure represents is the benign, protecting power of destiny." [2]

The experience under Anna's skirts constitutes a peripetia and transformation for Koljaiczek which he cannot disregard.[3] Though fitted with certain divine qualities himself, he has discovered the *axis mundi,* that sacred place where heaven and earth and all contained therein meet in a timeless harmony, and he is captivated by it just as Oskar, who later asks of himself: "What does Oskar search for beneath the skirts of his grandmother? Does he want to emulate his grandfather Koljaiczek and take advantage of the old woman? Does he seek oblivion, his home, that infinite Nirvana?" (p. 144). Then he goes on to answer that there are continents under those skirts–cities, huge rivers, and streams there; winds blow, but tranquillity reigns; it is dry but there is rain, ships collide, and God sits next to Oskar in warmth and comfort watching angels playing blindman's bluff, all beneath the skirts of Anna Bronski where summer, Christmas, Easter and All-Saints Day were celebrated; nowhere was it any more restful and tranquil than under the skirts of his grandmother (pp. 144-45).

Another important image that presents itself in this scene is that of the seated grandmother. According to Erich Neumann, "the Great Mother is often represented sitting on the earth. This 'sedentary' character, in which the buttocks form the antithesis to the feet, the symbols of free movement on the earth, represents a close bond with the earth, as can still be seen in the symbolism of language. The symbolic character of sitting is still evident in such terms as *sitzen,* 'to sit'; *besitzen,* 'to possess'; *Besitz ergreifen,* 'to seize possession'; and *besessen sein,* 'to be possessed.' Similarly the *Sitz,* 'seat,' and *Wohnsitz,* 'home' or 'seat,' of a tribe refer to the region whence it came or where it became *ansässig,* 'settled.' In ritual or custom, to sit on something has the significance of 'to take possession' of it." [4] Finally, Anna Bronski is not merely seated; she is rooted to the earth itself: "My grandmother sat as if she had grown there," and then, after the danger had passed, "my grandmother arose so slowly and painfully as if she had struck root to the ground, pulling up [as she arose] fibers and pieces of earth, thus interrupting what had just begun to grow" (p. 20). Anna Bronski, therefore, in form, costume, position, and also in color, is so closely identified with the earth as to be an integral part of it.

Grass presents a compact, highly symbolic vignette of a mythological nature, one in which a fateful adventure of a hero succeeds in unlocking the miraculous protective and creative powers of the earth goddess. In the classical tradition she tends a golden fire, blends with the elements, and becomes the receptacle for new life amid the vast barrenness. "Insofar as the brown maternal orb has the ascent position in this universe, we must assume that the mother is the ruling power. . . . In a thousand ways brown is the colour of participation. It is the colour of the earth, the original Mother. All the mystery-cults of the antique world were primarily chthonic in character, and the essential mystery of Eleusis was the *hierosgamos*–i.e., the rite of sacred marriage, in which the priestess was identified with the fruitful earth-mother."[5] Her passive reception of the fleeing animal-man and firebug, Joseph Koljaiczek, produces a new flow of life into the world. Through Anna Bronski a new genealogy of earth gods, of mythic heroes, is propagated that reaches a high point in the life of Oskar and continues on in his gifted son, Kurt, who like Prometheus also deals in flint and fire. The termination of the hectic chase and the replacement of the last fire by human sexuality (Eros) clearly indicate the end of existing chaos and the creation of order. Whereas the extinguishing of fire punctuates Anna Bronski's newly found dominance over Koljaiczek, the firebug, the chase itself is a reenactment of ritual combat or the hunt in primitive myths of creation where a particular force or entity escapes the power of chaos or of the primordial serpent (the unnatural, the latent unknown, the undifferentiated).

In a dramatic and precise fashion the events narrated here parallel the configuration of characters and events that are found in a number of myths of creation. In a work as distant in time as Hesiod's *Theogony*, for example, we find Chaos, Earth, and Eros to be the basic components of cosmic creation; and now, in a work as modern as *The Tin Drum* we again encounter the personification of earth resolving life out of chaos. If one reads and visualizes this scene a number of times, one is chilled by the conceptual reconstruction of archaic timelessness preceding the birth of measurable history and human destiny. The earth is bare and empty except for the great goddess and the ghostly dance of frantic men flitting about at the last moment preceding the hour when a new order will come into being. All together under the veil of approaching night and darkness, they skirmish in disarray, unaware that a new cosmogenesis is about to take place. Then, in the midst of confusion, Eros prevails. Joseph Koljaiczek and nature procreate in unison, in a kind of cosmic harmony, and a light rain begins to fall.[6] Here a further synthesis of form occurs to confirm the presence of a sacred union: the rain extinguishes the fire and the spirit—"smoke of the slowly dying fire enveloped my grandmother like a spacious fifth skirt, so that she too with her four skirts, her sighs, and her holy names, was like Koljaiczek under one skirt" (p. 20).

For good measure, the author bestows the name of Anna Bronski upon Oskar's grandmother, Anna being the name of the mother of the Blessed Virgin according to the apocryphal gospels, and Bronski a combination of the German word *Bron* and the Polish suffix *-ski.* Most German readers would automatically associate *Bron* with "a fountain, source, or spring," but Jacob and Wilhelm Grimm carry the concept further in their *Deutsches Wörterbuch* and claim that "*Bron, Bronne,* and *Born* are all coexisting forms of *Brunne,* a fountain or spring. The root of *Brunne* is *brinnen,* to burn, shine, or glow (after the concept of a warm fountain out of the interior of the earth). . . . *Brunne* is also a hedged, walled, or enclosed [by skirts!] *Quelle,* a fountain or source."[7] And beyond that there exists an intimate relationship between *Bron* as birth (the earthly origin of life) and eventual death and return to the earth. C. D. Jerde reflects on the "womb and tomb" character of Anna Bronski and formulates the effect on Oskar's sense of mystery in precise terms. "The grandmother motif represents both source and end of life. In *Hundejahre* the narrator says, everything comes from grandmother, and grandmother's lap and the space around grandmother's feet are the nursery of the bloom embodying legends and the superstitious teachings which set up the repetitious cycle of existence. At the same time, however, the grandmother is the everpresent hope of death; thus, in *The Tin Drum,* Oskar constantly tries to crawl under her four skirts to be close to his origin; yet the skirts remind him of a coffin and he watches the genital for signs of those who have died."[8]

Speculations such as this on a cosmogenic source are subsumed for good reason under the titles of "Mysteries" and "Ancestor Worship" in religious ritual. And if that seems at first glance too bizarre a conclusion for a modern novel such as *The Tin Drum,* then let us, at the risk of unnecessary repetition, once again review the archetypal pattern of events in this first episode before we make some attempt at extending and analyzing its purpose: The Kashubian Potato-Goddess, the Demeter of the North, has cleared her fields and has seated or planted herself on the earth; she, like Demeter whose symbol is a torch, tends a fire with a hazel scepter; a chase of cosmic proportion, extending back and forth over the horizon, ensues; the hero-victim of the chase is a firebug who is rescued by the grace of the goddess and then enjoys the supernal warmth, comfort, and restorative powers of her wide skirts; he then impregnates the goddess as the rains and darkness come to cloak the world; after which the two of them, as hierophants, the firebug and the Earth Mother, leave their sacred roles to return and unite with society: "If the hero in his triumph wins the blessing of the goddess or the god and is then explicitly commissioned to return to the world . . . the final stage of his adventure is supported by all the powers of his supernatural patron." [9]

To a striking degree these acts, as well as the novel as a whole, also parallel the vegetation or seasonal cycle of creation. All the components are present: the traditional representations of Earth, Chaos, and Eros; late autumn or the time of nature's death; man's need of ritualistic assurances that life will be renewed; the fire of the *daduchos* is present as the life symbol and sexuality as the act of creation; the nourishment; the unifying rains; the darkness to presage the death of the old order; and finally the reunification of the gods with society: "She had changed her name with the help of a liberal priest into Anna Koljaiczek and followed Joseph, if not into Egypt, then at least to the provincial capital on the river Mottlau" (p. 21).

It is entirely conceivable that Günter Grass should cast Oskar's grandmother in the role of a *tellus mater,* a potato goddess, a Kashubian Demeter. Sir James Frazer reminds us that Demeter, whose name may mean "corn or barley mother," is envisioned in various regions in accordance with the plants or vegetables that predominate there. In northern Europe, according to Frazer, the Potato-Mother (*Axo-mama*) and the "Old Potato Woman" are common legend.[10] There too a pattern of *hierosgamos*, the sacred marriage and fertilization of the Earth-Mother, was established in much the same manner and mood as in the Greek Eleusinian mysteries, where the rites also took place underground (under the skirts!), in late autumn: fires were extinguished, blackness reigned, and the ritual of love was performed. "Is there not the gloomiest descent, and the most solemn communion of the hierophant and the priestess, between him and her alone? Are the torches not extinguished, and does not the vast multitude regard as their salvation that which takes place between the two in darkness?" [11]

The purpose of such a ritual, the control and influencing of nature, and the underlying dynamics of magic are explained in detail by Frazer in *The Golden Bough* as the principle of sympathetic magic. "Homeopathic magic is founded on the association of ideas by similarity: contagious magic is founded on the association of ideas by contiguity. Homeopathic magic commits the mistake of assuming that things which resemble each other are the same: contagious magic commits the mistake of assuming that things which have once been in contact with each other are always in contact. But in practice the two branches are often combined; or, to be more exact, while homeopathic or imitative magic may be practiced by itself, contagious magic will generally be found to involve an application of the homeopathic or imitative principle."[12] The incomprehensibility of mystery of homeopathic ritual does not lie in the performance of rites, such as those performed in almost every chapter of this novel, but rather in the "unnatural" effects which they eventually produce; so the question of just how unnatural the Bronski-Koljaiczek pattern of action is must eventually be answered in terms of effect: i.e., the transformation of chaos (Koljaiczek) into order, the sanctification of a city or a region, and the creation of beings who to some degree achieve the status of divinity or semidivinity. All of this comes to pass with time; yet not only consequences but immediate appearances as well reveal Anna Bronski's variable and yet immutable nature. Anna Bronski constitutes an absolute starting point from which there is a gradual falling off into figures of lesser goddesses, into corruptions or distortions of her nature, until finally the literally absolute reversal of her presence—the antithetical Black Cook—appears and succeeds in dominating the destiny of the hero.

*The Black Cook: The Earth Mother's Alter Aspect*

The essential feature of the Great Mother is transformation. Throughout the novel the *tellus mater,* Anna Bronski, hovers invisibly over many scenes while her visible aspects continue to manifest themselves to the hero as changing forms or masks, as the feminine principle of life alternately disguised and revealed, different always and still eternally the same. Like organic nature itself that remains one while transforming in seasonal cycles, the Great Earth Mother moves elusively through countless stages from life to death and back again, her essential nature being too dynamic to fix in a single image. Although the mythopoeic mind may try to comprehend her in this aspect here or in that mask there, she remains hidden behind the mixed forms which expose her presence but conceal her real nature. Only in extremes, at the poles of creation and dissolution, does the Great Mother appear to reveal something of her endless power over man. At those extremes she is literally identified with the earth, first as the agricultural principle of the creation and growth of vegetation from which man lives; and secondly as the earth tomb which receives man and beast alike after death. This double relationship to the earth originally dominated the mythologies of man as symbolic points of contact with a transmutable and yet constant reality that lay beyond one's comprehension. We recall, for example, that in Greek mythology Gaia was the first and foremost goddess of creation and that the name means earth. Even after the fall of her first husband, Uranus, she remained as mother and wife to the gods that followed, Chronus and Zeus. By that time, however, particular aspects of her vast nature were being isolated and deified in the form of other, lesser goddesses, such as Rhea, Hera, and Demeter (a variant *Ge* = *De* + *meter,* or mother). Demeter, perhaps the best known of the earth goddesses and the goddess most likely to have influenced a modern author in fact or by vague association, personified in her double nature the human conceptions of fertility and death, especially of the mystery by which they flowed from one into the other and back again. Whereas Demeter represents birth, nourishment and growth, her alter aspect, her daughter Persephone (or Kore), signifies death and barrenness because of her annual return to the underworld as the wife of Hades. Neumann points out that "well-known reliefs, finally, show Kore full grown and almost identical with her virgin-mother Demeter. . . . The goddesses with the flower and the fruit are scarcely distinguishable from one another. Demeter and Kore are worshipped in one as 'the Goddesses,' and in the pictures where the two appear together one cannot make out at first which is mother and which is daughter–it is only their attributes that make the distinction possible. . . . This unity of Demeter and Kore is the central content of the Eleusian mysteries."[13] In other words, as a double function of a single goddess, Demeter is the creative giver of life and the daughter Persephone-Kore takes the gift of life again and returns it to the earth.

And in much the same way, it is this second aspect of the Great Goddess, the Black Cook that looms up like Persephone to close in on Oskar at the end of *The Tin Drum* for a fatal last embrace. Oskar senses only the deathly horror of her presence, but he cannot fathom her existence. "Don't ask Oskar who she is! Words fail him. What was following me before, what later kissed my hump, is now and forever in front of me, coming closer" (p. 711). Thus, in the essence of the mystery, Oskar's atavistic self is to be dissolved again into the formlessness that prevailed at the beginning of the novel, and with that dissolution the heroic cycle will have been completed.

This novel, then, begins with Oskar's grandmother, Anna Bronski, the creative and sustaining Earth Mother, and ends with the Black Cook, whose polar affinity to Anna Bronski-Koljaiczek is confirmed by Oskar himself as he returns to the surface of the earth on a Parisian escalator: "Up above where the escalator gave out, I would have liked, rather than a policeman, to see the exact opposite of the Black Cook: my grandmother Anna Koljaiczek standing there like a mountain ready to take me and my retinue under her skirts, into the mountain, at the end of my upward journey (p. 419)." Whereas the grandmother represents birth, shelter, nourishment, peace, and harmony–Oskar says it is "always summer" (p. 144) under her four skirts–the Black Cook represents terror, dissolution, and death. And, in keeping with archetypal patterns, it is only right that Anna Bronski should also reside in the East, the land of sunrise and birth, while the Black Cook is associated with the West, the land of death.[14] Literature and mythology include a vast number of female figures which resemble the Black Cook: the Hindu goddess Kali, Hecate, Lilith, Circe, and the Gorgons. As they do, the Black Cook also has her symbols and special places, her harbingers and transformations. Although her leitmotifs—dark or subterranean enclosures, cemeteries, eels, gulls—are too numerous to mention at the moment, an examination of the horde of dark figures which the Black Cook sends out into the world before her is absolutely essential in order to comprehend the vast dimension of her otherwise formless realm.

Not only adults but also children (whom Oskar refers to as brats and cannibals) contribute to his unusual education. One incident, for example, takes place when Susi Kater (her name literally means tomcat, the traditional animal of mystery and black magic), develops a game which might be called the "witches' kitchen." Susi and her little friends, described as evil henchmen, whip up a brew composed of the most vile elements one can imagine, but Susi not only determines the ingredients of her concoction, she decides that it must be fed to Oskar. Her gang forces it upon him, whereupon he becomes deathly ill, crawls away, and regurgitates what he has swallowed. Immediately thereafter he senses the urge to sing out to some windows several blocks away and discovers that as he sings, the distant glass shatters effortlessly. As a result of the vile brew Oskar uncovers new possibilities in using his voice to shatter glass. This vile soup, which might have been fatal to an ordinary person, becomes in reality a boon to the hero; what sickens him on the one hand strengthens his supernatural powers on the other.

Along these same lines, and of continuing significance, we find the development of another variation of the Black Cook in the figure of Luzie Rennwand. Among the chalices, the patens, and the few candelabras which Oskar and his band of delinquents, "The Dusters," have plundered from one church after another, one item especially gains ominous significance: a colored tapestry on which was woven a young maiden who seemed prim, proper, yet deceitful and threatening, and with her the mythical unicorn. The lady's smile, as Oskar and some of his men observe, reminds them very much of Luzie Rennwand, the sister of the Rennwand brothers in Oskar's gang. The tapestry also hangs on a spot which was previously dominated by death's-heads, black hands, and figures of destruction—replacing them in form rather than content. Oskar has the feeling that Luzie, as well as the maiden-unicorn motif of the tapestry, soon begins "to dominate all their deliberations" and is even successful in turning him (who is in his own way "fabulous and unique") into a human unicorn. She is maidenly and pure yet conniving, deceitful, possessing a strange power that can master a unicorn and eventually destroy a gang. Luzie does become the informer who brings the police down on Oskar's criminal disciples, and she also forces them to confess their sins at the bar of justice. It is also not difficult to recognize the similarities in the names of *Luzie* (related to the word Luzifer) and *Susi,* that devilish little girl, at whose command Oskar was forced to drink a foul and despicable brew. The Dusters hate Luzie in no uncertain terms, and Oskar is terrified of her up to the very end of the book where she is again transformed in a progression from Susi, to Luzie, then to Lux, the black hound of Hecate who is the Black Cook herself.

Luzie repeatedly displays an insatiable hunger. Especially in periods of crisis she continues munching on a sandwich or a biscuit. Even as the boys are arrested in the church, Oskar in a strange action picks up a lunchbasket, walks over to Luzie, and offers her a biscuit. He describes how she picks him up, holds him in her lap, and clamps the food between her teeth: "I observed her burning, beaten, forceful face: the restless eyes behind two black slits, the hammered-hard skin, a chewing triangle, doll-like, a black cook, swallowing sausage with peelings, getting thinner as she gobbled, hungrier, more triangular" (pp. 457-58). She is indeed the Black Cook who wears different masks but retains the same diabolical pleasures and intentions. Her face is an inverted triangle, symbolically suggesting, considering the Christian context of these few chapters, an inverted pagan or terrestrial trinity, a *chthonic unio mystica.*

Oskar fantasizes the trial of the Dusters in court as the image of a high springboard with his disciples diving, at the insistence and encouragement of Luzie, to their own destruction. And when it is Oskar's turn either to confess or withdraw, he looks up to see Luzie tempting him, as Satan did Christ, to jump from the tower and be saved by the hand of God: " 'Jump sweet Jesus, jump,' whispered the young ripe witness Luzie Rennwand. She sat on Satan's lap, something that emphasized her virginity even more. Satan pleased her by giving her a sausage sandwich. She bit into it but nevertheless remained chaste. 'Jump, sweet Jesus!' she chewed and offered me her undamaged triangle" (p. 462). Grass, here as elsewhere, begins to pile up, with almost a pleasurable sense of free association, a series of ideas that reinforce each other. The triangle concept, repeated here after first having been introduced into Oskar's conceptual world as Maria's pubic triangle, is presented again with overtones of chastity and seductiveness. The geometric figure, repeated in the triangular shape of Luzie's face, is offered to Oskar as a tempting tidbit which was given to her by Satan himself. In a veiled erotic allusion Luzie offers Oskar her consuming chastity in the form of a sandwich, an "undamaged triangle," which, in keeping with the tradition of the black mass that Oskar had just enacted, is also a host; for Satan "used a black Host—or sometimes a slice of turnip, also black. He consecrated, and if he wore a horned headdress he sometimes elevated it, by thrusting it on a horn."[15] The horned and mythological animal, as seen on the tapestry and repeated in several situations, reintroduces the unicorn, Luzie's pet, a wild animal of such evasiveness that it can be caught only by a virgin according to mythological traditions. After the advent of Christianity Jesus was sometimes represented as a symbolic unicorn that had been caught in the Virgin's lap. But the virgin here does not symbolize the Immaculate Conception. Luzie seems to be chaste only as death is chaste. Like Persephone, the daughter of Demeter, she enters the hero's life as the terrible chaste queen of Hades, whose purity tempts the hero to self-destruction. But Oskar declines. Instead of jumping off the tower, he hops onto Luzie Rennwand's lap like the proverbial unicorn, assumes the position of a helpless and victimized child, and finally, masquerading as the young innocent, he is exonerated and brought home in a kind of artificial deceitful victory. Prior to the episode with the Dusters, Oskar had refused to follow the Christian God, and with that Oskar rejects Christianity. As a result of his experiences with Jesus, the church, the Dusters, and by relinquishing all claims on the eternal salvation which the church has to offer, he conjures up the inexorable vision of the Black Cook. Up to the very end of the novel Oskar fears "that Luzie Rennwand will return in the shape of the bogyman and the Black Cook and bid me to jump for the last time" (p. 464). Now the Black Cook, the reverse image of the Earth Goddess, is entirely free to pursue Oskar and acquire him for her "soup" that boils in an endless cauldron as large as the circle of Nature itself and whose ingredients are supplied by the remnants of all life on earth.

*Agnes: Aphrodite or Persephone?*

If the story of *The Tin Drum* does in fact begin with the creation by the Earth Mother and end with the approach of her alter-aspect, the Black Cook, then it should be no surprise to learn that the remainder of Oskar Matzerath's matriarchal world should also be populated by female figures which resemble and are interposed between both visions of the Great Mother. "The universal goddess makes her appearance to men under a multitude of guises; for the effects of creation are multitudinous, complex, and of mutually contradictory kind when experienced from the viewpoint of the created world. The mother of life is at the same time the mother of death; she is masked in the ugly demonesses of famine and disease."[16] Indeed, only by viewing the female figures in this novel as transformational composites or masks of the universal goddess does it become possible to circumscribe *The Tin Drum* with a fairly comprehensible conceptual framework. Oskar's mother Agnes, who gives him birth and provides him with his tin drums, who lives a life of excess, and who is finally called to her death by a mysterious death's-head from the sea; Maria, who is Oskar's sister, lover, wife, and mother; Signora Roswitha Raguna, the ageless mother and dwarf lover of classical origin; and the nurse Dorothea, whom Oskar worships and whose finger becomes the relique of an occultistic obsession; and many others all dominate Oskar's life for a period of time and by attraction or aversion stake out the path which he must follow.

Most of the leitmotifs that prevail throughout the novel originate with experiences and impressions that Oskar receives from his mother Agnes. He first becomes aware of her as she remarks at his birth that when he is three years old she will give him a tin drum. Later on Oskar carefully studies and dwells on the photographs of his mother as a nurse. She is large in stature and uncontrollable in her appetites—for sex as well as for food. On her bedstead is a cameo of Magdalena, the prostitute of the Bible, a representation of the sexual mother. Like the gold leaf background of the religious image, Agnes's bedroom is golden in color, the canopy over her bed is light blue; and, contrary to the usual work for canopy bed in German, *Himmelbett* (a word describing a bed with a canopy spread like the heavens over it), Oskar chooses to call his mother's bed a *Betthimmel,* a bed which is itself the blissful heaven.

Agnes is a goddess of love in the outside world as well as at home. She never loses a game of cards in which hearts are the leading suit. Love is lavished on her by Matzerath, her legal husband, by Jan Bronski, her first cousin, and by many others from casual acquaintances down to the owner of a toy shop where she purchases the tin drums for Oskar. That, however, is but one aspect of her life and one side of her nature. The other is brought to light later on in a horrible and dramatic way—in the appearance of a black horse's head from the sea.

The incident occurs on the afternoon of Good Friday, the day of crucifixion. Agnes, Oskar, and her two males, Matzerath and Bronski, make an outing to *Neufahrwasser* on the Baltic Sea; and there, walking and climbing on a jetty from granite block to granite block, they follow the breakwater away from the mainland. At its end they see an elderly man fishing. He is holding onto a long clothesline leading out into the water. The gulls are swarming, a distant Finnish ship is sailing in towards the harbor, and the waves clap against the stones. Agnes walks up to the man, addresses him as *uncle*, and inquires what he is doing. But instead of answering, the "uncle" spits, waits a while, and soon begins to pull in the heavy line dripping with water and weeds out of the Baltic Sea. At the end of the rope is a black horse's head teeming with large and small eels gorging themselves on its brains. He extracts the eels from the horse's head and throws them into the potato sack filled with rock salt that causes the eels to clean themselves while squirming to death. Agnes is immediately captivated and yet horrified by this nocturnal shape that collides with daylight reality. She wants to flee, yet some terrible fascination holds her there. She seems to know that this apparition from the sea is her symbol, a message for her; and she must remain to witness it. She becomes first deeply engrossed, then transfixed, and finally ill as she watches the fisherman dislodge the grimy eels from the grinning mouth, the ears, and from the brain of the water-soaked horse's head.

The fisherman, having finished his project, slings the potato sack over his shoulder, hangs the rope—dripping water like seaweed—around his neck, and strides off as would an oceanic god that has just arisen from the sea. He exhibits tremendous inner strength and certainty, knowledge of the waters, a commanding stature among the elements, and an intimate acquaintanceship with the arriving

Finnish sailors—the men who make their living on the sea. The object which he hauls onto shore, however, is less significant for him than for Agnes, who sees in its presence the oracle of her own destiny. The shiny black horse's head hauled grinning and silent from the sea, saturated with long green and black eels, is a uniquely traumatic symbol that carries with it all the horrors of erotic lasciviousness as well as the grotesquerie of dismemberment and death. In the iconography of the Middle Ages the gates of hell were frequently represented by the mouth of a black horse's head; and although that image may be applied here, there are other parallels in mythology, especially those of the Black Demeter of the Greek cycles, that add greater clarification to this episode, which is certainly one of the most dramatic in the whole novel. "The Black Demeter," according to James Frazer, "was portrayed with the head and mane of a horse on the body of a woman. . . . It was said that in her search for her daughter, Demeter assumed the form of a mare to escape the addresses of Poseidon, and that, offended by his importunity, she withdrew in dudgeon to a cave not far from Phygalia in the highlands of Western Arcadia. There robed in black, she tarried so long that the fruits of the earth were perishing, and mankind would have died of famine if Pan had not soothed the angry goddess and persuaded her to quit the cave. In memory of this event, the Phygalians set up an image of the Black Demeter in the cave; it represented a woman dressed in a long robe, with a head and mane of a horse."[17] Whereas Demeter the mother gives birth at one point in the life cycle, she withdraws it as Persephone (or Kore, her daughter) at another. It follows then, as in classical mythology, that Agnes reads as her destiny that she must prepare to take the black horse to Hades, and that she is to emulate the devouring character of the queen of death even before descending. "The mysteries of death as mysteries of the Terrible Mother are based on her devouring-ensnaring function, in which she draws the life of the individual back into herself. Here the womb becomes a devouring maw and the conceptual symbols of diminution, rending, hacking to pieces, and annihilation, of rot and decay, have here their place, which is associated with graves, cemeteries, and negative death magic."[18] It is not by chance that the same images prevail in this incident as in the classical concept of the death mysteries: the huge ominous maw of the black horse's head as underground orifice or cavern; its grinning teeth like those of Cerberus, the three-headed dog at the entrance to Hades; the squirming demise of the eels as the last struggle for life; the nausea and fear one feels; the regurgitation and spittle on which the seagulls feed, like Harpies or Sirens; the rot and decay in Agnes's own womb (it is discovered that she was pregnant at the time of her death), and finally the significant fish-coffin in which she herself is devoured.

After her experience at the pier on Good Friday she literally eats herself to death with eels, crustaceans, and any other fishfood she can find. "She began with sardines for breakfast and two hours later, if there were no customers in the store, she attacked the plywood case with the Bohnsack sprats, demanded for lunch fried flounders or pomuchel in mustard sauce and in the afternoon there she was again with the can-opener in her hand: jellied eels, rollmops, fried herrings, and if Matzerath refused to fry or boil fish again for supper, then she didn't waste any words, she didn't grumble, she got up quietly from the table and came back from the shop with a piece of smoked eel" (p. 184). In frenzied hunger she even seizes the sardine cans and drinks the oil, all in preparation for her descent into the realm of death. Erich Neumann remarks on the universality of such rituals: "Here belongs also the blood-drinking goddess of death, whose hunger can be appeased only through the slaying of innumerable living creatures, whether like Kali in India she must be satisfied by the killing of men and animals; whether as goddess of war she perpetually demands the blood of men, or as goddess of death destroys all living things without distinction."[19] On experiencing the episode at *Neufahrwasser* Agnes identifies herself completely with the negative aspect of the Great Mother (the Black Demeter) confirming her transformation by mimetic participation in the homeopathic ritual of devouring life while life and earth, in return, consume her.

Agnes's most personal symbol, at this and subsequent points in the novel, is, however, not the horse's head which comes only as *kerygma* from another realm, but instead the fish (most specifically eels) as the symbol of pure sexuality.[20] The eels, as well as other fish, literally gratify and destroy Agnes. When sexuality, as initially practiced as creative ritual by Anna Bronski, becomes profaned by desire only for personal satisfaction, its presence in this novel acquires a death-bringing rather than a life-giving significance. While

Oskar notices the Finnish ship[21] coming into the harbor, Agnes continues to stand horrified and spellbound on the pier watching the strange process of fishing for eels, but it is only when the fisherman pulls two huge, parasitic eels from the throat of the horse's head—one no doubt for Matzerath and the other for Jan Bronski—that Agnes disgorges her breakfast. Even after that, as a grand finale, the fisherman reaches into the ear of the horse's head and pulls out one last, repugnant eel representing Oskar;[22] and at the sight of that one even Oskar's father, the sturdy Alfred Matzerath, turns green.

It is perfectly clear that Agnes begins her story as the genuine daughter of her divine mother in the form of an Aphrodite, as a kind of goddess of love, the queen of hearts, a Magdalena and a verifiable reaffirmation of the productive maternal principle. Michael Grant in his study of mythology informs us that "accompanied by Eros and with his aid, [Aphrodite] is the irresistible force impelling procreation and production, who 'strikes fond love into the hearts of all, and makes them in hot desire to renew the stock of their races.' " "Her birth proclaims an end to the era of unproductive monstrosities, and introduces a new order and fixedness of species."[23] But, by contrast, the very opposite events would occur following her death. Agnes, in the very manner of her death and departure, foreshadows the dissolution of the family, Danzig and Poland, and she also divines the insatiable and monstrous hunger that finally consumes all of Europe as it once was. Her death brings with it as well a loss of harmony, satisfaction, and peace in the Matzerath household. "In those years there was no more eroticism under the table, let alone love" (p. 249), although the men occasionally mechanically attempted to play cards wearing "fishbone pattern trousers." The binding force of love was gone and the card games clearly took on larger, politically significant overtones that anticipated the battles that would soon take place between Poland and the Third Reich. By a circuitous but nevertheless tight chain of logic, the death of Agnes, who united the opposing political positions of Matzerath and Jan Bronski, allows divisions to occur which eventually lead to far greater destruction.

Still, the complexities of this scene are far from exhausted. For one thing the flying seagulls swarm and scream about the heads of the characters throughout the whole incident. Unlike higher-flying birds that soar and carry significance of a spiritual or inspirational nature, these are earthbound birds, scavengers, fragmented and broken in their flights and terrifying in their vast number. Repeatedly they swoop down on the smaller eels and dart away with them. They are portrayed most like the Harpies, daughters of Poseidon and the sea, who rush to devour any and all food. Their hideous and dynamic nature relates them classically to the Erinyes, the Gorgons, and Nemesis—vicious monsters of retribution and horror, admonishers of guilt, and purveyors of punishment. The hideous terrifying noise and vision of pursuing Harpies not only terrorize Agnes in this case, but also her lover, Jan Bronski who fears the gulls and puts his hands in front of his blue eyes. His fear of being blinded by the gulls certainly recalls the punishment of Oedipus; and Jan Bronski, with all his inherent cowardliness, runs in the face of that *aletheia,* the truth divinely exposed. Whereas Oedipus, on discovering the death of Jocasta, blinds himself, Jan prefers to cover his blue eyes and flee before the pursuing gulls of Nemesis along with his presumptive incest-bred child, Oskar, who is holding onto and protecting "something else" in his pocket.

Oskar is consequently correct in saying that the Black Cook was there when "the eels demanded my mama and my poor mama demanded eels" (p. 711). Her death is a blood sacrifice to the funerary side of the Earth Mother and brings with it desolation and destruction on a large scale; but all such blood sacrifices are also fertility rituals that give birth as well to a new dimension of life, in this instance for Oskar, who says: "She died for me. She didn't want to stand in my way. She sacrificed herself for me" (p. 186). Oskar's comment, presumptuous though it may be, strengthens the argument that her death is a sacrifice that in turn opens the constricting magic circle holding him in childhood. Once liberated from her, Oskar has the opportunity of experiencing still other manifestations of life's maternal principle and responding to them in a more independent manner.

### *The Masks of Maria and Lina Greff*

In Book 2 Oskar must come to grips with feminine figures who, each in turn, lead and instruct him—Maria Truczinski, Lina Greff, and Signora Roswitha Raguna, all of whom again reflect in some measure the dual aspects of the Great Earth Mother. Oskar's own mother, Agnes, with her penchant for Catholicism, seems to be divided between the Christian and pagan world from the start, but Maria Truczinski arrives on the scene as an almost purely Christian figure, of whom Oskar says, "She wasn't only called Maria, she was one" (p. 213). In tone and respect, as well as by direct statement, Oskar identifies her with the Virgin Mary, an appropriate association, for it is she who leads him to his direct encounter with Christian mythology and the Christ child.[24] Whereas Agnes identified herself with Maria Magdalena, the sexual mother, Maria Truczinski assumes for Oskar the appearance and nature of the Virgin Mary, *but only initially;* for as she progresses through the novel, she changes masks several times from protectress-sister, to sexual teacher and mistress, to temptress and bride of Alfred Matzerath, then to mother of Oskar and mother of his child. This is all in keeping with the role of the goddess, as Joseph Campbell says; for the goddess "is mother, sister, mistress, bride."[25]

As a mother surrogate following Agnes's death, Maria begins by caring for Oskar and supplying him with his drums, but she also rejects him as lover to marry Matzerath and become Oskar's legal mother. As we shall see, she also takes him with her out of the realm of the good mother, the sacred grandmother Bronski-Koljaiczek who remains in the East, to the land of the dead, the West, the land of the Black Cook. Maria thrives in the West again as a transformed person. For a time she sells honey, the vital essence, the supreme nutriment of the plant mother; but the honey she sells is artificial, and she sells it on the black market, which is quite unlike the open country market in which Oskar's grandmother sells her nourishment.

Before Oskar meets Maria his world is dominated by a consciousness of the sexes rather than by sexual consciousness; for although he recognized the differences between man and woman at an impressively young age, he could not observe the compelling forces which attracted and unified them. It is only with the advent of the fizz powder and his love relationship to Maria that Oskar is led over the threshold into the new and dominant realm of sexual turmoil. Once there, for the first time a feeling of guilt, confusion, and anxiety overwhelms him, and he begins to cry (p. 319).

The discovery of sexual desire leads to the obviation of Oskar's unified concept of existence and thrusts him into a state that suggests the Fall of Man and the loss of innocence. The Fall begins when the powder, which Oskar licks out of Maria's hand and later from her navel, becomes the basic ingredient for a provocative rite of passage and a ritual that excites and instructs Oskar on the nature of sexual drives. Maria first holds some fizz powder in her cupped hand as a receptacle, and Oskar's spittle must moisten it. At first Oskar regards the practice as a silly game, but in time he gets caught up in the excitement of the activity and becomes conscious of his own genitals that respond to the game, "assume a will of their own," and are able to perform an act similar to but more satisfying than the fizz powder routine. Fizz powder, associated here with fruits (lemons, oranges, raspberries) and with woodruff, a sweet smelling herb, is related to fruits and pollen, ingredients that have been used in primitive societies for love potions. In a progression, then, the receptacle and the fizz powder which Maria provides ultimately become Maria's body and seed, while the tongue and spittle which Oskar contributes to activate them represent the organ and the seminal fluid that Oskar with some experimentation and experience learns to produce. This simple but frightening performance leads to a long diatribe of some significance by Oskar that might well be entitled, "Ode to My Masculine Organ" (see p. 332). By becoming aware of his phallus, Oskar leaves a shell of infantilism behind him and acquires all of the problems and disturbances that accompany such a change. With the arrival of sexual needs Oskar finds that he must often relinquish decisions to a stronger and more demanding drive over which he apparently has little or no control.

Maria's numerous roles (together with the mythic allusions used to describe her) place her squarely within the ineffable mysteries of a nature goddess. Oskar calls her in fact "a child of nature" (p. 217); and when at the beach he discovers the smell of earth beneath Maria's other odors (p. 220), he is reminded that she, as all women in this novel, draws her strength from earth itself. Oskar compares her hand with a volcano (p. 324), its bulbous mound with the moon, its fatty tissue with Mercury, and makes special mention of its hard Venus belt (p. 326). Elsewhere, during Oskar's first major exploration of Maria's body, he regards her navel as a seething volcano which for her "was farther away than Africa or Tierra del Fuego. . . . I, however, sank my tongue in Maria's bellybutton, looked for raspberries and found more and more, lost myself while gathering them, wandered into regions where no foresters asked for picking permits. . . . And when I found no more, I accidentally found mushrooms in other places. And because they grew deeply hidden under moss, . . . instead of drumming on tin, I drummed on moss" (p. 332).

Unfortunately, however, once Oskar succeeds in establishing a satisfying and pleasurable relationship with Maria, he is shunted aside by his legal father, Alfred Matzerath. Alfred is the next to seduce Maria; and when it is discovered that she has become pregnant, they marry. With that Oskar is again pitched into the background reserved for children, but this time he generates a terrible hate against Maria for her apparent betrayal. He wants to punish, to destroy the source of his former pleasure; and he attacks her and her yet unborn child with a pair of scissors. But Maria subdues him, and Oskar must withdraw with the knowledge of an irretrievable loss—that his victories are not of a permanent order and that failure as well as success must be mastered.

After Oskar's father marries Maria, Oskar's relationship to her changes radically. He loses interest in her, begins to look around for a replacement, and soon discovers Lina Greff, a woman of strange habits and of ample size. Lina Greff at first glance appears to be only a neurotic and apathetic middle-aged woman; but the description of her physical nature and domicile, her willingness and success in conveying several kinds of knowledge, even wisdom, to Oskar, and her growing capacity both to give and accept satisfactions, rapidly elevates her to the status of another mythic deity. Mrs. Greff is married to an ascetic, clean-cut, muscular Spartan who also happens to be a homosexual, unconcerned with his wife's needs. Oskar sums up their relationship with his own brand of rhetoric: "It may be that his wife, Mrs. Greff, a sloven with greasy brassieres and holes in her underwear compelled him [her husband] to seek a purer measure of love among wiry and clean-cut boys. But maybe on the other hand another root of that tree could be dug [found] on whose branches Mrs. Greff's dirty underwear blossomed in every season" (p. 349). Oskar associates Lina Greff with a tree, a huge, neglected tree on which her own soiled, torn, repugnant underwear hung. In a certain respect Oskar is comparing Lina Greff with his grandmother, who also was rooted to the earth and who promised, for him who sought and found the roots, a degree of unsuspected pleasure and illumination. At the feet of Lina Greff, Oskar notices that she, like Anna Bronski, also has a "personal fragrance which outcried, swallowed, killed that vanilla [odor of Maria] immediately" and "I [Oskar] decided from now on and every day I should carry my helplessness to Mrs. Greff" (p. 363).

Mrs. Greff is not a mere replacement for Maria: she is an overwhelming improvement. As a wonderfully comic Rabelaisian kind of woman, she is huge, soiled, formless, and motherly. It was Mrs. Greff who "made a man of him," who gave him the "broad epic breath which enabled Oskar to speak of military victories and bedroom successes in a single sentence." Whereas Oskar identifies Maria sexually with the harmonica, he says of Lina Greff that she placed him "directly at the conductor's stand; for Lina Greff offered me an orchestra graduated so wide and deep just as one can find in any case in Bayreuth or Salzburg" (p. 364). With her he experiences all of the instruments, all of the subtleties and potential rhythms of a huge musical body, the pleasures and satisfactions of this mountainous earth woman.

Only when Lina lures Oskar into her room on the day of her husband's suicide does the sight of Maria watching him call Oskar back to his senses—away from his pagan orgy—and causes him to flee and abandon their temptresses just as mythological heroes like Orlando in Ariosto's *Orlando Furioso,* Rinaldo in Tasso's *Jerusalem Delivered,* Odysseus, Aeneas, and others fled when reminded of their quests. Oskar himself does not hesitate to refer to his departure specifically as a "flight."

*Signora Roswitha Raguna*

After Oskar's mother dies and he again meets his so-called Master Bebra and his minimistress Roswitha, Oskar describes his reaction to Roswitha Raguna in the following way: "I was almost overwhelmed by dizziness. I grasped the blood-young, ancient hand of Raguna, the Mediterranean Sea beat on my coast, olive trees whispered into my ear; 'Roswitha will be your mother, Roswitha will understand. She, the great somnambule, who sees through everything, recognizes everything except herself, Mamma mia, only not herself, Dio! " (p. 198). Roswitha is indeed the Mediterranean Sea, and her whispers sound like the sound of olive trees, the voice of an earth mother of the South. Her small stature and her somnambulistic powers punctuate her supernatural role, but her real divinity is underscored mostly by the repeated mention of her agelessness: "How old is she anyway, the signora, I asked myself. Is she a blossoming twenty-year-old or, if not that, a nineteen-year-old girl? Or is she one of those graceful ninety-nine-year-old ladies who still a hundred years from now will embody indestructibly the small format of eternal youth?" (p. 366).

Roswitha, like the previous heroines, offers a mixed conception of a goddess interwoven with white and black threads. On the one hand she gives Oskar the most appropriate love of any woman he encounters, for she is his size and she apparently does love him. On the other hand Roswitha is clearly a temptress who wants to hold Oskar in her grasp by means of sexual satisfaction and material comfort. Her love is consuming, diverting him from other goals; she takes him out of his own world and into the world of the Black Cook, into the cosmopolitan world of Paris in the West, the city where he sees the Black Cook for the last time. Even Roswitha herself indicates that she is tempting him when she uses the word *verführen* (to seduce or lead astray) while trying to convince Oskar to go to the West with Bebra's theater (p. 383).

It is also significant that Roswitha tempts him with the aid of a theater in which he may perform, for in traditional myths the temptresses often entice the hero out of the real world into a world of illusion and externals: the courtiers in Alcina's palace in *Orlando Furioso,* for example, change clothing and appearance in theatrical play several times a day, and Alcina's beauty turns out to be the result of skillful makeup. But besides living and working in an illusory world, Roswitha's illusion of agelessness relates her to traditional temptresses, many of whom appear to be young and beautiful but are not. Duessa, a seemingly beautiful enchantress in Spenser's *Faerie Queene,* is found to be an old, filthy, and disgusting hag when she is seen in her bath. The author himself does not fail to notice the similarity between Roswitha's role and that of the mythological temptress Circe: "I hope it doesn't occur to the educated people among you to see in my poor Roswitha the female enchantress Circe just because of her former somnambulistic perfection" (p. 415). However, the author's purpose in such a statement here as elsewhere in the novel forces a mythic comparison on the reader and calls attention to that relationship which Oskar claims to deny.

There is little doubt that Circe in Homer's *Odyssey* plays the role of a holdfast and sexual temptress who magically reveals to the men who gaze upon her their true and often repugnant animal natures. Yet Odysseus succeeds in becoming her true lover for a period of time; and though Circe is a temptress of a negative sort who would hold him in her power, fixing or ensnaring him there with her, Odysseus learns and grows as her lover by experiencing the sexual and material pleasures until he can move beyond them to become his own master once more. Circe therefore becomes another example of an evil incarnate which, contrary to her desires, creates good. And what of Dido in Virgil's *Aeneid;* though it is not quite so clear that she is an evil temptress, she does try to hold Aeneas in Carthage and prevent him from completing his quest and fulfilling his mission to found Rome. Such temptresses, though they may have the best of intentions, have not been lost to modern literature. Hermann Hesse in *Siddhartha* creates the character Kamala, the beautiful courtesan who consciously chooses to initiate the hero in the rites of love, transforming him into one of the rich men whom he originally despises and holding him fast in the snare of sensual pleasures. This is all a necessary part of Siddhartha's education, just as these experiences with Roswitha are an integral part of Oskar's education by giving him insights into aspects of life and providing him with first-hand experiences of pleasures which would otherwise remain for him only in the realm of fantasy or ignorance. He is doomed if he does not engage the temptress or if, once having participated in the pleasures she has to offer, he fails to transcend them. Then he, like the little songbird which Kamala keeps in a golden cage, would be imprisoned in a fixed state, standing in clear opposition to the basic assumption that life must continue to grow and evolve in expanding stages. It is the mission of the mythological hero to experience and to learn so that he may go beyond the sensations which life offers in order to reach the human fulness and divine awareness which are ordained for him. Without being forced to move beyond relationships such as those to which Roswitha subjects Oskar, the hero, as any man, is permanently contained at a given stage of growth, wallowing in memories of childhood and living a life of infantile and imaginative satisfactions.

The farcical yet strangely significant episode that registers the deep connection between Roswitha and the Black Cook is manifested in the chapter "Inspection of Concrete, or Barbaric, Mystical and Bored," when Bebra's troupe of players visits the pillboxes and bunkers along the Atlantic Wall just before the Allied invasion. The immense fortification, at first regarded as a commendable feat of engineering, is gradually unveiled as the stage of a huge stone altar on which a sacrificial ritual in celebration of the terrible aspect of the Great Mother shall take place. With only minor variations the occurrences that happen on the pillbox Dora Seven can be seen as a life-and-death ritual having those same five archetypal traits that Erich Neumann enumerates as part of the "Blood sacrifice and dismemberment [that] belong to the fertility ritual of the Great Mother": 1) "it always has to do with death and rebirth relating either to life after death or to the mysteries of initiation"; 2) "it is almost always connected with a cave (or more rarely a constructed dwelling"; 3) "in those cases where the ritual has been preserved the labyrinth itself, or a drawing of it, is invariably situated at the entrance to the cave or the dwelling"; 4) "the presiding personage, either mythical or actual, is always a woman"; 5) "the labyrinth itself is walked through or the labyrinth design walked over, by men."[26] Bebra refers to rebirth when he goes through the breakfast ritual on Dora Seven, speaking of the seabreeze, the cradle of birth, saying, "Her soul is revealing itself" (p. 408). But soon the birth revelation blends with other elements into the configuration of a blood sacrifice, beginning with the burial of dogs or puppies in the cement of every bunker and ending with the slaughter of countless people. The dog is one of the few animals that was regularly sacrificed to Hecate, the Stygian goddess called the Queen of the Witches by Shakespeare in *Macbeth;* and, in the scene under discussion, human blood in murder and sacrifice is spilled in rich abundance: the five nuns are killed by Lankes, Roswitha herself dies, and finally the massive slaughter of warring troops begins the next day. What little regeneration there is must belong solely to Oskar, who with a greater sense of maturity and awareness soon returns to the East. Roswitha's death is reminiscent of rituals of transition, like the Greek nature mysteries or the Aztec harvest festival in which, like so many goddesses of mythology, the goddess herself is sacrificed for the sake of the hero. Accordingly, Oskar's new and authentic refrain is that Agnes and Roswitha have both died for his sake.

The caves or the constructed dwellings mentioned above are of course the bunkers or pillboxes themselves. There is also a symbolic mosaic of a labyrinth above the portals, an intricate design made of shells into strange patterns with inscriptions. And it is there that Roswitha presides over the ritual, the last breakfast, the sacrificial feast which she pulls out of the basket marked with names of strange languages and places, decorated with bows and, significantly, "artificial" paper flowers. She also substantiates the significance of this as a ritual feast when she speaks of the meal as "the holy arrangement of eating" (p. 406). And, finally (in keeping with Neumann's last principle), the participants do not walk through Dora Seven but choose to eat on top of the bunker directly over the sign of the labyrinth. This feast emphasizes the devouring of exotic foods, recapitulating in effect the monstrous devouring of whole countries by Germany during the war. As such it is also a concession to that slaughter which commences the next day with the invasion of Europe and ends with the final capitulation of Germany. In full context, then, the ritual meal actually appears to presage or even to produce the subsequent bloodbath. To that degree Roswitha is certainly an oracular priestess doing the biddings of the Black Cook. As for Oskar's relationship to her, he has learned some of her secrets, her rituals, and her mysteries—all of which help him over the next threshold and prepare him for the next round of adventures.

### *Nurse Dorothea*

Dorothea alone among Oskar's goddesses does not appear to belong to the sphere of the Great Earth Mother. If anything she stands in opposition to the women who have been Oskar's tangible progenitors, teachers, and sexual partners. Contrary to those women who seem to have grown directly out of the earth with all its subterranean darkness, fertility, vegetable odors, and ferment, Dorothea (whose name literally means the gift of God descends onto earth in all the white, radiant brilliance of her nurse's uniform "like a dove." Agnes, Oskar's mother, wore such a uniform before she married Alfred Matzerath, while she was, so to speak, still a virgin mother. And Dorothea, in contrast to all the other women in Oskar's life who provide him with drums, actually causes him to forget about drumming. He falls in love with her without ever having seen her. After having heard that she exists, the mere thought of her begins to obsess him. "She was very beautiful, but I never saw her" (p. 661) as he says (except, one might add, as an exalted fantasy of the unattainable goddess).

Only once do the two meet and exchange words, but that happens in the black of night in what appears to be the context of a bizarre satyr play. While still living next door to Nurse Dorothea in Zeidler's boarding house, Oskar trundles off one night to the bathroom of his house to relieve himself, but as he flings open the door in the dark he bumps into Dorothea. This is the first time he has actually encountered her, and the little scenario which follows is a grotesquely comic one indeed. Oskar, wearing no clothing but holding the cocomat in front of him, bumps into the knees of Dorothea as she is sitting on the stool. Her natural response is a frantic question: "Who are you?" Oskar playfully responds that she should guess; and Dorothea, feeling the coconut fiber material in front of her, responds, "O God, it's the devil!" Oskar with a giggle answers that he is in fact Satan who is visiting Nurse Dorothea and that he is in love with her. An attempted seduction then takes place, one with the humorous ironies reflected in Dorothea's ambivalent feelings that express fear of Satan and at the same time an uncontrollable desire to experience him sexually. Oskar, for all his desire and professed love of her, cannot function. He is suddenly impotent and asks Satan what is the matter. The response of the Satan in Oskar is simply that he doesn't feel like doing anything right now. So virtue triumphs, if only by default; and the "pure" white that Dorothea symbolizes for Oskar as the etherealized goddess of nurses's white uniforms remains unblemished. This is the second time that Satan has deserted or misled Oskar; the first time was in Oskar's attempt to shatter the church windows, and now it is in his failure to seduce Dorothea. The necessary conclusion is that both the church and nurses reside in a domain over which Satan has no power, a realm of unassailable purity. Such purity seems to stand in the metaphysical picture at the opposite end of the scale from the sinful soul, the forces of dissolution, and the realm of death.

One difficulty in writing a story which is essentially a pagan myth of the twentieth century is that its symbols will come into conflict with those of Christianity; and as we have seen, the gods of one mythology do not necessarily have power over those of another. Satan cannot help Oskar break church windows or seduce Dorothea, just as Oskar cannot finally be saved in the Christian sense of the word once he rejects the offer of apotheosis which Jesus makes to him. The two faiths, though existing side by side in this novel, simply cannot be reconciled. Yet Oskar attempts on other occasions to imitate Christ by gathering disciples, playing God in a black mass, and submitting to trials and temptations, as well as trying to establish the nurse, especially Dorothea, as the feminine principle of his own order. It is she whom he aspires to attain, and it is her ring finger that he worships later on as a holy relique, contained in a preserving jar that becomes for Oskar a vessel-symbol on par with the Holy Grail. In any case Oskar must face up to his failure. Dorothea rushes to her room, locking the door, and Oskar comes to the conclusion that the woman whom he had idealized and desired the most has left him; a woman that symbolized a soul of purity and transcendence, of salvation and grace, has slipped away. It is no accident that immediately after his abortive attempt at seduction Oskar's friend Klepp appears with the third member needed for the organizing of a jazz band, a guitarist, whose name is Scholle (literally a clump of earth or dirt), and claims Oskar.

In an obscure manner (which is evidenced by the end result), Oskar's failure to bring Dorothea into his domain by sexual conquest leads him to perplexity and a pattern of erratic behavior that indicates schizophrenia to the modern reader. Having been cast into one world and exposed to the compelling forces of another, Oskar has little alternative but resorting to madness of sorts. As a would-be Messiah he must first find lasting reconciliation between the forces of light and dark within himself, but how can he achieve such reconciliation when the symbols of the celestial and earthly realms which he must master are irrevocably split off from one another? To step into the church, to be a follower of Christ, as he is in fact invited to do by God himself, would mean that Oskar must reject his own natural earthbound greatness, and that he cannot do. Oskar must turn his back on the Christian principle in order to retain that deep affinity between himself and his terrestrial ancestors, for in more ways than one "his is the problem of Antaeus, who preserves his gigantic strength only through contact with mother earth."[27]

After Dorothea vanishes, Oskar remains in Zeidler's boarding house and takes over her room, her earthly domicile which paradoxically carries with it all the signs and symbols of the Black Cook. The room, except for the big armoire or closet, is singularly unattractive. It smells of vinegar, a preservative which is reminiscent of the spicy smells emanating from Anna Bronski, Maria, Roswitha, and others. Everything in the room is in disarray or marked with signs of ruin, disintegration, and impending death. Yet, in contrast to this, there stands a closet of the most orderly and holy appearance that Oskar has ever entered. Once he encloses himself in its darkness, his thought associations draw him back to the breakwater, the horse's head incident, and the eels. He "sat unafraid in the closet but then again not in the closet. He stood unafraid in the windlessness on the breakwater at *Neufahrwasser*" (p. 595). Also Oskar recalls the Black Cook by name, of whom he later says: "In all of the cupboards in which I ever squatted, she squatted also" (p. 711), a clear indication that her domain is all chthonic darkness. In this last episode of withdrawal, the blackness of the Cook evolves fully in the symbol of the black belt, the eels, sexuality, and death. It is interesting to note, in consideration of Dorothea's belt which Oskar held onto in the closet, that Kali too, the Hindu goddess to whom many human sacrifices were made, is also girdled with snakes or serpents and is depicted as black but smeared with blood.[28]

Now, having implied that possibly every death in this book is a kind of blood sacrifice to the Black Cook and that Oskar is related as a nature god who becomes initiated, renewed, or reborn through the sacrifices, and yet remains in terror of the Black Cook, we must postpone the examination of Oskar's final encounter with the forces of decay. As with all of the feminine figures the Black Cook herself is paradoxical, for where evil appears as a challenge, goodness also frequently results. If that statement holds true, then Oskar's final encounter with the Black Cook may yet prove to be his most regenerative experience. In the mythology of the seasonal cycle the experiencing of death is of course horrible indeed; but at the same time it presages the advent of rebirth, spiritual and physical vigor, and new hopes for future greatness. The last chapter of the book, which we must later examine in its entirety, might then in that light possibly be considered a positive experience for Oskar. A complete and opposite transformation certainly takes place from beginning to end, between grandmother Koljaiczek to her opposite pole, the Black Cook; and if that is the case, then the reader must also recognize that corresponding transformations occur in the hero who is a child of nature, an earth divinity of sorts, and certainly a mythic hero of a chthonic order who is destined to make his way through the bizarre conditions of a supposedly civilized world.

# THREE *Mythic Birth & Supernatural Aids*

The story of Oskar Matzerath begins where it ends, in an asylum, a place of "inviolable refuge for persons fleeing from the pursuit of avenging tyrants, gods, spirits" or, in the case of Oskar Matzerath, from the punishment of the courts and temporarily from the Black Cook. Tricked by a glossy black hound of Hecate and now haunted by the Terrible Mother herself, Oskar sits on his white, altarlike bed whose high bars offer him further protection from the external world and the black goddess. In addition, just as in classical times when all holy shrines were regarded as asylums and therefore guarded by special priests or attendants, Oskar has his brown-eyed guardian Bruno Münsterberg who ritualistically ties knots in simple strings and constructs elaborate white shapes out of them.[1] Like the *Prophetes* at the Delphic Oracle, Bruno watches over his *Pythia* or prophet, a *puer senex* marked both with youth and old age, Oskar Matzerath, who takes his drum in hand and beats up a state of creative frenzy to invoke the Muse Mnemosyne, the goddess of memory who will aid this poet-oracle to recall and formulate those inner experiences and external events that, when divinely blessed, give voice to the sacred and supernal verities of human existence.[2]

Similar to Odysseus, narrating the story of his many adventures at the court of Alcinous, Oskar relates the details of his exploits in relative security while his most threatening adventure still lies ahead of him. Following the epic tradition he relates events in an essentially chronological order from the third-person point of view, interjecting, however, personal comments, concerns, and attitudes at will into the story. Within the space of a paragraph or two, he might well switch the narrative stance from first to second to third person and back again, thereby providing himself with a flexible sentient center from which to relate events and develop dialogue.[3] Oskar is even empowered to become the omniscient author who may attend the rites of his own mother's conception.

We have already touched on the mythological grandeur of the female line in Oskar's family, and one must not overlook the male members of the tribe although their significance may in fact not be as far-reaching. Joseph Koljaiczek, Oskar asserts, was a firebug whose conflagrations were blessed by the presence of none other than the Virgin Mary herself; and if his actions resulted in destruction on the one hand, they were of a beneficent nature on the other, intending only to destroy the forces that divided Poland. In the eyes of many, his fires were rituals of miraculous significance: "Sawmills and woodlots provided fuel for a blazing bicolored national sentiment. As always where the future of Poland is at stake, the Virgin Mary was in on the proceedings, and there were witnesses—some of them may still be alive—who claimed to have seen the Mother of God, bedecked with the crown of Poland, enthroned on the collapsing roofs of several sawmills. . . . Koljaiczek's fires, we have every reason to believe, were solemn affairs, and solemn oaths were sworn" (p. 24).

Koljaiczek's fires in *The Tin Drum* manifest his strong desires to destroy an old order and replace it with a new one; and though they carry with them the sanction of God and the blessing of the Virgin, his ideological purpose is overruled by a fate that drives him out of the chaotic realm of revolution into the timeless sphere of mythology. Fate soon has him changing worlds, "climbing over the horizon," crawling into the fertile lap of another kind of creation. Koljaiczek is transformed through his union with Anna Bronski, and he becomes a raftsman working on the rivers, on water, a new element for him in which he apparently drowns. After his death, legends again arise, this time about his possible survival. Some say he escaped on a ship that was being christened at the time of his death, the *H.M.S. Columbus,* or perhaps he escaped another way and was now a multimillionaire in Buffalo, New York, with a special Phoenix guard (that is, a guard of the Phoenix, the legendary bird of Egyptian mythology that regenerated itself by bursting into flames and arising again in vigorous youth from its own ashes, an image that with time has become accepted as a symbol for resurrection and immortality).

Koljaiczek appears to be transformable and indestructible. Once he has served his purpose for the goddess, he may continue his activities elsewhere, for *The Tin Drum* is essentially a novel dealing with a relationship between a protagonist and the feminine principle of the Great Mother as expressed in her many masks and disguises. The male figures, potent and courageous as they may be, pass through the work like so many single threads that contribute to the creation of the fabric but fail to sustain themselves in a complete pattern.

After Joseph Koljaiczek vanishes below the surface of the waters, Anna Bronski-Koljaiczek settles down in Danzig with her daughter Agnes. In time love develops between Agnes and her first cousin, Jan Bronski, and continues even after she has married another man, Alfred Matzerath, a wounded soldier who has come to Danzig from the Rhineland, the Land of the West, which later on becomes Oskar's home also.

There is no contesting the fact that the strange circumstances surrounding the birth of Oskar himself stamp him indelibly with the mark of the mythic hero. First of all, astrological signs of the heavens are especially propitious for his arrival, and "a late-summer thunderstorm roaring like a high school principal" proclaims nature's universal participation in the birth of the hero. Then after freeing himself without aid, as Heracles had, from the womb of his mother, he is born clairaudient. He sees and understands all that is going on at the time of his birth and within minutes he is informed that he will receive a tin drum when he is three years of age, a statement whose significance is immediately punctuated by the beating wings of a night moth sounding out the rhythm of Oskar's future mission. Certainly Oskar's noble matriarchal lineage, first revealed in mystery and ritual under the wide skirts of his grandmother two generations earlier and soon to be reconfirmed in the archives of the gods—the "Photo Album"—cannot be doubted; but true to mythic tradition, Oskar's paternity can and will be questioned. Unlike solar gods Oskar is born under two sixty-watt lightbulbs, apparently one for each father who in both cases is ironically duller than the progenitor of a hero is expected to be. But as with other heroes Oskar's abilities and ambitions will lead him to lights of greater brilliance, to the highest of realms, out of the profane into a miraculous drumming contest with Jesus and with the fates themselves.

The message of the lights, as Oskar points out, is of less importance than the drumming rhythm of the moth: "I remember the play of light and shadows less than I do that noise that became audible between the moth and the lightbulb" (p. 48). Oskar regards sound as the central feature of his strange call to adventure. It was, our hero notes, as though this moth, in drumming, was bequeathing a last message to the bulbs, but the message fell instead upon Oskar's ears. That moth, he continues, was to become his idealized master, his sage, his symbol; for the moth had made him fall in love with the drum promised him by his mother just a few moments before. The moth was a drummer beating out universal images in sound, giving meaning to time and symphonic significance to all of nature, whose wild animals, woodpeckers, rabbits, frogs, and even worms drum their own syncopation with controlled passion. Also, as he notes, people drum on all sorts of materials and shapes; symphonies are created for the drum, the Negroes in darkest Africa drum, and now even a little moth in Eastern Europe drums to tell Oskar that life is composed of common rhythms rather than inert matter.

The point which Oskar is making is essentially a metaphysical one, for he observes that objects and entities in physical creation have their own time patterns, their own pitch, signature, and rhythm, and that time is the first principle of creation. And if all that exists has its own pattern of pulsations and Oskar has an ear for them, then he can also conjure up things and events by beating out a rhythm that forces them to oscillate and dance out of the past to the tune of his frenzied drumming. Shamans, witch doctors, and wizards use the drum to get the tribe or individuals and themselves into beat or "harmony" with a universal rhythm; and now, by extension of this practice, we see that Grass chooses to utilize the drum again as a magical instrument that can summon up ancestral visions and entities with the appropriate pounding. Or, to state the case less figuratively, the drum, at least as it functions in the *frame* of this novel, is the source of Oskar's capacity for artistic creation, for with it alone is he able to capture the rhythmic patterns of his past life at different stages and record them.

Although Oskar immediately decides to follow the path of the moth in its search for illumination, one question begins to plague him: "Who sent the moth to me and allowed it . . . to stimulate the desire in me for the drum my mother promised me?" (p. 49). The presence of the moth, to follow the implications of Oskar's question, apparently has tangible cause although it appears to be a chance phenomenon like the inadvertent picking of a rose in a fairy tale or the accidental dropping of a golden ball in a well, a chance incident that seems trivial in itself but nevertheless carries the magic power necessary to change the course of one's life. The moment communicates to the hero the special way he must go, but it also reveals the presence of an unsuspected and alien world beneath the veneer of the present one. "This first stage of the mythological journey—which we have designated the 'call to adventure'—signifies that destiny has summoned the hero and transferred his spiritual center of gravity from within the pale of his society to a zone unknown."[4]

The message is clear enough, and the "call to adventure" does not go unheeded even though Oskar is temporarily at a loss in understanding the purpose or authority of the call. In search for meaning Oskar later resorts to the family archive, to the "family grave that clarifies everything" (p. 50), the "Photograph Album" that actualizes Oskar's genealogy and birth into a meaningful present. From the photograph album Oskar receives assurances of his special origin and answer to his question: "What compelled me to seek and if you will, even find, mathematic and, oddly enough, cosmic references on this rectangular photo?" (p. 58), for the album in response becomes a testimony to the greatness of Oskar's lineage.

Of course the photographs record only the physical aspect of his predecessors, but Oskar is well prepared to recognize the unconditional being that hides behind the illusion of appearances. He notes, for example, that "even my grandmother Anna, who really was, by God, a person, hides herself on the photos taken before World War I behind a silly, assumed smile and gives no hint of the asylum which the circumference of her four layers of reticent skirts offers" (p. 55). And what is true here for the grandmother—that her universal and divine aspect cannot be photographed—applies also to the facial expressions and the artificial groupings of relatives and friends. Oskar even deduces the erotic parental triangle between Agnes, Matzerath, and Jan Bronski; he sees half moons in the women's hair, similarities between the women and the Madonna, and even confirms the deep bond of the Bronskis with the distant Kashubian fields of their origin. Oskar succeeds rather well in interpolating special significance in the family photos and in setting the stage with all of the main figures and supernumeraries who are to people Oskar's early life. In the form and content of pictures Oskar therefore discovers the signs that presaged his birth and identified his family with a special aura of meaning. But the pictures that please Oskar the most are those taken on his third birthday when he finally received his drum and rejected the society of adults in order to remain a three year old, in size at any rate.

If the moth beating against the lightbulbs at the time of his birth was a special message or creation *kerygma* for Oskar, then his decision to fall down the cellar steps on his third birthday may be considered Oskar's personal response and commitment to the call. Oskar observes that his father, Alfred Matzerath, has left the trapdoor to the cellar open, and he reads that immediately as an invitation to subscribe fully to a special destiny. The trapdoor demands an irrevocable decision from Oskar now, and Oskar accepts. Desiring to retain his three-year-old size and also to find a reasonable explanation for his cessation of growth, Oskar throws himself down into the cellar and in doing so crosses a major threshold that separates him from the normal functions of a routine world.

Oskar's disavowal of adult society and his commitment to the free and untrammeled domain of childhood is expressed conclusively in his determination not to grow. His decision to retain the stature of a three year old is more than an impulsive gesture: it establishes a necessary distance for the preservation of a physical state and mental capacity for viewing and synthesizing a world of opposites into a mythic unity. Therefore, it is Oskar's size, his attempt at immortalizing his childhood, and his final pathetic transformation into a dwarf (and not the tin drum which is exclusively a supernatural aid) that gives him and this novel its stamp of identity. As a divine child and culture hero Oskar sets out to mythologize his society and era; and what can actually be identified as mythical in the course of this work is the chronicling of Oskar's overpowering experiences as a child and a dwarf compelled to make his mark in the land of giants.

As in most myths of a traditional order it becomes a necessity for the son to retain his identity and assert his individuality in the face of leveling forces of a community that imposes conformity. Through guile the mythological hero is able to turn the table on a legendary "hold-fast," usually the father and/or king; and Oskar himself quickly recognizes the advantage of burdening his father with a measure of guilt, contrived as it may be. The trickster epithet applies equally well to epic heroes and gods alike, to Odysseus as well as to Hermes; so Oskar's subterfuge in displacing guilt here as he achieves his goal elsewhere is not without precedent. The conflict as a divinely inspired struggle between father and son (usually starting with an oracular divination) can be traced through countless well-known and obscure myths. Compare, for example, the myth of Oedipus, who is spirited away at birth because his father Laius tries to kill him and later returns to Thebes to kill his father, thereby repaying rejection and injury with patricide. Theseus, reputedly the son of Poseidon, is to be murdered by the guards so that his legal father, King Aegeus, may retain power. He too is whisked away only to return later on and cause the death of his father. Similar circumstances surround the lives of Romulus, Perseus, Jason, Dionysus, Apollo, Zeus, and countless others. But what begins with a special message for Oskar ends in physical distortion. He becomes a malformed "eternal" child by choice, a mythic hero by destiny, and, like others before him, the victim of those very forces that select him originally for greatness. Discussing such unique and yet nondescript figures as these, W. K. C. Guthrie poses a question which we must deal with in the last chapter: "What should we call these beings: gods, heroes or what?"[5] We must wait for the answer to that key question until we have traced in detail Oskar's ambitions, asserted by him to be "messianic" in purpose and aimed at nothing less that the apotheosis of self and the redemption of man.

By the end of chapter 4 Oskar has completed preparations for his mythic journey on a tin drum. He has aligned himself with the night moth and has decided to spend a good part of his life investigating the obscure, dark side of reality from which it came. Although the choice seems to belong to Oskar, his call to adventure, the symbols, and purposes of his journey have been determined by those incomprehensible forces that send moths with universal messages and goddesses with supernatural aids to their special, providential progeny. The gods are generous to those who have escaped the powers of the father or tyrant and have demonstrated strength and courage by crossing the first threshold voluntarily. They bestow upon the hero a magical charm or some special knowledge to offset the preponderant power of his enemies and help him fulfill his missions. Unbeknownst to Oskar as yet, the drum given to him by his mother is already a supernatural aid; and now, as if to confirm the magnitude of his special gift, Oskar is also endowed with a voice that can shatter glass. It first manifests itself as a protective weapon against those who attempt to rob the hero of his special talisman, the tin drum. "The ability to drum a necessary distance between myself and grown-ups with my toy tin drum developed shortly after my fall down the cellar stairs, almost simultaneously with the emergence of a voice which allowed me to sing, yell, or yell singing in such a sustained high-pitched vibrato that no one would dare take the drum away that was damaging his eardrums. When my drum was taken away I screamed, and when I screamed, valuable things were shattered to bits. I had the ability to shatter glass. My screams demolished vases . . . my voice cut through glass doors" (p. 68).

Oskar's special voice bestowed on him "shortly after his fall from the cellar steps" comes as a special boon from the concerned entities that are the custodians of such powers. If Oskar's fall into the cellar is his proven commitment to a great but yet unformulated destiny, then the gift of a glass-shattering voice becomes the corresponding validation of supernatural participation in his future. With time Oskar will put his voice as well as his drum and his size to other uses, but for the moment they are powerful enough indeed to permit him to vanquish the most formidable of enemies.

Oskar's first major victory establishes the efficacy of his aids as well as his dominance over his own parents. His incessant drumming exceeds all sensible bounds and grates mercilessly on the ears and nerves of adults. After unsuccessfully attempting in diverse ways to get the tin drum away from Oskar, Matzerath tries to take it by force; but at the crucial moment Oskar summons up his powers and releases a glass-shattering scream. To everyone's amazement the hero shatters the glass cover of a clock. All stand thunderstruck in the presence of a miraculous feat, and Jan Bronski, one of Oskar's presumptive fathers (recognizing the unearthly quality of the act), even begins to pray. The adults have tried to take away Oskar's noisy drum, but the battle is not over until Oskar "demolishes all four lightbulbs," plunging everything with a "killing scream into primordial darkness" (p. 73). Thus, at an early age and still almost unaware of his great powers, Oskar re-creates a state of cosmogonic blackness which terrifies the adults in the room. They too scream at first and demand light but soon reconcile themselves to the advantages of darkness. It is revealing that Grandmother Bronski-Koljaiczek should bring in the light, the controlled fire on a candle, with which order is restored. What the light reveals is an amorous and lewd state of affairs: the adults have paired off with one another, having exchanged partners to experience some of the erotic pleasures of love. The theme is reminiscent of much of the promiscuity of mythological heroes, gods, and goddesses. But grandmother returns "like an angry archangel" with the illumination of the candle to view the Gomorrah, calling it a disgrace; and the author himself compares their behavior to the wild pleasures of a Teutonic wood god, Rübezahl.

With light restored, Oskar withdraws to his special place beneath the table, below the surface on which the adults play their game of cards; and there, in effect, he is again in the cellar, in the world below, in a subterranean sphere. Oskar's place below the table is one of the many enclosures into which he withdraws for the tranquility and safety he needs to gather his thoughts and energies together again. The dark enclosures have, on occasions, the significance of a surrogate womb or a whale's belly, where powers of darkness may restore vitality by removing the disturbing forces of the external world. The result is that the hero gains assurance (as well as power) of what he is by comparison to the men who live only in a practical and profane world. On the surface of the table the adults are playing *Skat,* a card game that remains a major motif throughout Book 1, from the present scene to the grotesque card game played with Death during the destruction of the Polish post office. There, above the table we have the world, not as it is, but as a game and artificial product of human actions and engagement. The Skat game, in its varied contexts, provides an illusion of life, a sense-world of endless phenomena that conceals the absolute nature of being. But it is an order of things which the hero soon comes to recognize as a camouflage for a more significant and somewhat perverse form of behavior going on below the surface.

In the days following, on a September afternoon soon after his unpleasant encounter with Susi Kater, her gang, and her brick soup, Oskar learns to perfect the glass-shattering quality of his voice. He learns to throw it in quiet tones over long distances and to cut desired shapes and forms out of windows. After the soup episode Oskar, more alone than ever, makes his way to the top of an old tower from which he can look down over the city and experiment with his new long-distance glass-breaking voice. Interestingly enough his first major target is the municipal theater, "the dramatic coffeemill," as he calls it, a mechanical apparatus for grinding out art that is a mere semblance of life. The incident is not important in itself, but in another respect it marks the end of Oskar's final preparation for adventure. Now he has acquired all his supernatural aids, confirmed the truth of his special birth and divine ancestry, received his unique call to adventure, responded to the threats of society with a refusal to grow, and accepted the fact that there is a benign power everywhere that will support him in his travels. With the utmost confidence in his strength and with his premonition of prophetic greatness, he may now leave the protecting confines of the immediate family and engage external forces of evil. But there too, on the perilous path of adventure, he will repeatedly find special help waiting and unique powers at his disposal.

# FOUR *The Education & Early Adventures of the Hero*

By way of introduction to Oskar's public school education, the reader is first exposed to a short satyr play of political satire in which Polish and German kindergarten children beat each other. The main drama, however, takes place during Oskar's first and only day in public school, for it is here that he really demonstrates his skills and courage as a hero in combat against a monster of another world. Whereas in the kindergarten he had been harnessed and controlled with only minor flare-ups, Oskar's experience in grade school ends with a battle and a victory that does justice to the most glorious exploits of ancient gods and heroes.

On entering the strange and unnatural confines of the school building Oskar immediately perceives hints of impending danger in the frescoes of athletes, in the repugnant odors of the drinking fountains where boys guzzle "like so many pigs from a mother sow," in granite bowls with remnants of greasy saliva and bread crumbs lodged at the bottom, and in the cavelike halls that block out all memories of a living nature. Oskar is led up "monumental stairs, cut for giants" to an oversized desk surrounded by a horde of grimacing, screaming, hysterical children ready and willing to obey the dehumanizing Fräulein Spollenhauer, the first-grade teacher of dried-up mannish appearance with heavy glasses and deep furrows in a neck surrounded by a stiff white collar. Oskar at first observes the interplay of actions developing between her and "this mob of Barbarians," but soon he begins to accompany the singing class on his drum. For a moment the magic of his drumming induces Spollenhauer to "forget the teaching profession, to escape the prescribed caricature of her existence," and "to become human; that is, childlike, curious, complex, and amoral" (p. 87). Oskar has succeeded in transforming this mechanical official of society into a genuine, responsive human being, but only for the moment. Spollenhauer's inability to follow Oskar's rhythms soon forces her back into her traditional role as a brutal pedagogue and compels her to reestablish her power. Disturbed and challenged by Oskar's drum, she attempts first with mild blandishments and then with force to take it away, but Oskar counters by singing a scratch on one lens of her glasses. She tries to compose herself and regain control of the class, but when Oskar interrupts again with a few well-placed drum beats, Spollenhauer is unable to control her fury any longer. She changes literally into a beast that, "showing its claws," tries to seize Oskar's drum. In response Oskar emits a scream that shatters some of the oversized windows up above, as—from nowhere it seems—Spollenhauer conjures up a cane and slams it, with all the viciousness of a wild animal, first on the desk and then on Oskar's drum. "What kind of animal was this ready to strike? What zoo had it escaped from, what prey did it seek, what did it lust for?" (p. 91). Oskar, also furious now, responds with a full-bodied double scream that disintegrates Spollenhauer's glasses, blinding her as Odysseus blinded Polyphemus, the Cyclops, in his own cave. With bleeding eyebrows and empty spectacle frames, Spollenhauer retreats blinking, feeling her way backward, crying in pain and defeat. The children in the classroom cower back terrified by this battle of giants while their "mothers turn into furies" (p. 91) that in the confusion of the moment prepare to attack Agnes; but Oskar, with courageous presence of mind, grasps his mother by the hand and leads her out of this cavern of violence and confusion.

The mythic content and vocabulary of this episode are obvious enough. The school itself is described as a prosaic temple of society and a hall for giants. Spollenhauer is a "beast," children are referred to as "animals" and "Tartars," their mothers are "furies." But our hero willingly enters this temple of communal inhumanity dedicated to the propagation of organized conformity and engages one of society's giants in combat, vanquishes it by revealing its inherent blindness, and then saves himself and his mother from destruction. "I [Oskar] moved past the half-blinded Spollenhauer and found my way to my mother who was being threatened by furies, seized her by the hand, pulled her out of the drafty classroom, . . . echoing corridors, stone steps made for giants" (p. 91). On leaving the building Oskar takes the class schedule from his mother's hand and makes an "absurd ball of paper" out of it. Schedules, public schools, and formal instruction have lost all meaning for

Oskar; but to immortalize this victorious moment nevertheless, Oskar stops in front of the main portal of this huge temple of society and allows himself to be photographed.

The significance of this episode is far from obscure: the hero of the night world, whose birth was proclaimed by a storm and symbolized by a moth beating against two lightbulbs, who threw himself with courage and purpose into the darkness of the cellar over the first initiatory threshold, who possesses supernatural aids and is a child of the gods, enters a temple that is dedicated to the preservation a mechanical, depersonalized, faceless society. There he engages one of its demons in combat, vanquishes it by revealing its inflexibility and blindness, then saves himself and his mother from the furious powers of retribution. Beyond that we recall the strangely appropriate last words of Polyphemus who knew that his blindness was in fulfillment of a prophecy: "But I always expected some big and handsome fellow of tremendous strength to come along. And now some puny, good-for-nothing little runt fuddles me with wine and puts out my eye" (*Odyssey,* Book 9).

Still Oskar must receive an education somewhere. At his present stage of awareness, he is intrigued by the magic, runiclike figurines of written and printed letters which seem to carry so much significance for adults. In writing he sees a reflection of the apparent division of mankind, recognizing that there is a big alphabet for grown-ups, and so, he deduces, there must be a small alphabet for children and for dwarfs such as himself. Regarding illiteracy now as a glaring weakness in his education, Oskar resolves to go off in search of a reading teacher and soon hits upon the person of Gretchen Scheffler, the wife of the local baker who lives in an overstuffed, confusing but yet rich and colorful apartment. She loves children, but having none of her own, she lies in bed all day on embroidered sheets and pillowcases and knits children's clothing. Her cupboards and trunks, full of children's apparel knitted for no one in particular, attest to her excessive but pointless energy. For all the fabric she has crocheted, stitched, woven, braided, or knitted, she remains on the surface a lazy, self-indulgent woman, a woman archetypally reminiscent of the industrious and quiescent Arachne, the great spinstress or weaver of fate whose threads lead in all possible directions while she herself remains motionless in their midst.

Oskar cunningly succeeds in winning her over as his teacher.

Reacting to an inner voice, he chooses from among the volumes available for reading practice one about Rasputin and one by Goethe. Ambitious and intelligent, he quickly learns to read and comprehend the contents of these works which in time become the accepted antitheses of Oskar's contrasting values. Oskar admires the spiritual aspect of Goethe, the harmonious structure of his life and thoughts. In Rasputin he sees the opposing hero who is outside of society, a man in conflict with the given order and at home in chaos. Goethe, however, becomes for Oskar an expression of angelic completeness and eventually too highly structured, too well balanced, too resonant with life to be of great immediate interest. Rasputin, on the other hand, is the faith healer, the religious fanatic, the tormentor and yet savior of womanhood. He plays on the black side of mankind, on the nightside of life; similar to Oskar, he seems to draw his powers from the nether world, so for every hour that Oskar reads Goethe he spends three hours reading Rasputin. What results from this education with Gretchen Scheffler is a kind of hodge-podge of knowledge in which Rasputin appears in Goethe's *Elective Affinities* with Goethe's Ottilie and Olga sitting with him in his sleigh riding through the winter nights of St. Petersburg. In another respect, however, we shall soon see that these two ideals come to symbolize the outer limits of human endeavor. They represent for Oskar the dangerous extremes of Scylla, against whose granite hardness or rigidity one can be shattered, and Charybdis, the formless and chaotic powers that may overwhelm and swallow the unwary soul. Indeed the dichotomy eventually develops into a hybrid principle by which Oskar defines himself as "the little demigod whose business it is to harmonize chaos and intoxicate reason" (p. 386).

Oskar does not have to wait long for his first opportunity to "intoxicate reason" and institute disruption. In 1934 Alfred Matzerath, Oskar's German and legal father, joins the Nazi Party, hangs up a picture of Adolf Hitler, and begins to espouse "the forces of order." Tensions rise and tempers flare occasionally between Alfred Matzerath and Jan Bronski, who affirms his allegiance to Poland by going to work at the Polish post office. The situation degenerates even further when Matzerath manages to acquire a uniform and goes off parading every Sunday with his brown-shirted friends, leaving Agnes at home alone and waiting to entertain her paramour and first-cousin, Jan Bronski. Oskar soon finds his mother's clandestine affairs rather boring and decides to wander off with his drum to attend the mass meetings of the young Nazi Party in Danzig. Once there he recalls a bit of advice he received from his "master," the dwarf Bebra: "Oskar, never be a member of the audience! Never stand out front! The place for our kind is on the rostrum." On the rostrum Oskar is pampered, silenced, and finally removed, so one Sunday he decides to slip "past the nails that stick out like teeth" and enters the cavernous interior of the rostrum rather than join the audience out front. From there he observes the proceedings through a knothole and finds himself in complete disagreement with the artificial pomp and circumstance, especially with the drum and bugle corps that hammers out trite march music "blowing the fanfares of Sodom and Gomorrah." Picking up the rhythm on his drum, Oskar gradually transforms the banging and bellowing of the brown shirts into three-quarter waltz time, into the jazz syncopation of "Jimmy the Tiger" and the Charleston, and manages with the aid of his drum to release the tiger in man and replace ideological captivity with freedom, laughter, and dance. While the members of the Nazi Party have counted on drawing new members into their fixed order, Oskar drums a message of vitality and individual decision that in turn reveals the inner burden, even the absurdity of heavy-handed march music and military pomposity.

As Oskar transforms the military music into the waltzes and jazz rhythms, the people begin to laugh at the confusion and chase one another around on the lawns. "The situation could no longer be saved, the people danced away from the field. . . . The people lost themselves with 'Jimmy the Tiger' in the spacious enclosures of adjacent Steven's Park. There they were offered the jungle which Jimmy had promised; tigers walked on velvet paws; it was a substitute primeval forest for the people who had previously been crowding together on the meadow. Law and a sense of order went out the window" (p. 139). Oskar, therefore, creates a chaotic satyr play out of one of man's most organized events—a political rally. He transforms mechanical behavior into a spontaneous and untrammeled expression of nature, where men and women go bounding off playfully in chase through the gardens and woods, pursuing as they do the simple and natural pleasures which nature provides.

The disruption of the rally and the "belly of the whale" allegory are the essential motifs of this chapter. The two themes, however, are related to the extent that Oskar affects the external world by conveying his message from a superior, or *interior*, realm. From the inside, from the unique enclosure looking outward, his powers are more effective and revealing than they would be were he lost amid the faceless numbers of the crowd. As the mythological hero who can pass back and forth across the horizon of two worlds, in and out of whales' bellies, through earthly temples and subterranean caverns, Oskar can now surreptitiously transmit the forces at his disposal to disrupt, correct, "harmonize or intoxicate" the mechanical forces of a mindless society. It is significant to note at this point that Oskar refers to his hiding place below the rostrum as "my wooden labyrinth which was about the size of the whale's belly where Jonah sat getting stained with blubber," and then he comments further about "avoiding overhanging beams and protruding nails," which are compared to the leviathan's ribs and teeth; and when all is finally quiet, Oskar "emerged . . . from the bowels of a rostrum . . . which only happened accidentally to have the proportions of a prophet-swallowing whale" (p. 140).

Northrop Frye touches on the central significance of this episode while exploring the archetypal pattern of enclosures in general: "The image of the dark winding labyrinth for the monster's belly is a natural one, and one that frequently appears in heroic quests, notably that of Theseus."[1] By associating the belly of the whale with the labyrinth and with Theseus, Frye opens the way for an extended interpretation of the rostrum incident. Just as Theseus, Oskar is attended by a real sense of mission here: he must defeat the monster, the Nazi leader Löbsack, a misshapen hunchback presumably with an appearance similar to the bull-necked Minotaur of Crete; and by defeating him, the young Germans like the Athenian youth and maidens previously sacrificed to the Minotaur may be liberated. Theseus kills the monster with his special sword and frees his people from oppression; Oskar defeats the tyrant with his drum, his own supernatural aid.

By extension Frye associates this motif of liberation with that of the Old Testament where "the Messiah-figure of Moses leads his people out of Egypt. The Pharaoh of Egypt is identified with the leviathan by Ezekiel,"[2] another parallel for *The Tin Drum* considering Oskar's early messianic claims and his enclosure in the whalelike rostrum. And Oskar's zeal does not end with this incident: in rapid succession he leads countless others out of captivity by attacking with his drumming "the Reds and the Blacks, the Boy Scouts and Spinach Shirts, Jehovah's Witnesses, the Kyffhäuser Bund, and Vegetarians, and the Young Poles of the Fresh Air Movement. Whatever they might have to sing, trumpet, pray or proclaim, my drum knew better" (p. 143). And what Oskar the liberator cannot reach with his drum, he decides, he can shatter with his voice.

Oskar refuses to play one fixed role for long. Whereas in one chapter he envisions himself as a messiah liberating all sizes and shapes of people from organizational captivity, in the next he transforms himself into "the demigod of thieves" (p. 150) by assuming the sly and curious role of Hermes. With the aid of his supernatural glass-cutting voice he now begins to lead people (as a game for himself and a revelation for others) into temptation. As citizens from one walk of life or another stroll along the streets of Danzig and look into store windows, Oskar, hidden in dark doorways, cuts holes in show windows so that these people may reach in and steal whatever they wish. The victims are held spellbound when the glass falls out in front of them and the objects of their desire stand unguarded. At first they struggle against temptation, forced to make an active decision—to steal or not to steal. But inevitably (except in one case where love overrules greed) they take the item of their choice, suffer a guilty conscience, and as a result become disturbed and somewhat alienated from the fixed structures of a moralistic society. Here then, as elsewhere, Oskar seems inclined to force adults to acquire a new state of mind, one which may lead to a subsequent transformation of attitudes, values, and even character. Although Oskar first of all claims he was simply being devilish for leading these people into temptation, on reflection he adds: "Oskar, you not only fulfilled the small and medium desires of all those quiet winter-time walkers who were in love with some object of their dreams, you helped them to know themselves . . . to recognize the larceny in their hearts, . . . not to mention the changes made in self-righteous citizens who until that time had looked upon every small and incompetent pickpocket as a dangerous criminal" (p. 150). Oskar is again ironically dissociating the burghers of Danzig from a certain fixed state of mind, although his motives are perhaps less than altruistic in this case, for Oskar himself as a parody of "Hermes remains largely non-moral." It is a "fact that [Hermes] is god of luck and can give wealth, honest or dishonest,"[3] and no less Oskar, who, like this Greek god of wares, thieves, travels, educates pedestrians and increases their fortunes along the way. Oskar's contribution to the middle-class citizenry is the demonstration that there is really larceny in their hearts, and that with such knowledge one may develop new awareness, concern, and even tolerance, just as the district attorney who was tempted into thievery by Oskar. He did in fact become a better man for his transgression, a more understanding and moderate dispenser of justice, all because he was encouraged to steal by Oskar, who literally calls himself "the small demigod of thieves" (p. 150).[4]

Oskar also makes much of the fact that he spends his time in dark doorways, "a favorite dwelling place of evil." Hidden there, unseen in the black passageways as he once was within the bowels of the grandstands, he is able to affect the actions and alter the course of human lives at a safe distance. From a remote point he can cut through glass, thereby removing "from between two worlds" a transparent barrier that he refers to as "virgin glass," an untouched, mystical divider of realms; and to Oskar that seems reason enough in itself to act, for it is his self-proclaimed mission to unify what is divided and synthesize what is fragmented. The episode surrounding the glass-breaking and thievery as a social game comes to an end, however, after Oskar impulsively tempts his alleged father, Jan Bronski, to steal a ruby necklace. Again the event is framed in the language of the myth with Jan being referred to first as the creator, then as a monument, and finally as Parzival transfixed by the vision of drops of blood in the snow. Jan, unable to decide if this temptation comes from heaven or hell, takes the necklace nevertheless, and then instead of departing with his booty, he remains rooted to the spot. It is then that Oskar's playful curiosity leaves him as he thinks, "Oh father, son, and holy ghost! Something must happen in spirit if something is not to happen to Jan the father" (p. 153). With that Oskar opens his coat and begins to drum until Jan turns and walks toward Oskar, finding him in the doorway of a house.

The episode with Jan, the repetition of the phrase "*Jan*uary night," the allusion to Jan as a creator and a monument, the heavily emphasized motif of doorways and portals, the theme of coming and going, and finally the shift to Christian theology to identify Jan with "God and Father" prepare the soil for the possible growth of the concept of Jan as patterned on the Roman god Janus; but then after having developed the groundwork, Grass apparently chooses not to cultivate it fully. Certainly in Roman mythology Janus was the god of gods, *Janus pater* ("Jan Bronski . . . begot me in Matzerath's name"); the god of two faces *Janus bifrons* (cousin and secret lover!) that looks into the past and future (and is therefore ignorant of his real destiny which lies in the "eternal present"[5]); and he was also the god of all doorways, openings, and portals, which play such a prominent role in this scene. The relationship of a Hermes and a Janus figure in a single episode here is neither as bizarre nor contrived as one might first suspect. "While the Romans felt there was no Greek counterpart for Janus, Hermes seems to have been selected as similar in scope and character, and many are the features they have in common. Hermes, too, was a 'rector viarum,' the friend of travelers and guardian of gates and doorways and boundaries. Best of all he was 'a small god, intimately near.' "[6] Janus was also closely linked to questions of personal and national destiny, beginnings and closings of eras and war, concepts which pave the way to his disastrous presence later on at the battle of the Polish post office and the defeat of the Polish Guard. But for the moment, Oskar returns home with Jan Bronski to live in a slightly altered, more affectionate context while awaiting a new series of adventures on a different level.

Soon after the "Rostrum" and "Shopwindow" incidents, Oskar's mother dies and leaves Oskar in the care of the Truczinskis, a family of five including Maria–Oskar's future sister, lover, and mother. Maria's brother Herbert, a quiet man with the strength and appetite of a bull, abounds with energy, pugnacity, and courage. He is a veritable Heracles, who makes his livelihood maintaining order amid the violence of waterfront bars and cafes. Like Heracles he has stood a number of tests of physical strength and absolves himself on all counts until his last trial when he dies in a fiery passion equal to but a good deal more ludicrous than that of the Greek hero.

Oskar's initial fascination with Herbert stems from the complex configuration of scar tissue on his back (the result of knife wounds), about which Oskar speculates: "These are the parts of some girls and women, my own organ, the plaster of Paris watering can of the Christ child and that ring finger which the dog brought me just two years ago" (p. 205). As a pastime when Oskar touches one or the other of the scars, it becomes a signal for Herbert to relate the history of the origin of that particular wound; and so the scars chronicle a vast series of heroic acts born of blood and combat which, in the retelling, provide Oskar with some fascinating stories of titanic battles including one in which Truczinski kills a Lettish captain and falls into a state of remorse and gloom so deep that it robs him of all interest in life. He can do nothing but sleep and brood as Heracles did until the intervention of Minerva, who in her pity of him in his madness caused a deep sleep to fall upon him.

Reacting in a similar manner, Herbert Truczinski resolves not to return to his job at the waterfront but instead to become a caretaker for a mysterious wooden figure (then on exhibit in the maritime museum) that is steeped in legend of frightful destruction and disaster. This figure, Niobe, was originally carved as a prow figure for a large Florentine galleon, but from the time of her creation "this woman, the galleon figure brought only misfortune" (p. 216). The history of the people or even the cities and provinces that came into possession of this sumptuous, wooden, green naked figure have been marked by catastrophes such as murder, execution, suicide, drowning, fire, mutinies, and revolution. Nicknamed the Green Gal, Niobe terrifies and brings disaster to anyone near her or even to anyone vaguely cognizant of her presence.

In Greek mythology Niobe, the daughter of Tantalus, sustained the proud manner and the terrible misfortunes of an ill-fated family. Legend has it that Niobe had married Amphion, the king of Thebes, and gave him seven handsome sons and seven beautiful daughters of whom she was so proud that one day she even disparaged Leto, a minor goddess in the Greek Pantheon for having only two children, Apollo and Artemis. In retaliation, and at Leto's request, her children hunted down and killed all fourteen of Niobe's children, and, some say, her husband also. Heartbroken she ran away from her native land and finally persuaded Zeus to turn her into stone. In her misery, then, Niobe becomes immortalized according to legend as a crag of roughly human shape on Mount Sipylus in her last home in Asia Minor; and when seen from a distance, she seems to weep whenever the rays of the sun strike the wintercap of snow upon her peak. In another version of the story, "by Leto's contrivance Niobe's father fell incestuously in love with her and when she repulsed him, he burnt her children to death; her husband was then mangled by a wild boar, and she threw herself from a rock."[7] In any case the name in mythology refers to a woman whose very presence, it seems, leads to the destruction of all around her while she herself is petrified in stone, just as is Herbert's "Green Kitten."

The Niobe of *The Tin Drum* is carved out of wood but she has been treated with preservatives which render her indestructible. She has also been painted green, a color which conveys a balanced image of antithetical tendencies, for it is the color of vegetation and life on the one hand and of corpses or death on the other. The Niobe of mythology was also, it has been pointed out, productive and prolific as a life force, but at the same time she became a purveyor of death. It is not without significance that the Egyptians painted Osiris, their god both of vegetation and death, green. Extending the dichotomous significance of the color, Oskar and Herbert also find special attractiveness in her amber eyes as well as her naked figure. (The German word for amber is *Bernstein,* derived from *Brennstein,* meaning literally *burnstone.*) Indeed the amber eye of this green maiden becomes the center of a magic spell as it reflects the last golden rays of the setting sun (resembling the reflected sun on the snow-capped mountain which purportedly *is* the Greek Niobe turned to stone) that stream out to consume like fire the passions and powers of Herbert Truczinski.[8]

For a while Oskar and Herbert watch and wait and fear Niobe together; but concerned about the welfare of this child Oskar, the museum authorities forbid him to continue accompanying Herbert in his duties. Finally on a Wednesday morning (a day of misfortune in North Germany according to folk tradition, supposedly the day on which Lucifer was thrown out of heaven; compare Ash Wednesday, the reminder of "ashes to ashes," and human mortality), Herbert entered the fateful museum alone. And it is there, at the end of the day, that Oskar sees him again for the last time in the hands of an ignominious and absurd death. He has evidently attempted to rape the wooden maiden, Niobe, and in the process has torn loose a double-edged axe which embedded one edge of itself in the wooden figure and the other in Herbert's own chest so that he now hangs impaled, finding only death in his attempt to unite wood and flesh.

If union in the usual sense did not take place, then it did materialize in another way–by means of a sacrificial double axe. If not a purely sexual union, a union of violence and power and death does however occur. Herbert Truczinski may have been a giant of sorts, but he was not a god or divinity who could withstand the black powers from another realm. He had proven himself in combat over and over again in this world, but few are the heroes who can resist or overcome the woman figures that are temptresses or destroyers of life like Circe, the Gorgons, the Sirens, and Lorelei. It is also of significance to note (for our final task is to deal with Oskar and not Herbert Truczinski himself) that Truczinski's death occurs on the very first day that Oskar, claiming to be Herbert's "talisman and guardian angel" (p. 224), leaves his side. Herbert may have been stronger than most men, but he was not capable, as Oskar was, of dealing with forces of a supernatural order.

As for Niobe herself, Grass takes great pains to introduce her as a goddess of evil and witchcraft, "a bringer of destruction" who has left corpses strewn and cities ravaged in the wake of her travels. She is indestructible, immortal, timeless, frightening, bizarre in her proportions and color but yet sexually provocative. Oskar and Herbert spend a good deal of time studying and discussing her feminine charms, taunting and insulting her in the process. Herbert even picks up Oskar so that he can beat his drumsticks against her breast, and later, with a sensuously sadistic chuckle, Herbert drives a nail into her kneecap.[9] Attracted and yet terrified by Niobe, the two of them try to "make a game out of their fear of Niobe, to forget it, ignore it . . . and we might have succeeded if suddenly the afternoon sun had not fully struck her left amber eye and turned it into flames" (p. 224). The sun, first playing with the angels, flowers, and animals of the facade of the museum, finally enters the second-story room where the green galleon figure resides, "and illuminates an amber eye." Whether that symbolizes burning passion, the consuming magic of an evil eye, or solar union, is conjecture, although Herbert's immolation is certainly a reality, for he dangles from the axe that weds him in death to Niobe. "This Lady of the Double Axe must be the Mother Goddess herself, capable of appearing to her worshippers in various forms. . . . Deity, spiritual force, *mana* ['amber'?] call it by whatever name we will, was immanent in all things, animate or inanimate. All things, then, were upon occasion objects of death and respect, and they must be propitiated, otherwise no man knew how he could continue to live. The Lady, too, must be propitiated. The blood of the bull, shed for her, would cause her to descend from on high and enter the double axe, her alter ego."[10] These statements deal specifically with the divine consciousness of things, irreverence toward a goddess, the necessity of propitiation, the mysteries of blood sacrifice, or, in short, the concept of sacrificial death in mythology, the fundamental relationship of human sacrifice for symbolic union between the gods or goddesses and the hero.

Niobe's prowess is irresistibly erotic on the one hand and historically destructive on the other. She is considered dangerous by governing bodies and by individuals, for cities, states, and people have repeatedly paid for her presence in blood, and now again an erotic *hierosgamos* in death is performed. Oskar notices that Herbert and Niobe "are perfectly united up above" (p. 227) while below, "from his open trousers, stiff and without understanding," was proof of the incompatibility of "flesh and wood," of human instinct and divine powers, of a bull-like man and a terrible goddess. And though the whole episode at first appears merely ludicrous and absurd (Oskar checks his laughter on seeing Herbert hanging from Niobe), the reader, along with Oskar, is soon touched by the grotesque horror of this event that gains religious as well as cosmic proportions in the total scope of the novel. Oskar's last observation in the Niobe chapter focuses again on Herbert, hanging now like a lifeless member from a wooden statue (the tree of life and death?) and on his back, "the labyrinth of scars[11] which was to foreshadow, to anticipate, everything to come. . . . Like a blind man [Oskar] reads the script on that back." The cryptic messages of violence, sexual unfulfillment, sacrifice, and failure are in a way indications of the ultimate fate of the hero. And such incidents are common and even necessary for the epic hero who must at times become an observer in the arena of adventure and allow an alter ego, a double, a shadow to expose himself to forces that may destroy him. With Truczinski's departure a long series of deaths begins, each wrapped in an aura of mystery, each in communion with something beyond comprehension, and each reassuring as well as threatening for our hero, who views the mystery of death as a regrettable source of necessary liberation and retribution.

When the men whose fates are interwoven with the adventure of the gods and who, each in his own way larger than life size, are called to account for their actions, one encounters "what the Greeks called *nemesis:* again the agent or instrument of *nemesis* may be human vengeance, ghostly vengeance, divine vengeance, divine justice, accident, fate or the logic of events, but the essential thing is that *nemesis* happens."[12] Northrop Frye asserts here that *nemesis* must result from provoking the enmity of the god, certainly as Herbert Truczinski did by first taunting and then trying to violate Niobe. His death, therefore, simply reestablishes as a reality the power of death and destruction which Niobe has even over her most courageous victims, and Herbert provides the sacrificial blood that must flow to keep the reputation, awe, and horror of Niobe alive.

As a further example of the delicate balance of justice and *nemesis* established between men and the gods, Oskar begins drumming out a series of stories of death and destruction that begin with Niobe and surge out from her to inundate Danzig, Poland, and then all of Europe. "The woman [Niobe] did not die. She was sealed up and preserved in the cellar of the museum, allegedly to be restored. But you can't lock up misfortune in a cellar. It drains into the sewer pipes, leaks into the gas pipes, gets into every household with the gas, and no one who sets his soup kettle on the bluish flames suspects that disaster is bringing his food to a boil" (p. 229). Thus on the heels of the Niobe episode the specter of "Gasman" Hitler and the Third Reich falls over Danzig. A time of violence, harassment, political ambition, and callousness ensues. Small skirmishes and pitched battles are fought, prisoners executed, Danzig and most of Poland are annexed to Germany, and all the while Oskar is developing into manhood (though of miniature size) with the aid of Maria first and then of the earthy, overwhelming Frau Greff. Beyond that Oskar's story unexpectedly focuses on Frau Greff's husband, although "no friendship in spite of our familiarity ever developed between Oskar and Greff. Greff remained a stranger to me, arousing my interest at most but never my sympathy" (p. 370). It is hardly surprising that no real friendship does develop between Oskar and Greengrocer Greff, whose compulsive behavior, bereft of natural feelings, searching for operational balance, poses a frightening contrast to the passionate madness and death of Herbert Truczinski.

Although married to the huge, earthy, motherly, and overpowering woman whose sexuality Oskar compares to a whole orchestra, Greengrocer Greff is not tempted by her in the least, preferring as he does the company of young boys. In his short pants and agile frame he basks constantly in the reflection of his own muscular body and abstemious life as a heroic leader of boy scouts. At the outset troops of boys react admiringly to his handsome, heroic appearance, but as Greff gets older he sits, like Narcissus, (before and after bathing) next to a pool of water in the frozen Baltic Sea, reflecting and contemplating. When his favorites have fallen one after another in the war and he himself is no longer the handsome and heroic boy scout leader he was, he attracts no new admiration and with that his life purpose ends. He builds himself elaborate scales and machines (which function well but are usually out of balance); and finally, in resigned desperation, he constructs a complex scaffolding upon which he hangs himself with all the precision of a holy ritual.

So Greengrocer Greff executes himself and reconstructs in the nature of his death the circumstances of his life. That he *hangs* himself suggests the ideal of rejection of terrestrialness, of removal from the earth and anticipated immunity from its imperfections and its suffering. But though Greff seeks flight from the earth both figuratively and literally in death, he fails most ironically. The leitmotifs of potatoes, the figure four, wooden beams, vegetables and flowers, in addition to a slight miscalculation on his own weight, reveal his inability to escape the terrestrial powers. Even in Greff's attempt to balance off his own weight against a sack of potatoes, gravity prevails, his body slips down and his toes touch the ground. He does not transcend in death to some mystical isolation but sinks back to the earth. Four white pieces of paper, fragments of a police summons charging Greff with moral turpitude, indicate the disgraceful motivation for death; four lightbulbs and four whitewashed beams give off an intensive glow, and ironically, on the steps to the scaffolding Oskar sees a few asters, accompanied inappropriately by parsley stalks. "Apparently he had run out of flowers to strew on the steps for he had used most of the asters and also a few roses to wreath the four little pictures that hung on the four main beams of the scaffolding" (p. 377-78). The parsley stalks which Oskar refers to as inappropriate evidently recall for him the alternate meanings of the German word for stalk (*Stengel*, pistil of a flower; colloquial for the male organ), while parsley itself signifies productivity, success, and fertility.[13] The asters, on the other hand, do seem appropriate, connoting, as they do in Latin, stars, and suggesting perhaps the story of Asterius, the reigning king of Crete, who married Europa after Zeus had fathered three children with her. But Asterius's marriage with her remained as childless as Greff's, and their lack of normal sexual capacity was transmitted in turn to three adopted sons who feuded for the love of a young boy. Europa, Asterius's wife, also reminds one of Lina Greff in several respects. Europa received her pleasures by entertaining occasional lovers in her palace; and when discovered one day, she was driven from the kingdom. After a series of adventures she remarried and gave birth to Agamemnon, Menelaus, and Anaxibia, all of which indicates the great sexuality and fertility which was conspicuously lacking in her marriage to Asterius. Oskar becomes the occasional lover of Frau Greff, but her great adventure occurs during the occupation of Danzig when she is forced to submit to part of the Russian army, an experience that appears to be much to her liking.

The central concept which characterizes Greengrocer Greff's death is *balance*. The title of his chapter indicates the 165 pounds of his own body that he attempts to hang in balance against an equally heavy sack of potatoes. All is measured and weighed and offset by equal proportions. "Only now did Oskar comprehend the trouble that Greff had taken. The frame, the setting in which Greff was hanging, was selected in all extravagance. The Greengrocer had searched out an appropriate form of death, a well-balanced death. He who in his lifetime had had difficulties and embarrassing correspondence with the officials of the Bureau of Weights and Measures, he whose scales and weights had been confiscated several times, he who had had to pay fines for the inaccurate weighing of fruit and vegetables, had weighed himself to the last ounce with potatoes" (p. 376). Now it is interesting to note again that "the righting of the balance is what Greeks called *nemesis*,"[14] because the whole purpose of Greff's sacrifice of self is to establish and preserve in death what he could not attain in life. His death is in several respects a sacrifice to justice, an attempt to set the scales right again, to cancel out sexual deviation and unfulfilled ideals. Four pictures hanging on the four beams of the scaffolding–Baden-

Powell, founder of the boy scouts; St. George, victor over the vile and repulsive dragon; Michelangelo's David; and Horst Donath, a handsome young lad and the first object of Greff's love—reveal the essence of the dreams that Greff has substituted for a healthy and natural relationship to life. As a young man he was dedicated to his dreams; but once they vanished, only sacrificial death, dedicated to an idealized balance of justice, remained. And to that end he measures that hulk which was so prized as his body against a sack of potatoes, the aegis of the Earth Mother, that suspends Greff in air just as Herbert Truczinski was suspended by another symbol of sexuality and destruction, Niobe.[15]

Both Truczinski and Greff stand out by virtue of the fact that their stories are quite independent from the adventures of the hero. Each has his moment, sharing the spotlight with no one; and having created a world apart in which to live, each plays out his role on a separate stage, so to speak, on which the nature of death comes to reflect the type of life one has led. Both are closely observed, revered in some respects and feared in others as demigods might be; but where Oskar has a deep and rare sense of affection for Herbert, he maintains a feeling of cold detachment in relating the details of Greff's suffering and suicide. Oskar views Herbert's death at the bosom of Niobe with a feeling of admiration, humor, and, later, with regret; but Greff is dispatched impersonally in a pathetic and mechanistic ritual of his own invention. The two, therefore, posit antithetical avenues into the single realm of death, revealing in their *ars moriendi* the different quality of two lives that are subsumed in the uniting power of death.

Also running through the elaborate design of this chapter is the story of Old Heiland (literally savior in German), whose role as a former god has become pathetic in our time. A lamentable, sympathetic but misplaced person who spends his energy straightening, that is "saving" nails (that were formerly used to crucify him!), Heiland appears to be one of the many lesser gods relegated to impotence in the brutal struggles of the modern era. A number of the older, as well as vital, young heroes are sacrificed during the course of events in the first half of this novel, but the Old Heiland, who is in essence so harmless and even transparent in these times, lingers on and on only to be left behind and forgotten. Less prudent is the tender, profligate drunkard and lover of cats, the trumpeter

Meyn who "played just too beautifully for words." Unfortunately he decides to rehabilitate himself and join the Mounted SA, thereby sacrificing his inspired artistry, his sensitivity, and his love for cats. In order to join the Brown Shirts, he reorganizes his life and kills his four cats in the process. But he is reported to the SPCA and expelled from the SA, ironically even after having demonstrated "conspicuous bravery on the night of November 8, the Crystal Night" when Jewish stores were demolished and synagogues burned down. One of the stores also happened to be that of Sigismund Markus, the friendly toy merchant and admirer of Oskar's mother. Thus, in the less dramatic but equally inexorable fashion of lesser epic personages, he is ravaged by the growing forces of war and inhumanity; and subsequently the tender merchant of tin drums and toy soldiers, Sigismund, may be vaguely compared in the present catastrophe with his namesake, the Siegfried of German mythology, whose death was a signal for the collapse of Valhalla and for the passing away of the old gods.

Though these sacrifices of blood and individualism seem to hold only moderate meaning for Oskar, they certainly lend drama and significance to the sequence of events which they embrace: the brutal destruction of Poland, the Polish post office, and Oskar's personal discovery of love and sexual passion, each of which becomes a kind of sacrifice at the altar of nature. Just as Oskar is soon to be initiated into the realms of sexuality, divine powers, and inescapable destiny, he is also exposed by history and private circumstance to the horrors and comedy of death.[16] Whereas the Niobe chapter opened the doors for great suffering, slaughter, and destruction, the chapter following, "Faith, Hope, Love," one not entirely devoid of moralizing on Grass's part, tells the poignant and moving stories of good, of gifted, and of humane men who are ravaged by the rising forces of politics and history. But instead of describing the early stages of the disintegration of Oskar's world in a callous and realistic manner, Grass chooses to narrate this chapter that concludes Book 1 in the form of a fairy tale, beginning with "once upon a time" and ending with recurring refrains of a folksong or ballad. The framework of childlike irony here is certainly an effective device for a chapter that sounds for the most part incredibly barbarian and focuses squarely on the suffering and dehumanization caused by the monstrosities of history.

Ambitions and frustrations collide with political events in tragic and fantastic encounters that become ludicrous double talk when viewed in the light of a human reality: "An entire credulous nation believed there is faith for you in Santa Claus [Hitler], but Santa Claus was really the Gasman." The incidents that follow, all occurring under a banner of "Faith, Hope, and Love" (p. 239), range from the events of the Crystal Night to the episode of a once-lonely musician by the name of Meyn. So when Markus, the Jewish toy merchant, and Meyn, the ill-fated trumpeter and potential Nazi are both done in by a single brutal force, there is little left for Oskar to do but resign himself to the pleasant memory that "there was once upon a time a toy merchant whose name was Markus, and he took all the toys away with him out of this world. There was once a musician whose name was Meyn and if he hasn't died he is still alive and once again playing the trumpet too beautiful for words" (p. 240).

It is here, in the simplest language possible, that Grass also condemns with all bitterness the vicious hypocrisy of bombastic rhetoric and political language that produce hollow words and empty slogans "like sausages" to be swallowed without real satisfaction. He subsequently develops a string of puns that unravel as abstract and hollow words of morality much in the way they came from "the same butchers who filled dictionaries and sausage casings with language and sausage; there is no Paul, the man's name was Saul and he was a Saul [sow!] and as Saul he told the people of Corinth something about the priceless sausages he called faith, hope, and love, which he advertised as easily digestible and which to this very day in the forever changing form of Saul he palms off on mankind" (p. 239). Then Grass counterpoises real experiences of individual concern as a foil to the canned language and pompous abstract morality. He talks about the Jewish merchant who brings toys to children and the heartrending destiny of an inspired trumpeter who is driven to slaughter his four cats. The Nazis, political men blinded by their own ideology like the tyrants and mindless despoilers of old, arrive to vanquish beautiful dreams, to destroy artistic endeavors and simple human beings, demolish a sacred city, a revered and sentimental nation, the residence of Oskar Matzerath and the holy birthplace of his gods.

Whereas Book 1 describes Oskar's birth, development, and

initiation into society, Book 2 covers the war years and Oskar's trials as a warrior, lover, performer, a leader of "apostles," a conversation partner with Christ at one time and with Satan at another, an aspiring divinity, and a murderer who himself suffers symbolic burial, death, revival, and a journey to the West. His is a road strewn with corpses, destroyed idols, ruined cities, and fallen nations; but rather than interfering with the special destiny of the hero, these cataclysms open possibilities for new growth and adventure.

# FIVE *From Timeless Time to the Age of Iron*

Mythopoets tend to look back with longing upon some golden age which, formerly beyond time and in harmony with the gods, has since become fragmented, profane, and historical. *Illo tempore,* in that *Urzeit,* all events were still essentially sacred experiences reflecting in human action the light of a divine will.[1] Both Hesiod and Ovid have elaborated on the four ages of man, but they are not alone insofar as every mythology dealing with the origins of man presupposes a degeneration of harmony and happiness with the historical evolution of man. Initially, in the Golden Age, all life on earth enjoyed an eternal springtime and neither strife nor toil was necessary. In the Age of Silver the seasons were created and labor was essential to sustain life, but this was nevertheless still an age of courage and greatness among men, as shown, perhaps, by Oskar's grandparents in their human aspects. About the time Oskar is born a loosely defined Age of Bronze commences in which men learn to use arms, do battle with monsters, yet demonstrate heroism. The last period, the Age of Iron, was an era of crime and dishonor, a time when the gifts of the gods were misused and mankind sank into utter degradation. Whole civilizations were destroyed and plundered. Material wealth and human greed determined the measure of success, and conditions prevailed not unlike those which Oskar comes to experience after his trip to the West and his residence in postwar Germany.

Such stages of evolution are neither clearly defined nor separated, but one recognizes the essentials of their presence in *The Tin Drum* nevertheless. At the end of Book 1 profane history is slowly on the move. Politics have penetrated and begun to loosen the fabric of Oskar's timeless world as the story is told of the destruction of a world which Oskar experienced in *illo tempore*. Book 2 begins with a chapter that significantly announces the coming age of iron, "Scrap Metal," and ends with detailed descriptions of the history of Danzig, Oskar's illness (that coincides with the fall of the city) and his forced departure from the East. However, more than a country is lost for Oskar. Gone is the whole morning land of the East, the place of Oskar's birth, the mythic land of sacred thresholds and early adventures that shaped his life. Gone also, by the time Book 2 ends, are all those imposing and majestic figures that peopled Oskar's special world; and gone is Oskar's grandmother who remains in the East, in those mysterious regions "precisely determined by means of a wealth of long-vanished local place-names,"[2] yet echoing throughout the book like a ceremonial chant.

Change is inevitable, and Grass does not neglect the transition from sacred cosmogenesis to profane history. He examines at the outset "*a primordial event that took place in illo tempore,* the recital of what the gods or the semidivine beings did at the beginning of time. To tell a myth is to proclaim what happened *ab origine.* Once told, that is, revealed, the myth becomes apodictic truth; it establishes a truth that is absolute."[3] Then, subsequently, the early mythology of man and gods develops to reveal the stages of falling away from the sacred primordial realities onward into an historical and political Age of Iron in which materialism, fragmentation, and desanctification dominate the behavior and actions of mankind.

Although politico-historical events eventually begin to affect the course of the hero's travels, neither they nor social criticism ever become a central concern for Oskar. If anything they merely provide Oskar with new and interesting experiences. Even the pathetic destruction of the Polish post office, the central symbol of an old and beautiful tradition, becomes merely another threshold of experience for Oskar. His commitment to the realm of myth and mystery remains primary; and where profane history conflicts with his sacred mission, Oskar is quick to point out its incidental features, as, for example, when he hides his drum in a large letter basket in the post office.

> Already I regretted having made my drum at home in one of those movable laundry baskets full of undeliverable mail. Would the blood of these torn up and punctured postmen and postal clerks not seep through ten or twenty layers of paper and give my drum a color it had until now known only as a coat of enamel? What had my drum in common with the

> blood of Poland! Let them color their files and blotting paper with that vital juice! Let them pour blue out of their inkwells and fill them up again with red! Let them dye their handkerchiefs and white, starched shirts half-red and use them as Polish flags! After all, they were concerned with Poland and not with my drum! If they insisted that Poland, though lost, must be lost in white and red, was that any reason why my drum, suspect already by the fresh paint job should be lost too. (p. 264)

Though Oskar's and certainly Grass's sympathies lie with the political concept of Poland, they reject with a touch of admiration its temporal struggles, romantic sentimentality, and foolish nationalism. The Poles "were always kissing ladies' hands and never noticed until it was too late that what they were not kissing was a lady's languid fingers but rather the unrouged muzzle of a field howitzer" (pp. 272–73). We have already pointed out Oskar's opposition to mass rallies, fixed ideologies, and organizations in general, a point that reputable critics have seen fit to confirm.[4] Oskar's stand here has extended significance just as the subsequent "struggles, conflicts, and wars for the most part have a *ritual* cause and function."[5] Contrary to the Trojan War that had heroes and gods lining up on both sides, World War II at first appears to be a brutal and desecrating slaughter of short-sighted and foolish men. But the war and the struggle of clumsy and blundering patriots lends only superficial clarification to the battle of the Polish post office! What primarily deserves scrutiny here, in contrast to the dubious heroism of soldiers, is Oskar's experience in what becomes for him a grotesque journey to the Land of the Dead. Only those patterns of action performed as ritual have significance for Oskar, who, like Mircea Eliade, realizes that "the only profane activities are those which have no mythical meaning, that is, which lack exemplary models."[6]

The chapter "Scrap Metal" begins with a lengthy section describing Oskar's reminiscences and remorse at the passing of a golden and venerable age, but soon the action rises again and draws Oskar into a new and unusual series of adventures that covers the trip to the post office, the events that occur there, and his subsequent meeting with Leo Schugger. It seems that Oskar's drum is in desperate need of repair, and so he decides that his godfather, Jan Bronski, should take him and his drum to the janitor at the post office, Kobyella, who certainly would be able to put it in usable condition again. Jan, with strangely mixed emotions, agrees; but on the streetcar he sweats profusely, prepares to get off at each approaching stop, stares blankly into space, and smokes excessively until Oskar finally realizes the cause of his frantic condition. Jan, as a postal official, is supposed to help defend the post office from attack by the SS Home Guard; and he would have avoided that responsibility had it not been for Oskar and his drum compelling him to return to the city. The situation remotely suggests Peter's attempted escape from Rome when he encounters along the way a vision of Christ who exhorts him to return and be crucified. Oskar, too, brings Jan back to the post office for ultimate execution. It all seems natural and necessary enough to Oskar until the two of them arrive at the building which is soon to become the battleground for a life and death struggle between the inept Polish clerks and the clumsy German nationalists. As Oskar and Jan approach the building, they find a cordon of SS men posted there, who like Cerberus, the many-headed watchdog of Tartarus, allow men to enter the land of the dead but none to leave.

Once inside the post office building, escape seems impossible. The entrances are barricaded with furniture and sandbags, light is scarce, some rooms windowless, all reminding one of Northrop Frye's description of "the temple or One Building of the apocalypse, [where] we have the prison or dungeon, the sealed furnace of heat without light, like the City of Dis in Dante. Here too are the sinister counterparts of geometrical images: the sinister spiral (the maelstrom, whirlpool, or Charybdis), the sinister cross, and the sinister circle . . . the serpent, conventionally a demonic animal, gives us the uroborous, or serpent with its tail in its mouth."[7] The sinister uroborous that feeds upon death has already surrounded the ill-fated building in the form of a cordon of SS men; and once Jan Bronski enters that circle, his fate and fortune are sealed. Only three or four people will escape from it: Oskar among them, because he is a trickster and a Proteus who can disguise his form, and Viktor Weluhn, since he is half-blind and more a symbol of Poland's spirit than a man in his own right.

Oskar sleeps that night on "a mountain of mail gravid with news, a mountain which might have been the world," only to be awakened by gunfire that sounded similar to "the storm that accompanied my birth" (p. 259). Departing now, having rested on a "mountain," if only metaphorically, Oskar begins to wander through the dark and endless halls of the huge postal building, alone and in mortal danger, searching for Kobyella who, he hopes, will fix his drum. Moving cautiously past shattered windows, bursting shells, dead and dying men, clouds of plaster and piles of rubble, Oskar finally makes his way up the stairway to the third floor. In no uncertain terms we have, as Frye explains the archetypal situation in general, "the labyrinth of maze, the image of lost direction, often with a monster at its heart like the Minotaur,"[8] but the monster at the end of this maze turns out to be unique among the incongruities of literary annals as Oskar reaches his journey's end in a nursery! Lying there, among dolls, games, and tin soldiers, are both Jan Bronski and Kobyella, the latter firing his rifle at the enemy and the former curled up with fear in a catatonic state. There too an exploding shell that mortally wounds Kobyella lifts a new tin drum off of a high shelf and miraculously drops it into Oskar's lap. At the same time the nursery itself is demolished and along with it a good portion of Oskar's infantile ego. The fact that he receives a new drum in the nursery gives fulfillment to his purpose for going there, but it also demonstrates one ludicrous contrast among many that prevail throughout this sequence in which war is placed in a nursery to show by analogy how gallant games with tin soldiers become the game of frightened men playing with destruction. Meanwhile Jan Bronski, paralyzed with fright on the floor, whimpering and helpless, signals a dramatic reversal of roles between Oskar and himself. As Jan reverts in trauma to a pattern of infantile behavior, Oskar becomes a protective, reassuring, and courageous father figure.

The changing relationship develops dramatically in the stuffy windowless storeroom where Oskar spent his first night sleeping in one of the many mail baskets that now contain the bodies of the dead and dying defenders. The room is lit only by flickering tallow candles that add unreality to a place whose eeriness is already dramatized by a game of cards which Oskar initiates between himself, Jan, and Kobyella, who is in the last convulsive throes of death. Kobyella keeps bleeding, moaning, fainting, and occasionally collapsing on the card table; but Oskar just props him up again with a pair of suspenders and the game continues. The purpose of the game is to distract Jan from his own fears, an almost impossible task with shells exploding, the building shaking, and more bodies arriving. Terrified by fear of injury or death, Jan Bronski resorts to psychological withdrawal and escapes to earlier periods of life. Oskar must "warm him with his body," reassure him, and finally absorb his attention in a game of Skat. "When," as Oskar observes, "for the first time I lent my voice to adult speech and bid 'Eighteen,' " Jan was diverted and momentarily forgot his fears. Here, for the first time, Oskar drops his infantile role and leaves the containment of his own self-consciousness to engage adults in one of their own games. The experience is unique for him, for he is concerned now with someone else, intent on helping his alleged father overcome a fear of death. "It was I . . . who restored light to the world, lit a comforting Regatta for Jan, and pierced the darkness with flame upon flame," sticking two candles on the new drum. In that light "we three looked fantastic. Hitting us from below, the candlelight gave us the look of all-powerful wizards" (pp. 283-84). But then when Jan is dealt a "beautiful, sure-thing grand hand," it is still death that prevails, for Kobyella chooses that moment to collapse dramatically across the table, pulling the mail cart to which he is firmly secured and a flood of letters with him. Jan becomes desperate, then gains control, collects his cards, wipes off the blood and builds himself a card house of "rare and delicate beauty." In his preoccupation he is "enabled to forget the biting smoke and stench that crept, slowly and in coils, through the cracks in the door of the letter office making it seem as though the little room with the card house in it were directly door to door with hell" (p. 287).

Here, especially at the gates of hell, in the Orcus of death, Oskar blossoms and demonstrates the strength and determination which he possesses, while Jan Bronski, one of his early ethereal gods, "presents a picture of unmitigated helplessness and destitution. Such a figure is pathetic, and pathos, though it seems a gentler and more relaxed mood than tragedy, is even more terrifying. Its basis is the exclusion of an individual from a group, hence it attacks the deepest fear in ourselves that we possess–a fear much deeper than the relatively cosy and sociable bogey of hell."[9] The cozy and yet grotesque game of cards blocks out Jan's tragic lack of loyalty and courage by means of black humor and pathos. The most moving element in this scenario is not the defeat of the Poles but rather the helplessness and downfall of Jan, who is shot at by the enemy and vilified, beaten, and rejected by his Polish comrades. Finally all his loneliness and pathos is built into his "fragile house of cards." It is a delicate, sensitive, nostalgic house that he builds with the seven of spades and the queen of clubs, Jan's death card and the queen of Dis, as the foundation, and the queen of hearts (Agnes's card) and the king of hearts (his own card in life as first consort) at the pinnacle of the structure. Jan experiences only that one instant of bliss, a lonely, beautiful, and tragic moment; for at that instant the door is flung open by the invaders and Jan's house of cards is destroyed by the brutal harbingers of a new age, men whose "medium was concrete. They build for eternity." A new and callous age of iron and concrete is upon them, and from among the ranks of the old Bronski deities only Oskar, along with his grandmother and Maria, are able to survive and prevail.

Although Oskar has reached a new level of maturity and acquired a new drum at the Polish post office, he willingly deserts its defenders and his godfather (whom he delivered into the hands of death in the first place). In one respect Oskar fulfills an heroic obligation in this circle of hell, but in another he obliterates his triumph with trickery by reassuming his juvenile role and being driven home in grand style in an official car of the SS Home Guard. However, this double-dealing role of the hero is not uncommon in mythology: Theseus deserts Ariadne; Jason, Medea; Hercules slaughters his family; and Odysseus plays the undignified madman to avoid the obligation of going to war. In the mythological world it seems that trickery and cunning are completely compatible with heroism and nobility. Indeed, part of the grandeur of anthropocentric classical literature lies in the alternatives to the apparent moral imperatives. As occasion demands, the hero may become a willing victim like Achilles, Hector, and Amphiaraus; or one could evade catastrophe by cunning and subterfuge as Odysseus and then Trophonios did in his later fable. Often both tendencies were embodied in the same hero, and the question of which prevailed depended for the most part on the nature of the challenge and the mythic function of the hero.

For Oskar, at his present stage of development, self-preservation is of greater importance than moral principle, just as in classical thought continued life was certainly considered more desirable than a pointless and premature death among the shades and shadows. If Oskar engages now and then in deceitfulness and deception, he does so by authority of that same amoral behavior modeled by his deified parents and ancestors. If one must die in battle, that may be accepted; but it would be absurd to die uselessly for an abstract principle (such as a romanticized concept of the Polish post office), if one could escape by using one's wits. Still Oskar is not completely without conscience: "Even today, because I am occasionally ashamed of this disgusting behavior of mine, I say to myself: Jan didn't notice for he was preoccupied with his cards and . . . had gone off to the eternal realm of card houses and resided in a house where one may believe in happiness" (p. 291). So Jan, as Oskar rationalizes, was in fact not painfully executed but instead translated into a kind of special Valhalla for romantic lovers and Skat players.

In summing up the significance of these incidents, and assuming a certain consistency in Grass's mythological intuition, we see that Oskar experiences the extremes of chaos as his sacred world of the East, represented by the post office, is destroyed. We accept the fact, as Oskar does, that with the fall of the office, the *imago mundi* of the sacred idea of Poland for which Joseph Koljaiczek had also fought two generations back, is destroyed and that the invasion of Poland that follows is merely a mechanical anticlimax. Although the etymological path to the inner meaning of mythic thinking sometimes disturbs the bounds of credulity, we remind the reader of Eliade's assertion that in religious thought "a central post . . . is assimilated to the *axis mundi, i.e.,* to the cosmic pillar or the world tree, which . . . connects earth with heaven. . . . *cosmic symbolism* is found in the very structure of the habitation. . . .the tent pole or the central post of the house is assimilated to the Pillars of the World and is so named. This central pole or post has an important ritual role; the sacrifices in honor of the celestial Supreme Being are performed at the foot of it."[10] Accordingly the sacrifice is made now at the Polish post, that spiritual center of national communication where the last patriotic defenders of the Polish nation and ideal are slaughtered. Thus neither we nor Oskar experience merely the demise of some ineffectual and short-sighted patriots but rather the ritualistic destruction of a sacred institution by the multi-headed Cerberus, the metaphorical dragon, the archenemy of a sacred land that has returned in ruthless brutality to crush a small band of clumsy but well-meaning defenders of a noble ideal.

Meanwhile, in the bowels of the post office and in the midst of this battle between a sacred ideal and a primordial monster at the gates of Hades, Oskar experiences an inner transformation, gaining knowledge of how to act in the teeth of crisis. He is moved back through time to a nursery where he miraculously receives a new tin drum. There he observes the sustaining infantile bond between the fantasy of play (that is, tin soldiers, dolls, rocking horses, etc.) and the actions of men (that is, warfare and destruction, families and children, Polish cavalry, etc.). He also faces up to the challenges of the moment, to the horror of death, the suffering of men, and becomes a source of consolation to his blue-eyed "sky" father during his last moments on earth.

The observation which Susanne Langer makes about the cunning of culture heroes in general fits Oskar equally well: "Despite his greatness he slips back frequently into his role of folktale hero, and plays the trickster, outwitting human enemies, local ghosts, or even a venerable ancestor"[11] and so too Oskar eludes the monster of Nazidom that devours Jan and his fellow Poles. The hero-trickster in mythology is often unfairly cunning and in possession of a special disguise or trick with which he may save himself from harm. With the escape of the hero at least some semblance of hope is preserved, even where all else has been lost or destroyed. Oskar uses his size again and again to dupe others, but, as already mentioned, he is hardly dishonorable in the usual sense of the word. As Paul Radin claims of the trickster in general: "He knows neither good nor evil, yet he is responsible for both. He possesses no values, moral or social, is at the mercy of his passions and appetites, yet through his actions all values come into being."[12] This role is also retained in his next adventure, where he does in fact become an official amusing trickster on Bebra's stage. During his ensuing travels with Bebra his gifts, as he well realizes, are exploited and corrupted for the sake of entertainment, but Oskar is willing to go along with that for purposes of travel now and of further exploration.

There is a sequel, however, to the fall of the Polish post office that moves the adventure totally into the realm of the mysteries of transitions and death. Shortly after Oskar's hospitalization, a necessary cure for the episode at the post office, he is approached one evening by Leo Schugger, a former and bizarre seminarist who haunts funerals and cemeteries in a benign way. Even his name is foreboding, suggesting *Schuggels* (North German for "scarecrow").

He frightens Oskar with his long, gaunt figure, his crow costume, his coat of black with long and flowing tails, his clawlike fingers and hands covered with yellowish, skinlike gloves, all poised there like an ominous bird while "the spittle flowed from Leo Schugger's mouth and hung down in threads" (p. 302). Though his image resembles that of a vulture, he is a concerned, friendly, solicitous creature who spiritually feels reassured and content in his proximity to death. Grotesque in appearance and possessing the ability to sense when death approaches and where the dead are buried, he also seems to incorporate the contradictory balm of death with its promise of peace and fulfillment.

Leo serves a double role here—as a message bearer and psychopompus, a conductor of souls to the land of the dead. His message is never spoken directly but whistled in avian tones through an empty cartridge case which once housed the pellet that ended the life of Jan Bronski. Tooting on the casing and running on ahead, occasionally hanging the cartridge case by suction from his lower lip like a strange beak, Leo coaxes Oskar onward along a path dark and noisy with sirens and foghorns. Before the psychopompus or shaman, Leo Schugger, the intermediary between the world of men and the realm of death, can lead Oskar further into that mystic penumbral sphere, Oskar too must be transformed. Leo "following a sudden inspiration, flailed wildly with his arms, removed his long-tailed coat, and threw the heavy cloth that smelled of moist earth over my head and shoulders. . . . As soon as Leo saw Oskar staggering along in the coat, he burst out in a laughter that ended in the manner of a raven crowing and, like a raven, he flapped his wings. I must really have looked like a grotesque bird, if not a raven then a crow, especially with those coat-tails dragging behind me wiping up the asphalt highway like a train" (p. 300). Oskar, who himself will later become a shaman of sorts for others, assumes the costume of mysterious flight necessary to penetrate a forbidden realm. Like the shamans of the North, he "is clothed for the adventure in a magical costume representing a bird or reindeer, a shadow principle of the shaman himself, the shape of his soul. His drum is his animal—his eagle, reindeer, or horse; he is said to fly or ride on it. The stick he carries is another of his aids."[13] The purpose of such a journey is sometimes to cure the sick but more often to obtain some special information unknown or lost to the world of men.

> The ravens, the birds of Odin, are closely connected with battle and the devouring of the slain, . . . but the ravens have names of a different kind:
>
> *Huginn* and *Muninn,* Thought and Memory,
> fly over the world each day.
> I fear for Thought, lest he come not back,
> but I fear yet more for Memory.
>
> The birds here are symbols of the mind of the seer or shaman, sent out over vast distances.[14]

It is the knowledge of the sacred place of Jan Bronski's death and burial that Leo seeks to impart to Oskar, a spot that is marked by Jan's fateful card of death, the seven of spades. This information is important because "for some peoples, only ritual burial confirms death; he who is not buried according to custom is not dead."[15]

Having accompanied the shaman to that sacred spot and back again, Oskar must now communicate his knowledge of Jan's death to the clan mother. A few days later he goes to visit his grandmother, Anna Koljaiczek-Bronski, at the marketplace. He approaches her as a child, walking backward like a crab to the place where his grandmother is sitting, gives her Jan's death card, and shows her the golden buttons on his sailor's suit. His real wish, however, is to move backward in time "like the crab," regressing to childhood so that he may reenter the warm security beneath her skirts. Instead he makes the mistake of showing her his gold button, the sun symbol which he now bears proudly as the sun-deity principle for having demonstrated in battle the courage and maturity of the developing hero. And the sailor suit? An indication that he, too, like Odysseus and Aeneas, has embarked upon a long voyage of mythic adventure.

At the behest of another of Oskar's *male* teachers or guides—certainly his most important one, Bebra—Oskar is induced to leave Poland for his next adventure and travel to the West. We recall that Oskar's first meeting with Bebra, a musical clown and a leader of a troop of dwarfs, a wizard of sorts with great knowledge about "small people," constituted a major event in Oskar's life. Bebra, an aristocrat and royal leader of a group of Lilliputians, older and more experienced than Oskar in the world of transforming myths, was immediately recognized by Oskar as his new master or spiritual father. At their first meeting, when Oskar was only nine and a half years old, Bebra warned Oskar that the time of military tyranny was coming and that many grandstands and podiums would be built to glorify an inflexible ideology and preach the destruction of little people, so Oskar must always be sure to be on or under the stage and never out in front with the audience. Then, to seal the bond of kinship between them, Bebra gave Oskar a ritual kiss of acceptance and brotherhood that welcomes him into the cult of small people. With that Bebra drifted off in one direction and Oskar in another.

Since that time, however, Oskar has pursued his own special kind of primary education and traveled his own particular road to adventure. After his experiences under the grandstands, in doorways, with shopwindows, at funerals, cemeteries, and at the Polish post office, Oskar discovers sexual love with Maria and with Frau Greff, and he observes the departure of old friends like Truczinski and Greengrocer Greff to another world. After the death of Greff, but before meeting Bebra for the second time, Oskar embarks on a long harangue about history and the political events of the day. In keeping with the transitional quality of Book 2, he also discerns a displacement of values in the remote world of political and historical events; but by and large he views them as compulsive exercises that carry little significance for a person of special destiny like himself. Then, once again, Bebra arrives in Danzig, this time encouraging Oskar to join his theatrical group and come onto the stage among the performers rather than remain hidden in the background. Thus Bebra succeeds in removing Oskar from the relatively secure environs of Danzig and inducing him to explore the expanding empire of the Third Reich. So Bebra, here as on other occasions, entices Oskar over a new threshold, out of one world or state of mind and into another of different proportions.

Oskar refers to the production which he is invited to join as Bebra's "Miracle Play," recalling, of course, the miracle plays of the Middle Ages that portrayed events from the life of Christ and of the saints. But the acrobatic stunts, the glass-shattering, the mind-reading and prophesying which occur during the show cannot be considered serious miracles of a religious order. They are presented only for the sake of amusement, yet within a longer sequence of events they do prepare the way for the more genuine series of miracles that will follow after Oskar returns home from this journey. These performances offer sham miracles on stage and teach Oskar with time to distinguish between the artificial and the real thing.

Later, for example, when Oskar is a musical performer in the West, he will experience and recognize the false gimmickry of clarification in the Onion Cellar before embarking on his own mission to restore vitality and life to people that have become calcified in nature.

Now, after insisting like some figure of a fairy tale that "a good and wise nature [voice of a bird he hears] advises me, revered master [Bebra] to accept your suggestion" (p. 384), Oskar prepares for his trip west, to France, for the purpose of entertaining the German troops, but not before he literally holds a dialogue with "his gods Dionysus and Apollo." It is only fitting that one should consult the gods before embarking upon a long and dangerous voyage, one that in an oblique fashion duplicates some of the adventures of Odysseus. Both Oskar and Odysseus travel to the distant West, pass the destructive wall of Scylla, and sail safely by the treacherous currents of Charybdis. Along the way Oskar finds his Circe in the form of Roswitha, and listens with her to the sirens as they make love underground during an air attack. They dine on exotic foods and live in the comforts which as the modern day lotus entice men away from their human purposes and into the soporific apathy of bourgeois comfort. They suffer bombardment by the Laestrygones of modern warfare, and finally even after the crew of players has dissolved, Oskar makes his way back to Danzig only to discover that he "was no Odysseus because when he returned home he found everything the same" (p. 415). Yet Oskar continues to establish parallels by denying that Maria was no Penelope, Roswitha was no intoxicating Circe, and his presumptive son Kurt was no Telemachus. But Oskar's disclaimers only succeed again in focusing the reader's attention on that sphere of mythic thought where the author, by virtue of his classical allusions, literally places it.

Once he embarks upon his journey with the miracle troupe, Oskar becomes more concerned with his relationship to Roswitha than with his success as a performer or his role as a hero. Taking her as his recognized but unofficial wife, while the father figure Bebra looks on with nodding approval, Oskar, like Aeneas in Carthage, spends a pleasant and satisfying year with his Dido, who, when the time comes for him to depart, also goes up in smoke. Both Dido and Roswitha die from inconsideration on the part of the hero, one consumed in a funeral pyre and the other blown up by an enemy shell in the land of the bunkers and pillboxes.

The pillboxes on the Atlantic seaboard that hold a strange fascination for Oskar also achieve a mythic dimension by assuming the form of flattened turtles lying between sand dunes. Their observation portals and gun orifices resemble a tortoise face looking out onto the ebb and flow of the sea. And it is on top of the concrete shell of such a tortoise that an incongruous pageant and feast takes place. The bunker, as Grass develops it symbolically, is not merely an accidental stage for the highly symbolic ritual which Roswitha performs as high priestess; it is also a very special monument or temple dedicated to the goddess of death and destruction. Its name, Dora Seven, a short form of Theodora or Dorothea (*theos* God + *doron* gift), suggests at once the feminine and sacred conception it must have had in the minds of its designers. Grass calls its observation portals *Sehschlitze,* literally "seeing slits," again suggestive of a turtle's eyes. Of these concrete turtlelike shells the men of the German army say: "In concrete. That's all we have faith in, and nothing more" (p. 398). In keeping with the whole militaristic and defensive purposes of these structures, we also find that the turtle, where it is found in mythologies, carries the sense "of material existence and not of any aspect of transcendence. . . . In short, then, it would stand for turgidity, involution, obscurity, slowness, stagnation and highly concentrated materialism, etc."[16]

The entrances to these bunkers are decorated with seashell mosaics in intertwined forms resembling pretzels, just as a labyrinth. Historically a monster is usually pictured within the labyrinth; sometimes he seems to be one with it, to be himself the labyrinth. Along with the sign of the labyrinth we also have the proud confession by the German soldier Lankes (who is eventually identified as the monster of the labyrinth) that the men are rather superstitious and "have cemented a live puppy into each pillbox," a blood sacrifice to the goddess of death and destruction. The ritual of dog sacrifices immediately brings Hecate to mind, the terrifying chthonic Greek goddess of night, superstition, and death. She appears in most illustrations with snakes wrapped about her in a labyrinthine fashion and is constantly accompanied by her howling hounds that feed on the corpses of the dead. However, by carrying out blood sacrifices and rituals that are pleasing to Hecate, one may placate her enough so that she will withdraw and restrain her hounds and hunger for a while.[17] However, the dog sacrifice is only the beginning of a series of blood sacrifices (following them are the seven innocent nuns, a good part of the German and Allied invasion armies, and Roswitha herself) that feed the hunger of Hecate: "This Terrible Mother is the hungry earth, which devours its own children and fattens on their corpses."[18]

On a separate level these pillboxes also reflect the whole defensive and materially ponderous style of life that is coming to dominate the Western world. Oskar not only perceives in these structures mythological and sacred significance but also a profane effort to combat insecurity, ennui, discomfort, and death through the everlasting medium of concrete; and he also discerns here the beginnings of "the present apotheosis of bourgeois comfort" which in every respect will indeed be "barbaric, mystical, and bored." The connection between military life and bourgeois materialism is also apparent to Oskar, who has always been prepared to divest pedestrian heroism of its false mystique. The refrain of the poem, "On the Atlantic Wall," in which Oskar writes of the parochial activity, emphasizes the constrained, orderly, materialistic mentality of the present moment and predicts the times to come as he repeats the line: "We are approaching the Biedermeier" (bourgeois style and era), and then, as if to prove its material abundance, Roswitha produces a basket of food with fabulous and exotic morsels for all to devour. The conceptual progression of Oskar's poem is developed by antithesis and resolution. Each stanza begins with a three- or four-line description of military hardware of destruction only to shift focus suddenly to the world of middle-class comfort and security. The modern soldiers are not heroes but only displaced bourgeois, and like all good materialists they are really preoccupied with possessions first, preservation of wealth second, and with life and death afterward. True heroism, then, to cull the implications from Oskar's poem, is not to be found in armies or war. The huge and supposedly impressive Atlantic Wall is little more than the outer perimeter of a middle class, Biedermeier state of mind that is intent on preserving itself with all the insensitivity, superstitious ritual, and determination at its disposal.

The overtones and effect of the poem are equally interesting, for Oskar succeeds in dramatizing a military-bourgeois relationship and making it sound doubly absurd by *not* lending a gloomy or ponderous tone to this glorified apparatus of doom. Blind irony is indeed intended as Oskar writes more as an impartial observer than as a critic of vapid humans who are willing to gamble lives for the mindless seduction of bourgeois comfort. Reading the poem in retrospect, after following the events at its heels, one can also posit there a degree of *mythic* irony in its emphasis on the kind of self-surety, egocentricity, and smug security that is bound to provoke the fates, nemesis, the force that demands due respect to the gods. Because men do not realize that they are offensive to the gods when they become comfortably indifferent, that they overstep the limits of acceptable wealth when they take nature's gifts for granted, and that their excessive sense of indestructibility will only cause divine anger, they unconsciously open the door to the trauma of fate and the agonies of retribution.

But these constructions on the western wall of the German empire are just the beginning of what one will find in West Germany after the war. This period proclaims the onset of materialism and excessive technology, developing not merely for historical reasons but in faith that such armaments provide a barrier by which one can secure life from direct attack by the gods and man alike. We can catch a glimpse of this in the midst of the dawn of civilization where ruthless powers attempted to conquer, override, and insulate themselves from the fluid forms of demand of life. An example is personified in the mythical figure of Gilgamesh, the cultural hero and founder of the thick-walled town of Erech. He was the dictator who forced his people to labor, suffer, and even die in order to build a vast citadel. Finally it was only through the intervention of the gods that a counterforce in the figure of a primordial man (similar in certain respects to Oskar) was created who was able to confront Gilgamesh and force him to modify his brutal and autocratic exploitation of people. He, like other dictators after him, would gladly have spent a lifetime attacking would-be enemies and erecting barricades to insulate himself against his fellow men and the forces of nature. So we see here by implication and explanation that the military becomes a ruthless masculine power, not only as directed against an enemy but as a means of controlling and inhibiting the natural, vital energies of a subjective and personal order.

The arrogance of this callous order, the extravagance of its demands, the self-superiority of its mentality, and its impudent claims do not have long to wait before nemesis, the divine anger of the gods, descends. The day following the feast the Allied invasion takes place, causing disruption, devastation, the death of Roswitha, and the demise of Bebra's troupe. Bebra's last words of wisdom this time are: "We dwarfs and fools should not dance on concrete which was pressed and made hard for giants."

The high point of Oskar's travels is reached at the west wall, the western defense perimeter of the German army, for here he is able to observe that a bizarre admixture of sacred and mythic force still plays an important, although a corrupted, role at the extremes of human existence. He discovers, as Eliade explains, that: "It is highly probable that the fortifications of inhabited places and cities began by being magical defenses; for fortifications–trenches, labyrinths, ramparts, etc.–were designed rather to repel invasion by demons and the souls of the dead than attacks by human beings . . . during the Middle Ages, the walls of cities were ritually consecrated as a defense against the devil, sickness, and death. . . . In the last analysis the result of attacks, whether demonic or military, is always the same–ruin, disintegration, death."[19] Oskar soon discovers the verity of such observations, that here in the West superstition and dark fears as well as logic and technology have been an integral part of the construction of these military fortifications. Dogs have been sacrificed, blood offerings made to the goddess of death, ritual behavior is practiced, defenses assume the form of symbolic animals, mysterious signs of the labyrinth are constructed to ward off evil, and so it goes as far as Oskar is concerned until he writes his poem to show that the polarities of bourgeoisie and military defenses are little more than a mutated expression of man's attempt to protect himself in martial superstition from the inevitable forces of ruin, disintegration, and death.

Oskar has slowly but surely become wiser during the course of his adventures and therefore finds himself better prepared on his return to Danzig to explore and challenge the depths of the Catholic mysteries which the Truczinskis and the Bronskis had revered. Once, when Oskar was younger and less capable of dealing with the powers of the church, he rejected its rituals and idols out of hand. But now, as a world traveler, a mature hero, a rebel and actor of some experience, he can become a worthy adversary of even the Christ child, the cosmic drummer, who mocks our hero with an inspiring imitation of Oskar.

# SIX *Imitations of Oskar, Christ, & Satan*

Pagan mythology clearly dominates the world of *The Tin Drum*, but it is the challenge of Christianity that eventually drives Oskar to a point of frantic rebellion. Slowly, surely, and sometimes incongruously, Grass weaves into the fabric of his pagan story a Christian theme that begins with the mechanical Catholicism of Oskar's mother and ends with Oskar's deification of Dorothea and the adoration of her ring finger as a holy relique. But conflict becomes inevitable once a heathen mythological hero like Oskar has been born into a modern Christian world. The roots of Oskar's experiences and Weltanschauung are planted deeply and inextricably in his own mythogonic Kashubian soil; and although his resolved allegiance may subject him to frustration and even failure of sorts, Oskar remains loyal to his own mythic view of life until the very end. He accepts as gospel the sacred messages that greeted him at birth[1] and obeys unquestioningly the mysterious commands that direct him over spiritual thresholds into cellars, combat, travels, and special adventures.[2] And each episode becomes an additional augury and portent to confirm Oskar's special destiny as a messiah who will eventually in some measure reclaim and revivify a sacred quality of existence. When Oskar discovers, however, that the position of redeemer is already occupied by Jesus and that His godhead is unassailable, Oskar has no apparent choice but to rebel, establish himself as an antichrist, develop his own brand of theology, and acquire his own disciples.

Foreshadowing Oskar's impending conflict with Catholicism is an involved history of religious distortion by the forces of the Bronski paganism: the holy Virgin becomes for Koljaiczek the patroness of arson and ritual destruction; the image of Maria Magdalena guards the "heavenly bed" of the love goddess Agnes; confession provides license for the festive weekly ritual of food and love-making; and Oskar's Christian symbol, Satan (who appears as such *only* in

Christian contexts), becomes Oskar's spiritual guide in his personal defiance of the church. The name is invoked for the first time during Oskar's baptism when the priest asks Oskar if he renounces Satan, but before Oskar can refuse to renounce him, Jan answers for him in the affirmative. After various ceremonies are performed to rid Oskar of the Satan in his soul and to provide Oskar with his "pagan name," the first thing that Oskar does on leaving the church is to ask the devil in him: "Did you get through it all right?" Satan, in response, and knowing the shattering effectiveness of Oskar's voice, "jumped up and down and whispered: 'Did you see all those church windows, Oskar? They're all made of glass, all of glass!' " (p. 157).

In the context of this scenario a good deal of insistence is expressed that Oskar must receive the "pagan name" of Oskar, an indicator perhaps of the bitter contest between gods of conflicting realms, initiated during Oskar's first visit with his mother to the Church of the Sacred Heart. In a chapel at the side of the nave Oskar becomes intrigued with a plaster statue of Jesus, who was, as Oskar exclaims in astonishment: "My spit and image! He could have been my twin brother." The statue was also poised to perfection ready to beat a drum, if only it had had one. With sticks and a drum of his own, "it would have been me, the most perfect Oskar" (p. 162). The similarities extend beyond appearance and gesture to other surrounding figures in the church. There is a close resemblance between Oskar's sentimental and romantic "godfather, uncle, and presumptive father, Jan Bronski" and the mature Christ figure with his embarrassingly "stylized bleeding heart." Maria, too, looks as Agnes must have when she had been a seventeen-year-old girl.

Oskar is in fact so similar to this figure of Jesus confronting him that he is led to the implicit question of authenticity. Which is the real Jesus? Which of the two, the plastic image or Oskar Matzerath, is really the living God and spiritual redeemer? The ambiguity, he decides, can only be resolved through the act of drumming. The true Jesus must engage Oskar in a drumming contest to prove which of the two is really god, the cosmic drummer. So Oskar carefully hangs his drum on the statue, thrusts the drumsticks into the plaster hands, and awaits "the miracle: will he drum now, or can't he drum, or isn't he allowed to drum? Either he drums or he is not a real Jesus; if he doesn't drum now, Oskar is a realer Jesus than he is" (p. 164).

Christ does not hit the drum. Instead Oskar is discovered by the priest, cuffed, reprimanded, and pushed out of the chapel. The Satan in Oskar responds by hopping up and down, reminding Oskar to look at all that glass; and Oskar does. He aims his glass-shattering voice at a figure above and screams, but much to Oskar's amazement nothing happens. "Was that the miracle," Oskar asks himself on the verge of tears, that another god could counteract his magic? For the first time Oskar has failed miserably. He sinks down on the church floor and cries. He cannot shatter the church windows, and that must be attributed to the Christ child's intervention; for the moment Oskar must accept a standoff: although he cannot shatter Christian windows, neither can Jesus play his pagan drum, a clear indication for Oskar that he is to replace this god of plaster who cannot grasp the rhythms of life, who cannot deliver his message and therefore cannot redeem mankind. The matter rests there until Oskar has experienced a number of additional adventures, mourned the death of his mother, witnessed the marriage to his father of his sweetheart, the birth of his son, played in Bebra's "Miracle Theater," lived with Roswitha, and traveled to the western wall, the edge of the Land of the Dead.

Oskar returns home to Danzig on Kurt's third birthday in order to give him his tin drum so that he in turn might follow in his presumptive father's footsteps. But upon receiving the drum Kurt demolishes it completely; and to add injury to insult, he also thrashes Oskar soundly in a kind of burlesque of the Odysseus-Telemachus reunion to which Oskar had referred just before his return. It is only at that point that Oskar acquires a significant and sobering insight—namely that he was trying to direct his son rather than letting him work out his own destiny. From the outset Oskar's absolute principle has been one of self-determination. One must travel the way of personal discovery or one becomes a lifeless copy of one's father. Oskar rationalizes that he only wanted to instruct his son a bit, to teach him about his noble lineage, to let him view the parade of divine ancestors that could be conjured up under the skirts of his grandmother; but Oskar is rejected on each count—dramatic evidence that Kurt will go his own way at all costs and, as we shall see, become a leader in his own right.

After these early frustrations of his return home, Oskar begins to accompany Maria on her frequent visits to that same Catholic church he had once frequented with his mother Agnes. Nothing has changed, and Oskar again reconfirms the visual identity between himself and the statue of the Christ child. Again he decides to try to measure the drumming potential of this alleged divinity that had once failed to beat out the simplest of rhythms. Again Oskar takes his drum, hangs it around the statue of the Christ child and places his drumsticks in the statue's hands. Again he sits down, watches and waits until monotony sets in. Then, suddenly, the Christ child actually begins to drum!

The Christ child handles the drum deftly, first left and right and then with some elaborations. He drums out Oskar's biography, his most intimate experiences, and the story of his greatest adventures; he is even informed about the Rasputin-Goethe dichotomy of life, and he knows of the intimate secure feeling that Oskar had beneath the four skirts of his grandmother Anna Koljaiczek. Then slowly, as the initial impact of this miracle begins to register, Oskar suspects that he is being outclassed. Overwhelmed by Jesus's ability and superior knowledge, he reneges about the contest. He demands his drum back, insisting that the cross is sufficient for Christ. Oskar wants no miracles any longer—only his drum back—and he wants to flee "like ten devils" down the stairs, out of this Catholicism which seems to be enveloping him. Christ has played the drums and overpowered Oskar with his skill. Is Christ therefore really the cosmic drummer now? His drumming is genuine, moving, universal, and yet simple in form; and the information he drums out about the external events and inner secrets of Oskar's life confirm his omniscience. But instead of being flattered and impressed by this miracle, Oskar rejects the whole performance in extreme hostility and defiance, and his wrath bursts forth like a flood upon this god that has vanquished him. Three times Christ asks Oskar if he loves him and twice Oskar answers, "Not in the least," and the third time he explodes, "I hate you, you Bastard, you and all your hocus-pocus!" (p. 429). The breaking point comes finally when Christ "lifted his index finger like an elementary school teacher and gave me an assignment: 'You're Oskar, the rock, and on this rock I shall build my church. Follow me!' " (p. 430). Speechless and bristling with an uncontrollable rage, Oskar breaks off one of His plaster of Paris toes and screams that he will scratch his paint off if Jesus says that once more. But the rest is silence. Thrice has Oskar denied this god; he will not be the rock upon which a new church of Jesus shall be built; he simply will not complete the role of Peter which he is now asked to play.

Oskar, who was so intent on testing Jesus, has himself been put to the test. In the face of a miracle and a personal invitation from Jesus to join and even direct His church, Oskar balks and then explodes with determination to follow only the earth gods that have dominated his life. Before his dialogue with Jesus Oskar had been developing in accordance with epic necessity, but now a possible second path to achievement and salvation has revealed itself. Is he now to follow the god of Christian mythology, or should he continue on his own way as a chthonic demigod? Following the impulse that it is no doubt better to rule in hell than to serve in heaven, Oskar arbitrarily rejects a direct promise of Christian salvation, returning to the dark and undefinable limbo of the earth and assuming in his next adventure the guise of the devil whose sin consisted of a supreme effort to transcend his proper state and become like God.[3]

As he has threatened to do in the past, Oskar now goes out into the night world of Danzig and gathers disciples—the Dusters, a group of juvenile criminals that roam the city after dark. Through the miraculous skill of his glass-shattering voice Oskar gathers these young hoodlums into his fold. Before touching on that episode, we must return for a moment to the church following Oskar's defeat at the hands of Jesus and take up the voice theme that is initiated there. After His drumming performance and invitation to Oskar to join His church, Jesus reverts to a plaster idol again and rests in silence. Oskar, however, in uncontrollable anger and inner rage prepares to shatter one of the stained glass windows, but this time the intervention comes from Satan within him who warns Oskar that he should be careful or the Christ child may yet ruin his voice! Satan is most concerned for Oskar's voice, which is evidently a gift from the nether world and is essentially destructive. With it Oskar breaks forms, puts out lights, encourages crime, and achieves power over the earthlings, especially the Dusters. We also see that one of the first things that Oskar does after leaving the church is to test the precision and destructive capacity of his voice. He finds a shoe box containing four light bulbs which he proceeds to destroy. "Upon a fourth his voice inscribed JESUS in Sütterlin script, then pulverized both bulb and inscription" (p. 431). This sentence, like so many others that reader and critic may tend to pass over lightly, is heavily laden with implications that gain in clarity when regarded in a mythological context. The light bulb, reminiscent of the ones that Oskar's moth beat against at the time of his birth, may like fire or other forms of earthly illumination be equated with the central source of warmth and divine light, the sun. However, Oskar takes "several burned-out, but still pear-shaped bulbs" and writes JESUS in Sütterlin, the "pagan" script, on the fourth one and then shatters it. The bulb has been preserved in its original shape but the light has gone out of it, not unlike Catholicism as Oskar views it, which has retained its form but lost its power of illumination. That Oskar chooses to vanquish Jesus on the fourth bulb is no accident, although it may well be an unconscious choice. We recall the four skirts of the Great Earth Mother—the four winds, elements, and corners of the earth that in Oskar's system of symbolic numerology came to signify the terrestrial rather than the astral world; and now it is on his own ground—on the earth itself and in the realm of the physical forces—that Oskar will do battle with this Christian god.

The opportunity for revenge presents itself one evening as Oskar draws the attention of his future disciples while walking down the street "killing every third street light" (p. 435), each an association for him with the third member of the trinity. The Dusters, who roam the city, plundering whatever they can, corner Oskar and attempt to frighten and interrogate him; but Oskar reacts with his usual sangfroid and when asked, responds with deliberation, "My name is Jesus." Of course the young men take this to be a ploy of sorts and prepare to administer some punishment. At that moment the earthly and portentous forces which were unable to assist Oskar in his contest against the god of Christianity come to his aid.

When he says, with some alacrity, "I am Jesus," the sirens at the airport begin to scream, the sirens at the infantry barracks begin to scream, the sirens on the high school begin to scream, the sirens on the department store begin to scream, and the sirens at the Institute of Technology begin to scream, scream their foreboding of death and destruction from the sky; and simultaneously "like archangels taking up the glad tidings" (p. 441) they confirm the special validity of Oskar's claim. These sirens are of course identical with the sirens of classical mythology, for both are clearly sinister and terrifying harbingers of doom. Grass has these modern sirens sitting on top of tall buildings screeching their song of doom at the moon just as in the Odyssey, where these fabulous, frightening creatures sing to lure men to their death.

In spite of the sirens some of the Dusters are still a bit unsure of Oskar's powers, though the air raid's timely arrival gives them reason enough to believe. Now, to prove that miracles are no accident for him, Oskar demonstrates his ability to shatter glass windows in a distant chocolate factory, destroying the moon's reflection in them—or as he says, "I painted them black" (p. 443). With that he wins the allegiance and loyalty of this group of young criminals who "fought against everything," stole and demolished with Satanic pleasure, and opposed in principle any creative spirit. Oskar repeats now in essence what Jesus had once said to him alone: "Jesus will lead you. Follow me!"

Possessed by the illusion of deity, Oskar soon has his men robbing churches, stealing altar pieces, and, above all, taking the statue of the Holy Family. He acquires in very short order a vast assortment of Christian paraphernalia in the basement of a house, but he never has the opportunity to utilize what has been gathered. While stealing the Christ and Madonna figure from the church one night, he succumbs to the temptation of holding a black mass with himself as the figure of worship. He begins by sitting himself down on Mary's knee after the Christ child figure has been sawed away. While members of his gang don priests' robes and intone bits and pieces of the Catholic ritual, Oskar basks in the momentary glory, impressed with the atmosphere, the procedure, and the effectiveness of this black mass (p. 455). A travesty of the Catholic mass, this black liturgy parallels the ceremonies of the Luciferians, who, according to Charles Williams in his book on witchcraft, "carried on the semi-pagan dream of the unjust Creator and the just rebel—Prometheus Gnosticized." [4]

Although the English translation of Oskar's deification here rings with dramatic victory: "I had indeed taken the place of Christ," the original German text is a bit less vainglorious. *Die Nachfolge Christi trat ich an* indicates an imitation rather than a usurpation of Christ's divine role (p. 456). Oskar knows that he is acting here, that he is imitating; and therefore when he abruptly suffers a defeat in this moment of apparent exaltation, he does not succumb to humiliation or even excessive disappointment. Luzie Rennwand has informed the police of the Dusters's desecration and with that puts a dramatic end to Oskar's miracle play. The arrest brings about what Oskar refers to as "the second trial of Jesus" in which "Oskar, and hence also Jesus, is acquitted." Although Oskar avoids the punishment of the courts, he chooses a fate that is more terrifying. To escape legal punishment he jumps into Luzie's lap and perceives her as a vision he will never forget: "The Black Cook, devouring sausage with peelings, growing skinnier as she ate, hungrier, more triangular, more doll-like—that face stamped on me. Who can take that triangle out of and away from my mind? How long will it stay in me chewing sausages, peels, and people; and laughing as only a triangle can laugh and only women on tapestries who tame unicorns can" (p. 458).

The allusion to the women who can tame unicorns refers to the introduction of Luzie to the gang. At that time the Dusters were beginning to redecorate their basement with plunder from the local churches. From the Trinity Church they steal a colored tapestry, "showing a lady who seemed ever so prim, prissy, and deceitful, and a mythological animal known as a unicorn, who was very much under her influence" (p. 451). The tapestry is hung at one end of the basement on a spot that had been viewed as an altar of death: "The back wall of our cellar was formerly decorated with nonsense like death's heads, black hands, and other absurdities, but finally the unicorn motif dominated all our deliberations" (p. 452). Only Oskar perceives the foreboding relationship between the highly symbolic weaving, Luzie, and himself: "I asked myself why we had to bring in the second, woven Luzie, who turned your officers into unicorns, who alive or woven is essentially out to get you, for you alone, Oskar, are truly fabulous; you are the unique animal with the exaggerated twisted horn" (p. 452).

The tapestry of the virgin and unicorn as Oskar describes it, takes us back to the Christian legend as explained, for example, by Honorius von Autun in *Speculum de Mysteriis Ecclesiae:* "The wild animal with one horn is called a unicorn. In order to catch it, a virgin is put in a field. The animal comes to her then and because it lies down in her lap, it is captured. Christ is represented by this animal and his invincible strength by its horn."[5] The allusion to Christ as a unicorn jumping as symbol and spirit into the Virgin's lap is a frequent one in the figures of early Christian writers.[6] But Oskar is not the immaculate conception, nor is Luzie the Holy Mother. And yet the identification of Oskar with Christ and hence with the unicorn, the question of the Virgin's ability to hunt down and capture the unicorn, and the analogy of Oskar jumping into Luzie's lap all apply well to the context of the present dilemma. The Christian symbols have simply been replaced by their chthonic counterparts. The dark virgin of astrology represents the negative aspect of the earth with all its infernal horrors and enticements. The great attraction and terror for Oskar here is Luzie's face, an inverted triangle, an inversion of the sign of the trinity. Hers is a "black-framed triangle with slits for eyes" (p. 460) that draws men inevitably to their doom. Like the terrible devouring maw of the earth personified in the form of a hungry goddess, Luzie, the hungry virgin temptress, sits on Satan's lap biting into a sandwich. " 'Jump, sweet Jesus,' she chewed, offering me her triangle, still intact" (p. 462). Now, if we recall, Oskar did once jump at an inverted triangle. At the beach when Oskar saw Maria naked for the first time, she "frightened Oskar with her hairy triangle" (p. 257); and when Oskar jumped at it, he found himself lost for a moment in the earth, immersed in the odors of vanilla, mushrooms, and the dank smell of earth or soil. Now Oskar is invited to jump from a high tower and plunge into the devouring earth triangle from which his life once issued. The once productive Earth Mother is transforming with time into the Kali, the terrible earth goddess who sits ever ready to consume again the life which she once created.[7] Now she sits on Satan's lap, as Luzie Rennwand, who as a divine counterimage to Peter at the gates of Heaven, is positioned here at the portal of death. Certainly the image that Luzie creates in biting and swallowing sausages, tempting the Dusters from their tower into the "swimming pool" of destruction, or in capturing the unicorn, is open to psychological interpretation; but ultimately it is the mythological connotation of the chthonic Dark Mother rather than Oedipal symbols that prevails in this novel. Or, in Oskar's words, after refusing to jump at Luzie's triangle: "To this day I have not been able to break the habit of looking . . . for a skinny teenaged girl . . . who is constantly murdering men. . . . My horror is that Luzie Rennwand will turn up in the shape of the Black Cook and urge me to jump for the last time" (p. 464). For the moment, however, Oskar does not jump. He quietly climbs down from the tower, the high pinnacle he had created for himself with the aid of his apostles, the Dusters.

Oskar's ensuing difficulties, many of which persevere until the conclusion of the novel, are plagued by the frustrations of having failed to transcend certain limits of natural life; and where he reacts violently, he does so in defiance against some force or figure that threatens to obstruct him in his pursuit of his felt destiny. That, in fact, is the reason that Oskar gives for having caused the death of his second presumptive father, Alfred Matzerath: he was tired of dragging his father along with him in life.

As Danzig is being taken by the Russians, a group of three Soviet soldiers invade the cellar in which Oskar and his neighbors are hiding. As they go about the business of raping Mrs. Greff, Oskar hands Alfred Matzerath a Nazi signet pin which he attempts to hide by swallowing it. Unfortunately he begins to choke so violently on the open clasp that one of the Russian soldiers decides to put him out of his misery by emptying a magazine of bullets into him. At the same moment Oskar, who has been playing with a louse, crushes it unconsciously between his fingers, evidently crushing Matzerath's totem insect. Of course, as with Agnes and with Jan Bronski, Oskar takes full credit here for doing away with his father, the last member of the parental triangle. Ironically even in death Alfred becomes an obstruction. Oskar notices a stream of ants gathering sugar from a burst sack. Through no fault of his own Matzerath lies doubled up in the middle of their highway. The ants quickly discover a detour and industriously continue about their business. Neither the ants nor Oskar, it seems, can concern themselves with this dead hulk, for there is more work that needs to be done and a new path that must be followed.

Later, standing at the edge of his father's grave, Oskar remarks that funerals always remind one of other funerals; but this burial turns out to be especially significant for Oskar. On the way to the graveyard Maria was given a bird cage which contained a small Australian parrot, a Budgerigar; and while Oskar is standing before the open grave, Kurt throws rocks at the bird. Oskar reminisces on the many lives and deaths he has witnessed, and then from within him comes a compelling question which he hesitates even to formulate, let alone answer. He asks himself, "Should I or shouldn't I?" over and over and over again. Finally Oskar decides "I shall!" and at that moment Kurt hits the bird with a rock, causing it to scream out and making its feathers fly. Evidently, Oskar notes, Kurt too had been making some choice that depended on an augury or decision contingent on his hitting the bird with a rock.

Matzerath happens to be the last authoritative figure of this world in which Oskar has grown up and whose presence restricts the growth and freedom that he is searching for. Now free of his father, and all parental figures, Oskar is free to say "I shall," and with that he throws his tin drum into the grave onto the coffin so that it too might be buried along with his infantile existence. Then, suddenly, he begins to grow. The first symptom of his growth is a violent nosebleed. Cracking and grinding inside of him, his organs and his bones cause him to collapse. The old man Herr Heilandt aids Oskar momentarily, finishes filling the grave, picks him up, and carries him out of the cemetery.

It is there that they again meet Leo Schugger, the atavistic follower of funerals. Instead of demonstrating his usual control, cordiality, and sympathy, Leo begins to scream uncontrollably when he sees Oskar: "Look at the Lord, how he's growing, look how he's growing!" and then "he ran, danced, rolled, fell, fled, and flew with a screaming bird [in the cage]; he was himself a bird," screeching all the way: "He is growing, he is growing" until two young Russian soldiers, who have had their fill of the bizarre scene, shoot at him with machine guns only to have him, who thrives on death, elude it and continue screeching like a raven: "He's growing!"

Perceiving that Oskar is beginning to grow, Leo Schugger (one of the mythological shades–umbrae–or *manes*[8]) shouts out his name as "der Herr," the Lord. The statement is slightly ambiguous, however, because one does not know exactly where in the realm of darkness Schugger's allegiance lies. If Schugger is accepted as a funerary spirit or *manes,* then the Lord in his eyes must be a subterranean divinity or chthonic god who also reveres the forces of death and decay. "He is growing" is a terrifying observation for Schugger because growth implies life and therefore distance or removal from the realm of departed spirits and decaying bodies. The scene may well be a parody of the annunciation for the outside world that Oskar is coming, but rather than a dove of peace from the biblical scene we have a bird, a raven, or vulturelike figure whose surreal appearance aptly fits his message.

The abandonment of the tin drum and Oskar's decision to grow demonstrate a real effort on his part to change his direction in life.

In a symbolic gesture of renunciation Oskar throws his tin drum into the grave for burial, and with the loss of his drum Oskar also loses his ability to shatter glass with his voice. As a result he must now depend solely on his own human resources to make his way in this world. This all signifies rebirth for Oskar, who is described as covered with blood, seized in trauma, growing rapidly, shocked with pain, and taken by fever. In the process he relives a period of feverish infantile withdrawal and early fantasies; he is plagued by illusion and a degree of madness, only to be cured by Herr Fajngold, a kind of wizard who brings with him a lifegiving medicine he discovered when he lived among the dead in the concentration camp at Treblinka.

Oskar meanwhile is taken home, where he remains deathly ill for a time, in a coma filled with madness and visions, while he continues to grow physically. From a height of three feet he quickly shoots up dramatically to a height of four feet one inch. As we have seen, his transformation at the gravesite is clearly a rebirth of sorts with all the necessary bloody issue, birth trauma, confusion, fresh growth, and new awareness. Thus Oskar literally enters another realm, both physically and psychologically. But crossing the threshold he imagines he is trapped on a revolving carousel of children's objects and wild animals. He wants to break out of this turning circle of infantilism, but he cannot seem to get off the merry-go-round because God is standing there, paying for additional rides. He, the supernatural mover, insists that this revolving wheel continue to turn and that the children originally enticed there with a promise of amusement be held forever on a wheel of Ixion that pretends to be a source of pleasure. They pray a parody of "Our Father," asking that He should finally let the carousel stop so that they can get off, but to no avail.

The vision is related to Oskar's decision to grow and to give up his drum, to break free from the hermetic realm of infantile egocentricity, free from the dominance of the father gods, not just by means of momentary conflicts and rebellion but by really growing up and becoming an adult, by finding his place in a world beyond magic, mystery, and childish manipulations. But Oskar does not seem to be able to regain his health once he starts growing. He has been a child for twenty-one years, and the effort to break through his old form is excruciating. His fever chart resembles a horrendous mountainscape with sharp irregular rises and falls. Aside from the wild and domesticated animals he rides on—and besides God the Father, who always pays for another ride—Oskar sees other visions and faces. He notices that God has been replaced by Rasputin the next time around and that after him Goethe takes over as the purveyor of rides. They then begin to alternate—first "Rasputin intoxicated and after him Mr. von Goethe, controlled. A little madness with Rasputin, and after that for the purpose of reason, Goethe. The extremists surrounded Rasputin, the forces of order, Goethe" (p. 496). Oskar is torn in an endless circle of cadences between the chaotic, intoxicating power of Rasputin and the hard, balanced, granitelike character of Goethe. The pace increases, the revolutions continue, and Oskar seems to be thrown more deeply into madness and illness of a life of opposing forces, hopelessly turning from dissolution to stern rationality and back again. Then, when the fever and inner turmoil become unbearable, a certain Herr Fajngold enters and with his magic powder he envelops Oskar in an enchanted cloud ("of Lysol"), and with that brings Oskar back to earth. He also transforms or induces the animals (as medicine men and shamans have the power to do, Campbell claims, along with Eliade,) that have "appeared in vision, to become the guardians, initiators, and vehicles of the shamans, bestowing their knowledge, power, and spiritual insight,"[9] rather than allowing them to remain the bugbears of childhood.[10]

Herr Fajngold, a sympathetic, concerned, and forgiving Jew who has been made eccentric by his experiences in the concentration camp, has become the new owner of the Matzerath business since the Germans are disenfranchised by the newly conquering Russians. All of Fajngold's family and friends have been cremated in the ovens of Treblinka, yet he is still able to see them corporealized, and he converses with them about present incidents and past experiences. For his capacity to converse with the dead (yet to elude death at Treblinka), to avert even greater suffering as "sanitation man" at the camp, and now to bring Oskar back from the throes of madness and death, Fajngold must be placed alongside the other shamans and seers of this novel. He is a strangely mixed figure—a Jew and a Pole, an occupier and a protector, a reminder of the past and an eradicator of memories, a curer of disease and a spirit of death. He himself inhabits two worlds: he lives among the ghosts and memories of those who died in the concentration camps, and yet he gets along well in the world of immediate reality. In any case he can do with his disinfectant what the doctor cannot do with medicine: he can cure Oskar of his fever, rid him of his nightmares and the lice which he acquired at his father's death, and prepare him for his long journey west. This is not the first time, it will be recalled, that Fajngold has prepared the way for a Matzerath to travel west to the land of the dead. He was also instrumental in performing the burial of Alfred Matzerath by acting literally as a psychopompus who leads the casket and soul of Matzerath through masses of hostile Russian troops, through the ruins of a burning and plundered city and on to the graveyard where interment could take place.

Finally the decision is made that Danzig can no longer be the home of these Matzeraths who have been disenfranchised by military power and whose crucial moment of history has faded in importance from this scene. Maria, Kurt, and Oskar pack up and board a freight train leaving Danzig to the Germany of the West. As they look out at the platform they perceive the shrinking image of Herr Fajngold, who will remain in Danzig and vanish along with the world of the past.

In this chapter, "Should I or Shouldn't I," Grass offers the reader an historical examination of the city of Danzig, one which, like Oskar's description of the Polish cavalry, borders on a panegyric eulogy of the city that gave him and his forefathers their lives as well as their language and traditions. Praise of Danzig is a recurring and necessary theme throughout this book, for in Oskar's mind at least this city forms the central axis of the world around which all other places revolve at some distance. Danzig is Oskar's holy city,[11] his native soil, his immovable spot, the permanent home of the Great Earth Mother, Anna Bronski-Koljaiczek, and therefore his *axis mundi*. The city sits perennially at the center of his worldly awareness, just as some homeland concept does in every major myth. Once separation occurs, the mythic hero feels himself robbed of his source of strength and inspiration. When Oskar is transported from the city in feverish delirium, he leaves behind the holy sepulchers, the sanctuaries of childhood including his three-year-old size and the four skirts of his divine grandmother, his drum and his glass-shattering voice. However, he will find the graveyards again in the West; he will take up the tin drum and play it with greater effectiveness than before; his grandmother will visit him again as a cosmic vision; but the innocent childlike appearance which he possessed in Danzig is lost to him. Oskar changes as he travels west from a *puer aternus,* the child-adult and the naive mover of events, into a misshapen dwarf.

The dwarf concept of folklore also has its classical counterpart in the form of Kuretes or the race of Cabiri, sons of the underworld god, Hephaestus, the ugly and crippled god of the forge and the patron of all artists who worked with metal. To him are attributed the creation of the arms of Achilles and (at the risk of straining the imagination and our sense of chronology) perhaps, also, Oskar's tin drum, whose red field Oskar equates with fire. The Cabiri were simply "earth-god symbols, personified as little dwarfs"[12] that related to men primarily through special skills and magic, preserving much of the primordial instincts and cunningness of natural beings, and positing therefore a countervalence to the spiritual aspirations of civilized man. The name Cabiri is probably Phoenician and, if so, it means "the great or mighty ones." The figures were also dwarfs in the service of a nature goddess, probably Demeter or Cybele and closely related to the Idean dactyll ("fingers," which in *The Tin Drum* are associated with Tom Thumb, drumsticks, scarfs, eels, the phallus, and, finally, with Sister Dorothea's ring finger). These dwarfs were credited with working in metal, but they also apparently introduced music and rhythm (namely dactylic meter) to Greece and were the possessors of certain magical or supernatural aids. The child Zeus was once entrusted to these dwarfs, the Kuretes; and they created a legend by drowning out his crying as they drummed on their shields. Related to them in myths, dwarfs of Rhodes, the Telchines, also hammered metal; they were drummers and daemons of sorts, and they were the natural enemies of both gods and men, although one of their talents was the unusual gift of creating almost identical likenesses of the gods.

W. K. C. Guthrie in *The Greeks and their Gods* quotes Strabo to sum up the general qualities of the classic dwarfs and demigods: "The Kuretes are similar daemons or attendants upon gods, and are mixed up with certain sacred rites, both mystic and other. . . . There is much confusion in these accounts. Some declare that the Korybantes and Kabiri and Idaean Daktyls and Telchines are the same as the Kuretes, others pronounce them related and distinguish certain small differences between them, but agree that in general terms, and to name their prevailing characteristics, all alike are enthusiastic and Bacchic types, who in the guise of acolytes, by dances in arms with tumult, noise, cymbals, tympana and weapons . . . arouse the passions in the course of religious ceremonies."[13] The associations are all present in *The Tin Drum:* the semidivinity of Oskar the dwarf, the hammering on metal and typanium or the drum itself, the noise and tumult and rejuvenation that occurs in the cult of Oskarism in Book 3, the ecstatic dancing of Oskar's novitiates later on through the streets, the drumming fingers, and Oskar's own phallus: "Herbert's . . . promises, it was my drumsticks, from my third birthday on, which promised scars, reproductive organs, and finally the ring finger . . . beginning with the boy Jesus' watering can, it all promised me my own sex" (p. 206).

Through Books 1 and 2 Oskar has of necessity acquired the inevitable sins of the mythological hero who must destroy and make his way beyond the people and expectations imposed on him at birth. He regards his mothers and fathers as classical obstructions to his mission, and therefore the metaphorical dragons he slays are in some sense his elders, rivals, and enemies projected into the real world as challenging monsters and capricious opponents. And if the personages surrounding Oskar are by and large symbolic representations of epic forces and cosmic challenges, then Oskar himself also "presents to us not a specific person, but the human estate of such a person. . . . Though he is born of a purely self-centered imagination, he is super-personal; a product not only of particular experience, but of *social insight*. He is the envisagement of a vital factor in life; that is why he is projected into reality by the symbolism of religion."[14] If the child of destiny is himself to shine as a hero, he must surpass the power and position of his fathers even if the way to that end leads over their graves, a mythological truism accepted in the classical tradition from Kronos and Zeus to Oedipus and Romulus and then beyond in countless other primitive legends and myths.

The path to individual greatness inevitably leads also to long journeys of exploration and self-discovery away from home and the immediate protection of the local gods and goddesses. Bereft of his supernatural aids, the hero is forced to rely on his merely human capacities for a while and adjust to the demands of another realm. Oskar does in fact leave Danzig with only his memories, his photograph album, and none of his supernatural aids. This journey west may be compared to an adventure which Frobenius in *Das Zeitalter des Sonnengottes* chose to call the night sea journey, a concept that seems to have originated as an ancient notion that the sun runs a nightly course of travel on a subterranean sea in symbolic death followed by resurrection the next morning in the eastern skies. The ancients assumed that there was some third infernal region, some lower ocean or enclosed realm through which the sun had to travel a lifeless journey in order to reappear with the morning. In ritual practices and mythological stories, then, the mythic heroes, often identified in some way with the sun, were also required to reenact this period of removal and death by being shut up in a container of sorts, a chest, a cave, a coffin, or inside an animal or a fish. But the enclosure motif, or even the madness and illness which sometimes accompanies the hero, also suggests that this journey is but a transition, a dark threshold that simulates night and death but leads to rebirth and introduction to a new quality of life. Book 2 ends with a clear statement of recognition that Oskar can no longer regard himself as a child, that the war has ended, that a new phase of life must begin and new territories must be staked out, so that he can, in his own words, "begin a new, furthermore grown-up life" (p. 516).

Oskar, contrary to the direction of the sun on its nightly crossing, goes to the West, the land associated with death, instead of toward the East. He journeys now within the belly of a freight-car, one filled with bizarre spirits and stopped frequently by thieving and threatening partisans, occupied by the Black Cook as well as other sinister figures, to the land of the West. But the associations are not restricted to the travels alone, for once he is there he finds himself working as a stonecutter amid gravestones or preparing for burials and funerals in the local graveyards. Slowly it does seem that he begins to find a new and providential outlet for his talents, but the hope for a new life and human acceptance in the West is futile. If anything Oskar finds himself more deeply entangled than before in the symbols of death and deterioration. To go west, to the land of the setting sun, to the adult life, Oskar has sacrificed his drum, has been bathed in his own blood, suffered illness and madness, witnessed the endless circle of an infantile merry-go-round, been cured by the shaman

Fajngold, traveled the night sea in a coffinlike box, suffered the perils of sudden growth, developed a hunchback, and finally entered a hospital in Düsseldorf where with the help of the pure and hygienic nurses he regains his health.[15] So Oskar moves now from the hospital into a different world, into the encounters, boredom, reactions, and activities which the new life imposes.

# SEVEN *Unrest & Resignation in the West*

Although Oskar resigns himself to the demands of "normal life" in West Germany and seriously believes for the while that the specters of his past have been buried along with his tin drum in the East, the figures with whom he interacts in the West still function as mythic gods or earth spirits wearing human masks. Even within the ranks of his own decimated family, the mythological directions have not been lost, for now Kurt, Oskar's alleged son, also manifests great hidden energy and a special destiny as a hero of industry.

The first chapter of Book 3 is titled "Firestones and Gravestones," the former a symbol for Kurt and the latter one for Oskar. After the war there are no matches available, so Kurt with his aggressive genius for earning money, begins at six years of age to sell flints (literally firestones) on the black market and supports the family, whereas Oskar prefers to work in the region of the dead with a mason who carves, delivers, and erects gravestones. But Oskar's role is basically a passive one now while Kurt plays the figure of the dynamic young god who, ironically like an entrepreneur Prometheus, brings fire to the suffering people of the West. Kurt's emergence as a young god of fire goes back, like Oskar's decision to grow, to the burial of their father Matzerath in Danzig. Some Russians had given Maria a caged bird to carry along with her in the funeral procession; and when at the cemetery Kurt begins to pitch rocks at it, Oskar assumes he is carrying out an augury for the determination of future events. "After his bull's-eye he had probably arrived at a decision," but what it was, Oskar did not know. "The uncertainty was killing me. After all, it was my son who had decided for or against something. Had he decided at last to recognize and love me as his only true father? . . . Or was his decision: death to my presumptive father?" (p. 485). Then Oskar, *apparently* of his own volition, decides to grow and immediately suffers a violent nosebleed. But in the following chapter, "Disinfectant," Oskar relates another version of this same incident to his keeper Münsterberg. He says that is was only after that stone hit *him*, not the bird, that he began to grow. If so, then there is confusion of identity between the caged bird and Oskar, who, when accidentally (providentially?) struck by a rock, breaks out of his "cage" of childhood, that enchanted cage of the East, and decides to become an adult. The identity between the bird and Oskar is evidently important for Kurt also, who transfers to the bird the brutal hostility he previously exhibited only toward Oskar. Therefore, as Kurt strikes the bird and/or Oskar with a stone, his perverse ritual augury is complete. On the one hand he knocks Oskar out of his infantile world and stature of three feet with a stone; he forces him (according to the second version of the story, pp. 491-92) to lose his drum in the grave and his voice along with it; and on the other hand Kurt clears the way for himself to become the dominating figure in a new and loose trinity of Oskar, Maria, and himself. With Oskar's supernatural aids gone and his childlike appearance a thing of the past, the way is open for Kurt to move independently and in accordance with his own needs.

In keeping with the pattern of augury which Kurt used to predict his own future and free himself of his presumptive father, he becomes the demigod of "striking-stones," firestones, or flints that bring light and heat, two qualities which stand in diametric opposition to the dark, cold, and funerary realm in which Oskar dwells. Kurt's contribution reflects the solar qualities of the sun; but although the rising sun-god, like the heavenly source he represents, may be in the ascendency momentarily, it will be the forces of night, of earth, and of mystery that will in the end prevail.

While Kurt thrives, Oskar tries to adjust himself to Western civilization by eating a great deal and reading a bit, earning a very modest livelihood inscribing gravestones, exploring some mechanical amusements, visiting the nurses in the hospital, and having his little quarrels with Maria and Kurt. It is soon after he admits that he "had lost interest in grownup life" (p. 523) that Oskar goes to work for a strange gentleman by the name of P. Korneff, a stonecutter and mortuary sculptor, and once there he finds himself back amid familiar symbols of a chthonic order. Korneff's chiseled reliefs of Christ remind Oskar of the "Athlete on the Cross" in the Sacred Heart Church in Danzig, similar down to the drops of blood which once transfixed Jan Bronski in the snow and associated him irrevocably with the "bleeding heart" crucifixion. Oskar's job also takes him to the graveyard frequently, where one day he sees Leo Schugger again.

His employer then tells him that this is really Sabber Willem and that every graveyard has such people as Schugger and Sabber. In action and appearance the two are identical and apparently meant to affirm the presence of some benevolent spirit of graveyards everywhere. In a narrow sense, as we have mentioned elsewhere, these figures may be regarded as Latin *manes* or *umbrae,* shadows of solicitous protective guardians of the tomb. But Sabber plays a more minor role in Oskar's life then Leo Schugger did in the East. Of greater importance to Oskar are some of the daydreams that he experiences in the graveyard.

In one fantasy Oskar travels to the sea where the water throws a corpse onto the beach. Oskar bends over the body with the hope that it is Maria perhaps or the nurse Gertrud whom he has met at the hospital and would like to get to know better, but it turns out to be Luzie, clad in a number of wet, woolen jackets which Oskar proceeds to take off. Finally, beneath layer and layer of knitted jackets, Oskar finds her heart wrapped in a sport shirt of the kind formerly worn by a Hitler youth girls club. Her heart has petrified into a small gravestone on which is inscribed: "Here rests Oskar–here rests Oskar–here rests Oskar" (p. 535). Luzie's heart has become so firmly hardened with the obsession of Oskar's death that the two are now indistinguishable. The heart, center of human emotion, usually symbolizes warmth of feeling; but Luzie, an alternate image of the Black Cook and the woman who preoccupies Oskar's fears, embodies only hatred, desire for retribution, and death where Oskar is concerned.

The moment he discovers this gravestone which the Black Cook has set for him, Oskar is called back by Korneff, his employer, to the task of setting a different gravestone. The name Korneff is based on the word *corn* and is suggestive of the vegetation cycle, especially since Korneff deals with death and burial as an occupation. We recall that the corn goddess and the great potato mother are separated by geography rather than by concept and that the figures of creation and death are merely contrary aspects of a single cycle. Whereas the symbols of creation and life govern the beginning of this novel (ritual cosmogenesis, fertilization, growth, protection by the Great Earth Mother [the four skirts] and *nisus formativus*), the end of the novel is dominated by the symbols of death and the overwhelming shadow of the Black Cook. Korneff is the first mystagogue of Book 3 who introduces Oskar to the rituals of burial, or literally "planting the corpse." Besides his occupation with the monuments of death and his agreement to initiate Oskar into the ritual of burials, Korneff perennially grows huge grotesque boils that resemble kernels of corn on the back of his neck. In fact Oskar, after dreaming of Luzie, participates in a disgusting vignette in which Korneff lies down on a gravestone. While a burial service takes place at an adjacent gravesite, he squeezes Korneff's furuncles and drains them of their pus. With contrapuntal precision Grass combines the final mass of a burial ceremony and the removal of the boils in single concert. Every time Oskar squeezes another boil, the sound of "amen" comes floating across the graveyard as though a final mass were being said for each furuncle removed form Korneff's neck.[1] As Oskar goes about his work, Korneff recites the death liturgy. For the moment it is Oskar who performs as the healer of body by draining the boils of their poisonous fluid. And Korneff, who can be compared remotely to Osiris, Adonis, or other vegetation gods that are traditionally identified with death and resurrection, in turn teaches Oskar all he has to know about graveyards and gravestones, the monuments to death. The preponderance of such symbols in these early scenes of Book 3 sets the tone for Oskar's subsequent adventures and prepares the way for the final visit of the Black Cook herself.

Suddenly Oskar changes direction and goes out in search of life and immediate pleasure. Having earned some money, he now begins to dress as his former master Bebra did, and like Bebra he acts the part of an establishment dwarf. Of course Oskar has had a long history of love for nurses dating back to the picture in the photograph album of his mother as a nurse, and now he begins to preoccupy himself with the pursuit and conquest of nurses. Actually, however, it is the nurse's uniform and the Red Cross pin that entice him mostly, and he is extremely disappointed when he finally manages to arrange a date with the nurse Gertrud, only to have her appear in her civilian clothes. The absence of the white uniform robs Oskar of his enthusiasm, but still they go together to a remote quarter of the city, into a dance hall that carries the name of

Wendig (German for "fleet, changing"), but it also had the name of *Löwenburg* ("fortress of lions"). And by entering this club Oskar again leaves the overt world of the West and takes a step back over a threshold into a darker world of primitives and "Jimmy-the-Tiger," the theme song of his old master and mystagogue, Bebra.

Suddenly, within the confines of this subterranean den, Oskar becomes a suave and confident figure. He seems to be the master here, confident and superior, and he is even mistaken for Jimmy-the-Tiger himself. It is evident that the vital forces which he once had at his command in Danzig momentarily become his again and are greatly esteemed by the clientele of this club. But by contrast Gertrud feels awkward and out of place here. She bumps into things, trips over furniture, and finally beats a hasty retreat out of the club, leaving Oskar to sit there alone. But Oskar is not lost here in this place so reminiscent of arenas in which he fought some of his mightiest early battles. Then in his honor the band begins to play "Jimmy-the-Tiger." Some girls join him at his table and one asks him to dance, and as Jimmy-Oskar moves rapidly around the floor he seems to conjure up the strength and greatness of the wild and powerful image which he possessed in his youth. Oskar is again, at least for the moment, the possessor of special knowledge and power. His familiarity with the forces in play here give him the opportunity now of returning to a realm in which he is king; but that, unfortunately, would constitute a step backward, a return to a past state or lower step of development and prevent him from resolving the new and difficult trials he has experienced since his days in Danzig. Therefore he chooses not to dwell in the Fortress of Lions but to return to Korneff and his routine duties as a mason.

Working with Korneff at the cemetery one day, Oskar experiences another powerful moment of illumination similar to the moment when he discarded his drum. Looking out from the cemetery of Oberaussern (meaning above and outside), he is struck by the tremendous view. He suddenly sees spread out before him the new, hissing, billowing factories of Fortuna Nord, a huge center of industry for the Allied forces in West Germany. But then, as Oskar begins to dig a grave in the presence of this spectacular view, he finds the finger of a corpse, which has evidently been cut off by a shovel. It is this bone as a symbol of decay and death that Oskar opposes in eloquent hyperboles to the vast materialistic forces manifested by the city of Fortuna Nord. He proudly insists that "to me the head and the fingers of this woman were more human than the beauty of the factories of Fortuna Nord. Of course, it may be true that I enjoyed the pathos of the industrial scene, . . . but I remained nevertheless distrustful of such external beauties. . . . I admit, that the high voltage communicated to me a cosmic feeling similar to Goethe, but the finger of the woman touched my heart" (p. 550).

Oskar recognizes in this city of industry and order a lyrical harmony conceived as cooperation between man and nature, and in several respects his observations parallel the conclusion of the second part of *Faust,* where every effort is made through industry to reclaim the land from the sea. Opposed to such creative forces (and not completely contrary to *Faust*), Oskar finds at his feet some bones that immediately conjure up the ubiquitous forces of death and decay. In another literary allusion he identifies himself with Yorick, the jester—or rather with the skull of the jester that Hamlet found in the graveyard. Then other complex associations begin to confound his symbolic configuration which expands in confusion only to be reduced again to the polarity of Goethe versus Rasputin, order and chaos, life versus the degenerating forces of death. Oskar asks which pole he shall choose, for it lies in the nature of man that he may not embrace both. So, he says, I "made the town graveyard the middle point of the world, and the factory of Fortuna Nord into my impressive half-divine antagonist; and the fields were Denmark's fields" (p. 550). And there, amid a field of corpses that Oskar calls the "middle point of the world," he sits comparing the humming of high-voltage lines overhead to the thinking of Fortuna Nord as a "redoubtable demigod, my antagonist," and of himself as Hamlet as well as Yorick. Fortuna Nord, "that industrial landscape . . . possessed a surface beauty which I had always distrusted." Death, burial, and the forces of deterioration have more meaning for Oskar as he reminisces and remembers his earthly father Matzerath and heavenly father Bronski, both in addition to his grandmother and others. Oskar confronts past with present and stands indeed like Hercules at the crossroads, trying to decide if he should follow his messianic path of hardship, suffering, pain, but also of fame and purpose; or should he choose a life of ease, luxury, wealth, grateful friends, a happy home and children! "To marry or not to marry, that is the question."

Finally he decides: "For me, however, Oskar Matzerath, Bronski, Yorick, a new era began," and so he calls forth all the past gods and goddesses and experiences as authority for his new decision. Having worked for a good while in the land of the dead, he has come to the decision that he can indeed fit, like Matzerath, into life and society. He decides to marry and become a middle-class citizen, a *pater familias,* a man of wealth, happiness, and comfort; but unfortunately, when he finally comes out with the proposal, Maria turns him down. His momentous internal decision is overridden by external veto. The nail of fortune, the destiny of decision, has been struck by an external hammer, and with that the crossroads at which he had placed himself again become a single path. Marriage symbolized a commitment to a normal life for Oskar; but having failed, he retreats for the nonce into a remoter, less acceptable realm, the realm of the art and the artist.

"I would have really been a good citizen . . . but Maria turned me down" (p. 553), Oskar laments after his rebuff. Oskar had been ready to give in to temptation, to spend the rest of his life with his Dido, Circe, or Jocasta. Having come to recognize in the graveyard the unconquerable forces of death, Oskar wished to turn to life and become a bourgeois, a Holdfast of society, a comfortably married man. But as is frequently the case with the mythological hero when he tires of adventure and chooses to repudiate his mission, fate comes to frustrate him and spur him on along his destined path. Not all the choices belong to the hero; a good number are made by the gods. Even in Oskar's next adventure with the artists and the world of art, it is he who is passively chosen, while sitting on a park bench, to be absorbed into a new and asocial realm of thought and activity.

Oskar is invited to become a model, to expose his face and body to the scrutiny of the artist's eye. Oskar is no model of the usual vein, for he carries with him hidden significance which becomes a source of creative inspiration for artists who perceive in him a rich repository of evil forces, potential harmony, and mythological associations. Professor Kuchen, for example, whose name means "cake" and stems etymologically from *kochen* or "cook," is depicted as a sinister figure who regards Oskar as a model victim "deserving only of destruction." Kuchen, with his black beard, coal eyes, black hat, black chalk lines under his fingernails, and black chalk dust coming out of his nostrils, tells his students that they should consider Oskar as an enemy who "must be slaughtered, crucified, nailed onto paper with heavy black lines." His diabolical fervor can be compared only to Rasputin, who was also described as black and diabolical, while his degree of expressed hostility against Oskar equals that of Luzie. Not only this professor but also his students see the sinister aspect in Oskar: "These sons and daughters of the Muses have recognized the Rasputin in you to be sure, but they will probably never discover the Goethe who lies dormant in you" (p. 556).

Then Oskar becomes a model for Herr Maruhn, a sculptor and proponent of classical forms, whose name ("Maroon") suggests the dark red color of the brooch which Oskar repeatedly notices on nurses' uniforms. It is Maruhn who discovers the Goethean harmonious substructure of Oskar's being. "I learned to appreciate Master Maruhn who could construct such excellent skeletons that it was not necessary to hide the structure with cheaper stuff" (p. 560). It is he who shapes a perfect skeletal frame for Oskar, classically harmonious and balanced in every respect; but unfortunately he cannot add the flesh, the imperfect human coverage that is heir to passion and conceals the underlying harmony.

The third group for which Oskar models is composed of painters who see him consecutively in different tones and colors, first bluish, reflecting perhaps the color of his Bronski eyes, and then later as a deathly green (Niobe's color) or nauseating yellow (of the caged bird). Contrary to Professor Maruhn, who created Oskar's skeletal system with a degree of eternal harmony and permanence, these painters seem to see his skin colorations in different shades of macabre decay. What they bring to the canvas is confirmation that life is transient, marked for death.

Modeling for Oskar is, however, a passive experience. His observations of these people who paint him and try to capture his essence with success produces a number of short observations and critical commentaries on his part, but the implication is, of course, that he possesses the ultimate artistic genius which they all lack. But his genius is not quite ready to express itself; and Oskar willingly bides his time, now associating with artists, attending an artists' ball, thinking out problems, and observing life in the West, all of which seems to lead him nowhere until he accidentally runs into Corporal Lankes, the brutal and conscienceless soldier, artist, and former designer of the pillboxes of the Atlantic Wall. Oskar has not seen him since his tour with Bebra's theater. But of greater importance now is his bizarre relationship with a beautiful young girl named Ulla. She has come to the artists' ball with Lankes clad as an angel, but Oskar insists that this was no masquerade. She was a young, pure goddess of light and illumination and certainly one of the Muses.

A new phase in Oskar's modeling career begins with Ulla as he poses with her in different costumes and scenes, reflecting some part of his past history, present purpose, and future mission. One time they pose as the Faun and the Nymph, another time as Beauty and the Beast, and then even as the Lady and the Unicorn. But the picture which becomes most popular is entitled "Madonna 49," in which Oskar poses as a crippled and distorted Jesus, symbolizing the complete loss of hope in the year 1949. Then, one of the artists, Raskolnikov, insists that Oskar pose with a tin drum, but Oskar becomes evasive and tries to reject the offer completely. Oskar associates the drum with all the guilt-ridden experiences of childhood, so when Raskolnikov (whose name is synonymous with murder, guilt, and atonement) brings him the drum anyway, Oskar screams in histrionic travesty that he will never take a drum again, that that phase of life has ended for him. Raskolnikov continues urging him, saying, "Nothing is ended, everything returns, guilt, atonement, more guilt." Ulla bends over and kisses him. "I wept when the Muse Ulla bent over me: I could not, blinded by tears, prevent the Muse from giving me that terrible kiss. All of you who have ever received a kiss by the Muse will surely understand that Oskar at once stamped by that kiss was condemned to take back the drum he had rejected years before, the drum he had buried in the sand of Saspe Cemetery" (p. 568). That terrible kiss of the Muse rips away Oskar's facade as an establishment dwarf (see p. 538) and compels him to face again the destiny he attempted to bury in the grave of his father. The kiss, however, and *not* a feeling of guilt, convinces Oskar to accept his drum again; guilt for past events does not motivate the epic myth hero who lives for the future. And Lucy Johnson also observes that "for Grass, innocence has a special meaning–freedom from knowledge of good and evil and therefore of responsibility and guilt."[2] Oskar takes the drum in hand again–not to absolve himself from guilt but instead to go the way of the divine artist, the culture hero, the cosmic drummer. His attempt to avoid that fate by becoming a good middle-class bourgeois, by marrying Maria, and earning a modest living, has come to naught. Oskar is destined now to fulfill not himself but also the needs of his epoch. "The need of his times works inside the artist without his wanting it, seeing it, or understanding its true significance. In this sense he is close to the seer, the prophet, the mystic. And it is precisely when he does not represent the existing canon but transforms and overturns it that his function rises to the level of the sacral, for he then gives utterance to the authentic and direct revelation of the numinosum."[3] It is indeed "the need of his times" that forces the drum upon Oskar again without his wanting it, but once the muse kisses him (just as Bebra did in another era), his fate as an artist and prophet is sealed.

The kiss soon succeeds in bringing dormant forces into motion again and leads Oskar to resolve some of the aimless confusion that has plagued him since his arrival in the West. Oskar now moves out of Maria's house, leaving her and his presumptive son Kurt behind, and searches out a new residence which in turn becomes an important point of departure along a path that returns him to the chthonic world, nurses, Bebra, and employment as a Messiah of great revelation for the people of the West. Indeed Bebra's new booking agency is even called "West," and appropriately so for it serves to introduce and popularize Oskar throughout this whole land. Bebra also has been the dwarf of the West from the very start. He arrived in Danzig from the West, and it was he who enticed Oskar out of the East to travel the continent all the way to the western front and discover there the temple of death and the modern labyrinth. Oskar, as a result of his dealings with Bebra, will also make another pilgrimage to the West Wall in order to meditate there and perform a blood sacrifice before embarking upon his divine mission as a redeeming artist-prophet.

The Land of the West, as we have touched upon it several times already, finally comes to signify (in contrast to the East) a place of technology, materialism, boredom, bathos, or, in short, spiritual deprivation and human invalidation. If we are willing to regard this western land as an extended metaphor in the total mythos of *The Tin Drum*, then we may also come to recognize that these are not unlike the shores near Sodom upon which Oskar, like Jonah, has been spewed after having made the night sea journey in the belly of the whale. He has passed in darkness through the Western Gate, the portal of Hecate, into a kind of mythic waste land like Nineveh peopled by men of energy but without spirit, living unknowingly in the shadow of death. Details are less important here than the compelling truth that this western land of *The Tin Drum,* like Nineveh and countless other limbos of mythology, is a spiritual desert in need of saving. This was not at all the case in the East, where even holocausts and tragedy were dominated by some binding spiritual principle that lent them purpose and sanctity. Oskar is certainly the last representative of the East who may yet demonstrate those ancient revitalizing forces of another world, saving souls like other prophets or mythological heroes.

# EIGHT *The Descent to Trophonios*

On several occasions Oskar has made a dramatic and concerted effort to join the world of adults, as we have seen. He attempted to abandon his childlike stature: he gave up the supernatural aids of his youth—the drum and his glass-shattering voice, and finally he even asked Maria to marry him so that he might become a husband, father, citizen, and therefore an integrated member of human society. But in each case the fates contravened. His decision to grow turned him into a hunchback, his rejected drum was forced back upon him, and his effort for acceptance in the community was nullified when Maria shunned his proposal of marriage. Time and again providence appears to interfere with Oskar's attempts at leading a normal life, and each time that alternatives are denied him he is compelled to return to the mythological sphere that dominated his childhood. Whenever he is drawn back to the earth like Antaeus, he acquires the renewed inner strength and the endemic powers he lacks as he floats aimlessly through civilized society trying to become something less than a hero.

Having made a futile attempt to escape his mythic destiny, Oskar is providentially drawn back into the world of a subterranean order as he looks for a new place to live. He walks down a street of ruins and overgrown piles of rubble, past a large black slab of Swedish granite on an unfinished building, into the courtyard of a solitary house; and after glancing at the pile of empty coffins stored there and the sign "Undertaker, Schornemann" (low German cognate for "shovel-man"), Oskar enters the den of a man he refers to as the "Hedgehog" and takes up residence there. As the Stygian images indicate, Oskar is again departing from the surface world and reentering the infernal region of earth deities and chthonic forces. When Zeidler, the owner (whose name means "beekeeper")[1] appears at the door, "hedgehoggy" as Oskar says, he has a dense layer of shaving lather on his face which adds to his unhuman but nevertheless likable appearance. Zeidler is carefully depicted as a small, outspoken, erratic animal that likes to smash glasses against the iron stove when he gets angry, a practice which Oskar compares to his own former skill. Zeidler's front room is sketched in the tartan fashion of a Matisse painting, cluttered with strangely mixed pieces of furniture, somber and yet colorful, set off by four leather chairs upon a floor covered by four rugs atop one another, recalling the skirts of Anna Bronski; but here the large brownish one on the bottom is covered by a green one, then a blue, and finally a wine-red one. The two bottom ones, brown and green, suggest the arcs of nature's vegetation cycle, while the blue one that runs to the distant corners of the room is stretched over the others as the heavens might be. The bottom three—brown for the subsurface of earth, green for the vegetation world, and blue for the heavens—may also represent the three cosmic layers which have been united at this sacred spot where the fragments of Oskar's life will be integrated in preparation for his final adventures. The sequence also parallels the predominating color themes of the novel beginning with the brown firmament of Anna Bronski's fields, the paradoxical life-death greenery of Niobe, followed by the heavenly aspirations reflected in Jesus-Oskar's blue eyes. It is a wine-red rug, the color of passion in the red cross on the nurse's uniform that is uppermost, that dominates all others in the Zeidler house and takes Oskar back to one of the basic themes of the novel, his predilection for nurses.

The Hedgehog chapter begins with a literary allusion in which Oskar compares himself with the seeker of spiritual clarification—Parsifal. The comparison is based on the familiar moment at which Parsifal is transfixed by the sight of three drops of red blood in a pure white snow, which Oskar then explains in relationship to himself: "The snow, that is the professional uniform of a nurse; the red cross which most nurses wear in the middle of their collars to hold them together as a brooch, just as the nurse Dorothea did, appeared for me in place of the three drops of blood" (p. 570). This allusion to nurses, especially significant for the development of the color symbolism in the novel, serves as an introduction here for Oskar's decision to take up residence in this house when Zeidler tells him that one small apartment is occupied by a nurse. This is stimulus enough for Oskar's imagination. He is fascinated by the idea of living here under the same roof with a nurse and he begins to reflect on all of his experiences with nurses ranging from those he met after having fallen down the cellar stairs at the age of three to those whom he met in the hospital in Düsseldorf or saw going to work in their uniforms, leaving out only the allusion to his mother as a nurse. Now, without ever having met her or knowing one concrete thing about her, Oskar begins to epitomize all of his dreams of nurses in the form of this "Nurse Dorothea, about whom I only knew that she had rented a room at Zeidler's place behind a milk-white glass door" (p. 581). From this moment on, until the very end of the novel, it is Dorothea in counterpoint to the Black Cook who preoccupies Oskar's thoughts.

The closer the Black Cook approaches him on the one hand, the greater Oskar's efforts become to embrace and deify the Nurse Dorothea as a source of salvation on the other. A whole chapter is dedicated to Oskar's exploration of Dorothea's room and his fantasies in her armoire. After making some wish-directed references to figures that he has been modeling, such as Zeus's abduction of Europa or the Nurse as Temptation and Atonement for the Fool, Oskar tries the door to Dorothea's room one day and finds that it is open. Though Oskar conceives of Dorothea as ethereal and heavenly, her room is certainly of an earthly order. It seems to be a collection of broken, decayed, and unsightly elements. Half-packages of sanitary napkins, uncorked bottles, half-tubes of salves, bits of hair, soiled brassieres, and cheap detective novels lie about the room in complete disarray. The room smells of vinegar; it is spotted with dust and dandruff; and even her bed, which Oskar had so often imagined to be beautiful and enticing turned out to be of "the same hateful frame" as the one on which he himself had spent so many restless nights. Everything about this room appears to be hateful, distasteful, odious.

Then Oskar notices Dorothea's armoire, a commanding closet that opens itself almost like an act of grace to welcome and absorb him: "Immediately and without my help, the wood [door] opened widely with a sigh and offered such a view that I had to take several steps back in order to be able to observe it coolly with crossed arms. . . . Completely with a feeling of freshness like on the first day of the creation he wanted to greet the closet because the closet had received him with open arms" (p. 592). Contrary to the room that he has just examined, Oskar views the closet as vast, enticing, timeless, and unspoiled. He approaches it slowly in respect and awe; and as Oskar enters its confines, he steps out of both time and space, into a void that is plainly marked for him by the purity of its order and sanctity. He regards this closet as a container of Dorothea's "visible presence," a holy altar that promises to be a haven of tranquility similar to the one he had once found under his grandmother's skirts. Oskar's only objection to this armoire is that someone (a barbarian he says) sawed off its legs and put it flat but yet unevenly onto the floor, a comment which serves to imply that this armoire should be raised slightly from the floor's surface to give it the effect of elevation and etherealness.

Oskar enters the armoire, pulls the doors closed behind him, and sets out on the fantasy of free adventure. Joseph Campbell would assume that he has entered the "shrine or altar at the center being symbolical of the Inexhaustible Point. The one who enters the temple compound and proceeds to the sanctuary is imitating the deed of the original hero. His aim is to rehearse the universal pattern as a means of evoking within himself the recollection of the life-centering, life-renewing form"[2] And this is precisely what Oskar experiences. The odor of the closet is clean and pleasant, and as he lays his forehead against the nurse's uniform he suddenly feels that all the doors of past and the present history are open to him. Unconsciously he takes hold of a black leather belt that leads him in free association back in years to the fisherman, the seagulls, the black horse's head, and the eels which presaged his mother's death; but this time some of the images and perceptions are unraveled a bit further to reveal the significance that was hidden in the complexity of that original scene. Now the fisherman on the pier is magnified as he sits holding his clotheslines and potato sack that throbs with movement, while Oskar in the closet holds a black leather belt and recalls that at the time of the apparition from the sea he was holding something else "that was to be sure also black and slippery but still not a belt" (p. 595). Then he ruminates about how nice it would be if one could place all that was white into one category and everything black into another, to balance the Black Cook off against the whiteness of the nurse's uniform, the whiteness of doves against the black horse's head, and so on. He recalls that when two eels were pulled out of the horse's head, his mother had to vomit; and later on that she vomited from eating fish and eels. He recalls that seagulls have evil eyes, that they could not be driven away, and that Jan Bronski held both hands in front of his eyes to protect them, for it is generally known that gulls may pick out the eyes of an evildoer, and render him blind as Oedipus. Then he remembers the end of the episode when everyone thought that the fisherman was through pulling out eels, and to everyone's surpirse "he pulled one huge one out of the horse's ear and swung it about until the eel showed its lacquer and shined like a black leather belt, and with that I want to have said: Nurse Dorothea wore just such a belt" (597), the belt which Oskar now held in his hands. For the moment the black belt becomes an enclosing circle embracing the body of the white uniform, an uroborous, the snake eating its own tail, the symbol of the constantly rotating life-and-death cycle in which one aspect revolves into the other. The symbol signifies the eternal transformation of life and matter, for all organic life must in turn provide nourishment for other growing entities of nature.

Oskar interweaves the images of belt, eels, and men with recollections of his nurse-mother who began to consume fish of all kind until she had "had enough, not only of eels but also of life and especially of men" (p. 597). Agnes's overindulgence with sex and food, both of which she associates as a *single* erotic experience, in turn become a source of death rather than activity for the creation and maintenance of life. Oskar goes on to say that he has inherited from her the tendency of "not wanting to give up anything and on the other hand being able to get along without everything; only I cannot live without smoked eels no matter how expensive they are." Then the eels once again become the black patent leather belt that belongs to Sister Dorothea: "I just couldn't tear myself away from that belt; it was endless; it increased even; for I opened the buttons of my fly with my free hand and did something that allowed me to imagine once again the nurse which had faded a little in my vision through the intervention of the many lacquered eels and also the Finns that had docked. . . . and Oskar had to make an effort not to soil the full-length skirt belonging to Sister Dorothea that was hanging next to him" (pp. 597–98).[3] The black patent leather belt now substitutes for the eel and evolves into Oskar's own male organ as the recollection of the scene at the beach, and thoughts of his mother's relationship with men (and with fish) stimulate him to of masturbation. On that note the doors to the closet seem to swing open of their own accord and Oskar leaves the confines of the enclosure drumming playfully with his fingers, something he has not done for years. He also realizes that a forty-watt bulb (the father spirit, as we recall from his birth) that has been burning in the room all this time has been spying on him. In the closet he had withdrawn from the world of light, he had withdrawn from time and space; as a matter of fact he had traveled backwards in time, transformed his travels into a sexual resurrection, and then at the moment he experienced an orgasm the doors opened and he was once again like fresh seed spewed forth into the world of light. In the darkness, withdrawn from the world, he has relived the mysteries of creation, life, reproduction, death; and now a kind of rebirth, a regeneration of energy, allows him to return to the world with the knowledge that all of its external manifestations are merely symbolic transformations of a single continuum.

The clothes closet episode is one of the significant cycles of the Universal Round experienced in form as well as content; it is symbolized by circles, a series of small circles with one large embracing circumference of action that posits the basic epic structure of this novel. All epic narratives are characterized by such periods of active engagement punctuated by periods of rest in which the creative powers and life energies may be regenerated. Each cycle, from night and back to day again, or from the world of perceptible reality into fearful but yet revitalizing sleep, from engagement in the world to complete withdrawal and back again, completes a recurring pattern or Round. These are the measurable alternations from one state to another which can be conceptualized in the form of a revolving wheel (or a black leather belt and a white nurse's uniform). The small circles of the Universal Round or the cosmogonic cycles are of a microcosmic or personal order here; but by analogy, when experienced as ritual, they succeed in reflecting an all-embracing movement of the universe.[4]

A visual construct of this conception, the uroborous, is confirmed by the patent leather belt and the color imagery of this episode. The circular form of the snake devouring itself sets one of several possible images as the basic pattern of unity to define this novel. Like Oskar's world itself, the uroborous as an image is both time-bound and infinite. It feeds constantly on a segment of its own tail, growing at one end and vanishing at the other in perfect balance to create the timeless circle of life. The head and its adjacent arc are white, while the center begins to turn from light grey to a lifeless black. Organic life feeds upon death, for only by devouring life in an endless balanced cycle can life continue to survive. The conception that this image conveys provides the basis for the chthonic mysteries that are an integral part of every primitive and modern mythology of a transcendent order. Only Grandmother Bronski is beyond the Universal Round, for she encompasses and is synonymous with the Great Earth itself.[5] It is below her skirts, in Oskar's language, that all opposites and unities exist in timeless harmony. It is she who exists and orders life before Oskar's arrival and only she, as we will discover in the end, who can save Oskar from the Black Cook. However, she chooses rather to groom him for the inevitable destiny which must follow a natural course.

Now, having emotionally and intuitively experienced a degree of enlightenment, Oskar has reestablished a firm bond with the sacred and semidivine world of his origin. It is not surprising therefore to see that he is prophetically cast again in the role of mythological hero as he models at the studio—first as Vulcan, then as Pluto, and finally as a hunchbacked Odysseus. In these jobs as a model Oskar is constantly together with Ulla, whom he refers to as one of the Muses. She is the visual confirmation of inchoate inspiration and encouragement for Oskar to return to his real vocation as the drumming artist. His present profession as a model is indeed a pose, and when Oskar becomes clear on that point, he willingly leaves his job as a model to embark upon a final series of adventures in which he fulfills his destiny.

The point of departure for Oskar's great new adventure and cultural mission begins in the beautiful filth of Klepp Münzer's room. Klepp is described in detail as a completely soiled, earthy type—fat, sweating, lazy, superstitious, unwashed, apparently on the verge of death, smelling like a corpse, or, in short, in Oskar's words, "he was decaying in the best of spirits" (p. 605). He never leaves his bed; he cooks there and relieves himself there as well, making a life pattern and a ritual out of his phlegmatism.

Little by little, as Oskar becomes better acquainted with Klepp, after the two of them eat a meal of sordid spaghetti that resembles sludge or paste, which Oskar incidentally learns to appreciate, a conversation between them develops on the topic of music; and when Klepp challenges Oskar's authority as a musician, Oskar is compelled to run to his room, fetch his drum, and give Klepp a demonstration of his virtuosity. He begins to drum, relating in the rhythms of the percussion instrument all of his life experiences in their epic order, from the appearance of the mysterious moth at the moment of birth to the drum and the fall on his third birthday, the Pestalozzi school, the glass-shattering voice, the politics, the coffins, the eels, the gulls, the Polish post office, and on and on with the never-ending refrain of his grandmother sitting in her four skirts in the Kashubian potato fields while rain fell from above, conceiving under her skirts the poor mother who brought Oskar into this world. As Oskar beats out the rhythms of his life, Klepp joins him on his flute, and together they explore Oskar's grandfather's flight on the timber rafts and into the river, the pleasurable space below Anna Koljaiczek's skirts, and the apotheosis of Anna's husband, Oskar's grandfather, Joseph Koljaiczek. The episode breaks through a plane of reality to summon up spirits of the past that seem to have been shut up in Oskar's drum, and with them Oskar and Klepp embark upon an ecstatic journey to a new realm of inspiration.

Before the last tones vanish, Klepp experiences a dramatic transformation. He jumps out of bed, opens the windows, announces that an era of his life has ended; and he washes himself as Oskar perceives that "this was a complete purification" for Klepp: "He washed himself, he washed himself, Klepp began to wash himself. He dared to wash off everything 'till it was no washing any more but ablution . . . I suddenly realized that not only Oskar's drum had been resurrected but Klepp too was resurrected" (p. 612). Both Oskar and Klepp have become attuned to the rhythms of life again and decide to return to the world outside after their lengthy seclusion in the den of the Hedgehog. To celebrate the newly found feeling of purification and resurrection, the two of them spend the evening drinking beer and eating blood-sausages with onions. They agree to start a jazz band together, and Oskar officially proclaims that he will give up his modeling, a completely passive occupation, and his stone-cutting as well, to become the percussion man in the band.

After an event that again confirms the inaccessibility of nurses—Oskar's failure to seduce Dorothea on the fiber rug in the Hedgehog's house—he begins working with Klepp Münzer (whose first name refers to "stealing" [*kleptein*] and whose second name alludes to a German coin which, according to Brockhaus, was originally made of gold dust, "Feingold"–the name of the wizard from the concentration camp who saved Oskar from madness, possibly death, and then sent him along with Maria and Kurt to the West). Klepp also finds a guitarist named Scholle (literally a "clump of soil or a clod of dirt") to fill out the trio, and the three soon find a job playing in a bizarre restaurant, "The Onion Cellar." The place is actually less of a restaurant than a sacrarium where guests are introduced to secret rites and alleged processes for self-purification. Rather than food the guests of the Onion Cellar receive instruction in expressing emotion, dramatizing remorse, and overcoming frustration. The details with which Grass describes this cellar and the events that take place there reveal some special concern on his part.

Outside the restaurant an enamel shield hangs from a wrought-iron arm resembling the gallows. The only window is effectively blocked by nature's overgrowth. Having entered through an iron door painted red and watched over by a porter in a sheepskin, one finds five concrete steps which descend onto a three-foot square landing with four more steps that lead further down to where Ferdinand Schmuh stands–"The owner in person who welcomed every guest with extremely dextrous movements of the eyebrows and other gestures, as though he were initiating every new guest into a secret rite" (p. 628). And the Onion Cellar is a real cellar–quite damp, tubular in shape, extending upwards into the former first floor which serves as a balcony that can be reached only by climbing a precipitous "chicken-coop ladder," as Oskar describes it, that is really not a ladder at all but a precarious gangway that sways threateningly and makes one think of an ocean voyage, especially because the dangerously steep steps have only a clothesline railing. The cellar is also lighted by carbide lamps such as miners carry, and that too gives the effect of transporting the guests into a deep cavern or mine such as one might find "about three thousand feet below the surface of the earth."

Not everyone may enter the cellar, and those who do must display a certain degree of courage to counteract the natural fears imposed by narrow stairways, shaking causeways, a clammy subterranean atmosphere, and the terror of descending deep into the bowels of the earth. But all this is only by way of introduction to the actual rites which follow. Now Ferdinand Schmuh, the host, puts on his cobalt blue shawl, goes through a careful litany, and finally distributes the onions which, as the high point of the ritual, are sliced up in order to produce tears. He is greeted by the people as the "saviour" or the "miraculous uncle" since he leads them through an experience that borders on spiritual catharsis. His objective is a relatively simple one: after many tearless years, the guests are made to cry, to cry completely and without restraint, to cry freely and openly. The tears are hyperbolically compared to rivers that overflow and to cleansing dew.

The Onion Celler is also a kind of *axis mundi* or world navel, as in Greek mythology where the conception of a central point, the hub or navel, the *omphalos* was cast as a hemispherical onion-shaped excavation in the earth. The most famous was the one at Delphi that was supposed to have marked the center of the earth. The earth deity, Trophonios (literally the feeder), said to have built the first temple of Apollo at Delphi, was worshiped after his death, especially in a certain cave in Boeotia, where worshipers and inquirers went for purification and mystic experiences that might help them resolve their present dilemmas and predict the future. The following description of the purification rites in the name of Trophonius, formulated by Pausanias, not only concurs with the description of the Onion Cellar but also duplicates some of its rituals, fears and effects.

> As to the oracle, the procedure is as follows. When a man has resolved to go down to the oracle of Trophonius, he . . . . sacrifices both to Trophonius himself and to the children of Trophonius, also to . . . Demeter, whom they surname Europa, and say she was Trophonius' nurse. The oracle . . . . is surrounded in a circle by a basement of white marble, the circumference of which is about that of a threshing floor of the smallest size, and the height less than two ells. On the basement are set bronze spikes connected by cross-rails, which are also of bronze, and there are gates in the railing. Inside the enclosure is a chasm in the earth, not a natural chasm, but built in the exactest style of masonry. The shape of this structure is like that of a pot for baking bread in . . . . There is no passage leading down to the bottom; but when a man goes to Trophonius they bring him a narrow and light ladder. When he has descended he sees a hole between the ground and the masonry . . . . So he lays himself on his back on the ground,

> and holding in his hand barley cakes kneaded with honey, he thrusts his feet first into the hole and follows himself, endeavouring to get his knees through the hole. When they are through, the rest of his body is immediately dragged after them and shoots in, just as a man might be caught and dragged down by a swirl of a mighty and rapid river. Once they are inside the shrine the future is not revealed to all in one and the same way, but to one it is given to see, and to another to hear . . . . When a man has come up from Trophonius the priests take him in hand again, and set him on what is called the chair of Memory, which stands not far from the shrine; and, being seated there, he is questioned by them as to all he saw and heard. On being informed, they hand him over to his friends, who carry him, still overpowered with fear, and quite unconscious of himself and his surroundings, to the building where he lodged before, the house of Good Fortune and the Good Demon. Afterwards, however, he will have all his wits as before, and the power of laughter will come back to him. I write not from mere hearsay: I have myself consulted Trophonius, and have seen others who have done so. (*Pausanias* 9.39–4.14; tr. J. G. Frazer)

In general as well as in a number of specific details, we find numerous parallels here to what happens in the Onion Cellar.[6] The people do indeed learn to confront strong emotions, until one day, quite carelessly and impulsively, Schmuh gives his guests a second onion. And then terror, frenzy, and chaos break loose. An orgy ensues in which the self-oblivious guests become disgusting, violent, and too uncontrollable even for Schmuh himself. He pleads with Oskar and the Rhine-River-Three Jazz Band to do something, but only Oskar reacts by taking his drum and getting everyone's attention with a short ditty, "Bake, Bake, Bake a Cake," that brings them back to the actual "baking-pot" shape of this cellar. Then Oskar goes on to take complete possession of his audience by returning these adults to a state of childhood.

Oskar therefore achieves in fact what Schmuh attempted to accomplish with a shallow trick. The tears which the people cried for Schmuh were as mechanical as the rites which he had performed. Even Schmuh's inadvertently created orgy, Oskar observes, "was a dull, uninspired affair, hardly worth describing in detail" (p. 642). The tears and remorse of these people and the means by which they were achieved are thin or artificial, and Oskar is quick to recognize the bathos in which this presumptuous mystery play is immersed. As a result of the failure of the false prophet, Ferdinand Schmuh (whose name in German, *Schmuh,* means "swindle, unfair profit, or deception"), Oskar is compelled to become the special mystagogue who can direct these people through the depths and retrieve them again from the embrace of Trophonius. "First I put a harness on these postwar humans who were incapable of real orgy," Oskar says; and he leads them like "their Pied Piper" back to their childhood, drumming up the Black Cook and making her "rage through the Onion Cellar, gigantic, coal-black, inscrutable, and obtained the results for which Schmuh required onions; the ladies and gentlemen wept large round, childlike tears . . . they were terrified, they begged for mercy" (pp. 643-44). Oskar continues to lead them then through the length and breadth of childhood, returning them to the roots of their existence to relive a forgotten mythic dimension of their lives–childhood, when dreams and reality were still united in one well-integrated mythopoetic totality.

We recall that Oskar in his early development once revealed an inchoate gift for making adults "human, that is, childlike, curious, complex, and immoral" (p. 87). Now, more mature after his own many descents to Trophonios, to the world "underneath," he is able to perform a ritual which may transport others to the mysteries he has experienced. By plunging stiff, materialistic, self-commiserating adults back into a lost childhood state of mythopoesis, when all dreams were still realities and reality was yet an extended, vital part of one's self, Oskar returns them to the depths of their own sacred creation and to the horrible knowledge of their own mortality.

Having said all that, one must add that Grass seems more concerned with the graphic processes of transformation than with its clarifying results. Here, repeating a motif that has returned relentlessly throughout the novel, we find a new variation of the theme the Belly of the Whale, the Night Sea Crossing, the Valley of Shadows, or the Descent to Trophonios. Having left the world of apparent order and stolid rationality, the guests of the Onion Cellar, as well as Schmuh himself, become overwhelmed by the perilous flow of irrational desires and chaotic behavior. Panic ensues, fear and uncertainty prevail, and madness threatens. The powers of darkness and the mysteries of a subterranean ritual have released terrors that spring up from below to engulf the victim, and only he who has once been initiated into this realm of irrationality and is himself related to nonmaterial powers may guide and retrieve those who have not been psychically or spiritually prepared for the experience.

Whereas the guests of the Onion Cellar as well as the original visitors to Trophonios are subjected to psychic terrors that bring them to the verge of disaster, the intended result is precisely the opposite. The experience with the mysteries serves the purpose of making the initiate and his universe whole once again. The netherworld figures are released in caverns and cellars and shown to be a dynamic and living part of a total existence that must be held in balance. The Greek gods of the underworld, for example, were actually shadow figures of the Olympians, as the name Zeus Chthonios or the double image of Demeter and Persephone reveal. It seems to have been the purpose of the mysteries to reunite those levels of existence which rationality splits apart.

Whereas Oskar's drumming now has the effect of reintegrating his listeners with their own psycho-mythic origins, Schmuh had previously done the very opposite. In a sense the onions which his guests had cut up were symbols of their own psyches, dissected in a ritual that allowed one to preside homeopathically over his own death. The German word for onion (*Zwiebel*) also has a verb form *zwiebeln*, which means "to torture, pain, or mishandle someone," and in that respect one might surmise that the visitors to the Onion Cellar were indeed dealing in sado-masochism, practicing *mortificatio,* and simultaneously bewailing their symbolic victim. The experience in any case, as evidenced in the subsequent stories of frequenters of the Cellar, produces results that border on madness, a form of schizophrenia here that poses as an answer to the exigencies of reality. Where fragmentation and dismemberment become the apparent answer the result is, of course, disaster. Fortunately it is Oskar's drumming and not Schmuh's disastrous impulse that prevails. Oskar like Orpheus leads the souls out of the dissolution of the underworld. By drumming he conjures up old forms which integrate the tortured souls of those who can respond to his rhythm.

We have discussed the Belly of the Whale experience, and the concept applies again no less than it did earlier. However, whereas Oskar once jolted hollow men from their mechanical, military, rigid behavior in the grandstand episode, here he restores to health those who have become so loose and fragmented that they run the risk of being swallowed by chaos. In the first instance Oskar saves his listeners from Scylla, in the second from Charybdis. In the former episode he shatters the hard shell to release the human being within, and in the latter case Oskar "kindles" a tune with his drum, and with it he is able to lead those in danger up and out of the labyrinth by taking them, as one knows from Dante's inferno, through its darkest center.

Once Oskar accepts the role of mystagogue in this crisis, he must also accept the consequences. On the one hand he exposes himself as a person of supernatural power, as a deity of sorts, and he also becomes a cultural hero who is in turn required to fulfill certain unique functions in his society. Yet, by pursuing that course, Oskar further isolates himself as an individual and must, therefore, continue his way as he began it–in solitude. For the moment, however, we note that Oskar considers Schmuh's request to "save the situation" from total dissolution to be the "incisive experience" (p. 640) of his life, for now he demonstrates total mastery over himself and others, a mastery that will permit him to fulfill a mission which only he is destined to undertake. This chapter therefore constitutes a peripetia for Oskar insofar as he demonstrates his supreme skill as the cosmic drummer who with the aid of sympathetic rhythms can touch a "magic spring" from which the vital forces of life again begin to flow, encouraging stolid citizens to dance like children through the streets of Düsseldorf. Music, dance, and ceremony, as Sir James Frazer asserts, were supposed to effect this end: "Primitive man believed that in order to produce the great phenomenon of nature on which his life depended he had only to imitate them, and that immediately by secret sympathy or mystic influence the little drama which acted in the forest glade or mountain dell, on desert plain or wind-swept shore, would be taken up or repeated by mightier actors on a vaster stage."[7] The magic spring which Oskar causes to flow again is quite literally the flow of genuine emotion, without which one is little more than one of the walking dead. Oskar plays his music in this underground cellar where no food of any consequence is devoured, where only a ritual in the slicing of onions brings about the mollification of hardened personalities. But when Schmuh fails to take his followers beyond that point, Oskar makes his appearance as the real prophet of regeneration as a mystagogue who can provide a mode of redemption for people who have become lifeless bricks in the edifice of society. Thus Oskar's drum finds its social purpose, one that might well be viewed as the final purpose of its long history. But nothing stands still for the epic hero, and the completion of one task merely becomes the beginning of another. Where he might have reached his ultimate goal here in a lesser novel, he faces instead a bifurcation of the ways at which Oskar the demigod-hero and Oskar the mortal must part company. Whereas one choice fulfills his cultural destiny, the other dooms him to personal failure; whereas one aspect of his life grows to messianic proportions, the other, as we shall soon see, will become little more than an exercise in futility.

# NINE *Travel, Triumph, & Despair*

Just as the treasure of the conquered dragon or sorcerer is acquired by the appointed hero, Oskar assumes the unfulfilled mission of Ferdinand Schmuh, the false priest of the Onion Cellar. Schmuh's obvious limitations are exposed by his inability to lead his followers to any significant depth in the mysteries of Trophonios without losing them to the chaos that resides just below the formal surface of ritual. When Schmuh impulsively transgresses the set limitations of ritual practice and inadvertently releases some of the genuine undercurrents of man's own deep mystery, it is Oskar who must descend like Orpheus to the nether world and rescue the frantic souls that are beginning to dissolve there. Like the true shaman or culture hero that he now becomes, Oskar does not merely retrieve lost souls from confusion but also leads them back through the center of a maze of aboriginal monsters to social reality on the streets of Düsseldorf.

Susanne Langer points out the hero's function in *Philosophy in a New Key:* "The status of the culture-hero is thus very complex. His activities lie in the real world, and their effects are felt by real men forever after; he therefore has a somewhat vague, yet unmistakable historical relation to living men, and a tie to the locality on which he has left his mark. This alone would suffice to distinguish him from the hero of fairyland, whose acts are bound up entirely with a story, so that he can be dispensed with at the end of it, and a new hero introduced for the next story."[1] In the next phase of this adventure Oskar himself truly becomes a culture hero while Schmuh is effectively dispatched for his fairyland pretensions and flagrant disrespect of Eunomia, the goddess of wise legislation and order.

Schmuh's hobby is shooting sparrows, and until now he has spent a number of leisurely afternoons bagging a set limit of twelve; but on one fateful afternoon, after he has reached his limit of twelve, he returns to his car only to see an additional sparrow sitting nearby singing brazenly, whereupon Schmuh takes his rifle and shoots his thirteenth bird. That act and the events that follow belong as much to the mystery of folktales and superstition as to the realm of traditional mythology. As he is driving home from the hunt on a dangerous detour, hundreds of birds suddenly loom up out of the bushes, grass, and trees to envelop his Mercedes, bang against the windshield, terrify the passengers, and cause the car to go over a cliff and the driver to hurtle to his death. Thirteen is indeed the number of misfortune, and by shooting the thirteenth bird Schmuh provokes the revengeful forces of nature's justice. Whereas "twelve" is evidently linked to measurable time by virtue of the astrological signs and to space by its flexible arithmetical workability in dealing with measurements, "thirteen" carries with it the omen of misfortune or death that awaits just beyond the surveyable world of man. By succumbing to temptation and killing the thirteenth bird, Schmuh provokes Nemesis, the goddess who takes swift steps to punish immoderation and restore things to their proper and natural order.

At the cemetery where Schmuh is being buried, a certain Dr. Dösch introduces himself as a representative of an entertainment agency that would like to sign Oskar for a number of concert tours. Dösch had been a guest in the Onion Cellar and marvelled, he says, at the "impressive stunt" which Oskar performed there. Rather than signing this "terrific contract" indiscreetly in the shadow of death, Oskar puts off Dr. Dösch and travels west with his old acquaintance, Corporal Lankes, to reflect on past events and future possibilities.

The most significant incident that occurs once the two of them are again installed in the old pillbox, Dora Seven, on the Atlantic Wall, is the cooking and eating of a large codfish. Oskar prepares the fish like a superb gourmet, languishing artistically on the details of the culinary art. Then, waiting for the fish to cook, Oskar plays his drum in the sand and relives the experiences of former times in this same place with Roswitha, Bebra, and his troupe of players of the Miracle Show. When the fish is finished cooking, a long debate between Oskar and Lankes begins as to who shall eat the head of the fish and who shall have the tail. However trivial the incident may appear on the surface, one discovers on closer examination that its true significance centers again on a performance of a sacrificial ritual and a subsequent augury.

Oskar begins the ritual sacrifice with a mild invocation to the undifferentiated name of the double goddess, *Dora* Seven and *Doro-*

thea. As he thinks of Dorothea in cleaning the fish, the milt and the blood of the liver spurt out over his hands. In the mythic mode blood is at once associated with the process of life, death, and birth again, so instead of disregarding the milt and liver, Oskar carefully lodges them in the jaws of the fish. While scaling the disemboweled fish, Oskar also turns toward the sun, thereby addressing himself to its western descent and symbolic death. Oskar mentions that he stands protected from the wind by Dora Seven, the omphalos-shaped temple of death with its enigmatic mandala of shells and stones at its portal. The sun also reflects off the "head" of the bunker as it once did out of the diabolical amber eye of Niobe, who had taken Herbert Truczinski as her victim. Then, as Oskar bathes the fish in olive oil and lemon juice, stuffing the bowels with delicacies, Lankes begins to circle around the fish "like a hungry sea gull." Lankes certainly has a good deal in common with the seagull scavengers that once descended on the eels at Neufahrwasser-Brösen. The comparison here to that scene in "Good Friday Fare" is not wholly unwarranted. The seagull-Lankes equation and affinity for fish continues to be developed as a major motif of this scene that transforms eels into death sexual organs, fish into relentless hunger, and both into death from the sea.

Lankes's attitude, be it toward animals or human beings, can be characterized only in terms of unconscious, brutal self-satisfaction; and the only way to propitiate him is through diversion, food, or other forms of physical satisfaction, so for the moment Oskar succeeds in diverting Lankes from his hunger by drumming out another of his séance histories from the Kashubian potato fields up to the earlier visit to the West Wall. When the fish has finished cooking over the glowing coals to the sound of Oskar's drumming, Lankes, showing his sharp teeth and beating his apelike chest, proclaims his hunger; but he is again diverted from descending on the fish by Oskar's question: "Head or tail?" The question, it turns out, is not a simple one. Like Oskar's previous questions, "To grow or not to grow" and "To marry or not to marry," the problem of "head or tail" is debated as a crucial one upon whose outcome more depends than the mere satisfaction of hunger. Predictably at this point, Oskar is apportioned the tail while Lankes enjoys the head as well as the delicacies lodged between its jaws, the milt and the liver along with the corresponding *mana* which they contain. If, as Plato asserts in *Timaeus,* "the head is truly the image of this world," then Oskar's apportionment of the tail must carry with it the subaltern *mana* to prepare him for "that world" into which he as an Orphic drummer will lead his followers during the adventure which now awaits him. Lankes, too, will profit from this sacrificial meal that prepares him with the insight and inspiration necessary to make his way in this most materialistic of all worlds.

W. G. Cunliffe describes Lankes as "mean, tough, selfish, and brutal, but far from neurotic and not at all addicted to unnecessary bloodshed."[2] However, when such qualities become the definitive description of an individual, as they do here, they displace human essence. Oskar, recognizing these very same qualities in Lankes, expands on them with the nomenclature of a mythological half-man and half-beast, alternately attributing to Lankes the movements of a gull, the chest of an ape, the head of a wolf, the fangs of a predator, and the moral character of a monster. And Lankes's actions continue to supply ample evidence to support visual images as an animal incarnate. When Oskar asks Lankes if he remembers machine-gunning the nuns on the beach, Lankes, savoring and sucking on bones, replies that he does indeed remember them, even their names; and then, as in a miracle of sorts, a young novitiate who is in effect a reembodiment of the youngest nun which Lankes had shot down, Sister Agneta, comes walking up over the sandy beach and casually stands "above the backbone of the cod which was revealing itself more clearly." It is at that point that Lankes grins, shakes his "wolf's head," and offers Agneta some fish; but she is whisked away for the moment by a group of nuns while Lankes, lying down with his fork sticking straight up from his mouth, participates with Oskar in a teichoscopic fantasy that envisions nuns as fleets of ships out to attack the Puritanism of England with the flagship Don Juan at its head. Agneta, however, drops out of the fleet and returns, whereupon Lankes—Don Juan—promptly lures her in all her purity into the pillbox and seduces her while Oskar sits outside lamenting his own failures in the domain of love. While Lankes is defiling the "Bride of Christ," Oskar has painful reveries of Nurse Dorothea; gulls in white nurses' uniforms wave at him, and the sun burns like a glowing Red Cross pin. Agneta, following her reappearance from the pillbox, helps herself to a portion of the fateful fish (associating it, Oskar remarks, with the act that preceded it), walks down to the sea, and presumably commits suicide by drowning. While Oskar casts accusations of callousness at him, Lankes envisions a series of pictures that he will paint about nuns in "black, lots of black." Thus he succeeds in turning even death to his advantage. He does in fact return to West Germany after his participation in this experience to win fame and fortune, to gobble up even more possessions and people with efficiency and impunity.

Regarding this amalgam of prior motifs (nurse-nun, seduction, fish, and death), there can be little doubt that we are dealing here with an archetypical reenactment of the rape of Persephone by the black Hierophant in addition to the symbolic life and death of Agnes Matzerath. We recall that Persephone was considered as one aspect of a twofold image with her mother, Demeter, and that together the two of them symbolized the cycle of life and death. Persephone, too, like Agneta here, was kept under close watch by her mother (superior), but one day as she was picking flowers (as Agneta here picks up shells from the beach), the earth opens and Hades carries her off to his underworld realm. The subsequent ritual reenactment of this mythogem and other related incidents were formalized at Eleusis, where, as J. E. Harrison claims, a form of rebirth or redemption also took place. "Is there not there performed the descent into darkness, the venerated congress of the Hierophant with the priestess, of him alone with her alone? Are not the torches extinguished and does not the vast and countless assemblage believe *that in what is done by the two in darkness is their salvation?*"[3] But what may have been a process of salvation for the ancients of Greece or for Joseph Koljaiczek on the Kashubian potato fields in the East becomes a casual ritual in the West. What was once holy has now become polluted to the degree where Oskar, himself no great friend of chastity, is compelled to call Lankes an inhuman monster. Animal-men are common enough in all mythologies, and even "in the early Hellenic religions there are traces of animal worship and of a belief in animal incarnations of a divinity, ancestor, or hero. Apollo Lykeios was a reminder of the time when he was still a god of the wild and associated with the wolf, his sacred animal."[4] Such animal appearances or behavior in men generally associated the incarnation with the unrestrained creatures of forest and woodland which engaged at will in satisfying their appetites. Lankes, as well as the Lykeios aspect of Apollo, is characterized by just such rapacious desires and conscienceless lusts. And in the present scene, the object of Lankes's lust (after the hearty meal) is indeed the sacrificial lamb, Agneta (whose name, like Agnes's is derived from the Greek *(h)agnos,* meaning ritually pure, chaste, and possibly the Greek word *amnos* or lamb, *agnus* in Latin). To some degree both of them blend into a single image here, defiled by sexuality and condemned to death under the sign of the fish. The white nurse of the East has become the black nun of the West just as the rites of creation or cosmogenesis become the ritual of death and despair.

For the moment, however, let us regard the ritual as one of desacrilization through which Oskar appears to win a degree of liberation from the grasp of his sacred ancestors so that he may enter a realm foreign to their divine nature. Considering the sacred origin of the drum, the omen of the moth, and his mother's promise as well as his own disavowal of his father's world of business on the day of his birth, Oskar evidently feels the need to participate in a propitiatory ritual as a prophylactic against the powers of ancestral retribution; for as J. E. Harrison describes the mysteries, it is as though "The ghost below demands the *blood of the victim washed off from the polluted suppliant:* when the ghost has drunk of this, then, and not till then, there is placation and purification."[5] But that part of the ritual attends only to Oskar's anxieties regarding the past and fails to answer the central question regarding the totem of the fish sacrificed.

Grass, who is so attracted to both punning and to the development of new mythogems, also associates the fish with Dr. Dösch, the executive representative from the Concert Agency West who has invited Oskar into the "business" of drumming. In appearance and in his choice of language, Dösch has quickly become for Oskar the image of organized commerce. It was he who "generously" presented Oskar with the money necessary to make this trip to the Atlantic Wall, suggesting that Oskar take time to consider his offer carefully. At a crucial point in the ritual, as Oskar and Lankes are about to eat the fish, Oskar refers to the codfish in the dialect of Danzig as a Dorsch (p. 654) although he uses the correct German word, *Kabeljau,* elsewhere. The doublet form of *Dorsch* in that coastal area near Danzig is in fact *Dösch:* and as that is the case, a bond is established that allows an interpretation of sacrificial devouring by which primitive suppliants strengthened themselves with the body and spirit of their enemy to prepare for the ordeals to come. On the one side this serious thread of meaning seems to be consciously hidden by Grass under a bizarre and playful dialogue, yet the repeated pattern of initiatory rites has become an established practice in linking together Oskar's chain of adventures. In preparatory acts the hero usually receives some supernatural aid or some energizing nutrition, such as Suzi's repugnant brick soup, to help him through the coming ordeals. And now that the ritual here has run its course, the specters of ancestors are temporarily appeased, the spirit or *mana* of the fish has been ingested, and Oskar returns to Germany to become the commercial drummer and Lankes to paint pictures of nuns.

Oskar is hardly enthusiastic about the prospects in store for him. His attitude clearly indicates resignation rather than a desire to make a large amount of money. Oskar, it seems, would have preferred to go another way, but there are few choices really open to the mythic hero. At one point during the ritual Oskar laments that he cannot "find a way out of this concrete landscape, this vegetable called Rommel asparagus" (p. 661), referring to a serpentine pattern of tank spikes surrounding him in the sand. He is caught in a magic labyrinth of forces he cannot escape. Therefore, like a martyr moving towards a death which has long since been his destiny, Oskar reads in the signs of the times his own unavoidable fate as the "tail of the fish." He must continue to move along a predestined line toward the completion of a mission that now returns him to the world of West Germany to transform his experiences, as he says, "with the tin of his drum into the pure, ringing gold of the post-war era" (p. 664).

When Oskar first visits the main office of the Concert Agency West, housed in a huge mountain of steel, chrome, and brick, he discovers that its director is no one other than his old friend and master, Bebra, the establishment dwarf who as an officer in the Ministry of Nazi Propaganda took him on his first visit to Dora Seven. But this former master of Oskar is now old, indeed, completely paralyzed, and in the world of the West, mechanized, for he has a versatile, motorized chair which allows him to propel himself around mechanically and do business as usual.

Bebra, greeting Oskar more like a judge than an old friend, reminds him that he, Oskar, remains guilty in fact for the murder of his parents. And, as in answer to a judge, Oskar with tongue in cheek admits his guilt, ending with an histrionic and bathetic plea for mercy. Bebra laughs at the artificiality and dramatic effect of Oskar's words: "Mercy my dear master Bebra! Mercy!" But instead of mercy, Bebra, recognizing the willing role of mea culpa which Oskar is playing, pushes a button and a secretary enters with a contract for Oskar to sign. And no sooner does Oskar sign, than Bebra throws his electric wheelchair into high gear and disappears from the room, leaving Oskar behind to inform the reader that he has not really sold his soul to the devil. Yet a diabolical action seems to have occurred here. The necessity of a contract among old soulmates such as Bebra and Oskar appears out of place. Why should Bebra feel it necessary to manage this reunion so formally, emphasizing Oskar's crimes and stimulating his sense of guilt? And why should Oskar feel that the atonement and mercy which he "pretends" to desire will come only after he signs an agreement to work for the Concert Agency West? There seems to be little purpose for this whole scenario if Oskar does not atone for some of his early transgressions by now fulfilling the terms of a contract; but since that is not the case, one must assume that Oskar is in fact dealing with a figure of a superior nature while fulfilling his own wishes.

Actually there is little change in the relationship between Bebra and Oskar from start to finish. Bebra is Oskar's admitted teacher and leader from the outset. Forty-four years older than Oskar, he acknowledges that he could be Oskar's grandfather, but in appearance he is even older. "His eyes become as old as the hills," and Bebra, who claims to be a direct descendant of Prince Eugene, is also identified with the Byzantine general Narses, the misshapen dwarf and eunuch who was credited, along with other martial victories, with the destruction of the Sibyl's cave on the Phlegraean plain, a cavern reputed to be an entrance to the underworld and a domicile of Hecate.[6] By the time Oskar encounters Bebra for the third and last time, he has risen in position to become the boss of the concert agency. He speaks to Oskar like a lord to his quaking vassal; the effect of which is already implicit in Bebra's name (the homonymic *bebere*, meaning to tremble, quake, shake).

In this scene Bebra is described as ancient in appearance, immovable, physically "unhuman" (he can only speak and push buttons), and apparently omniscient, knowing as he does of Oskar's presumed murders of the fathers, Matzerath and Jan Bronski, and of Oskar's adventures in the Onion Cellar. Bebra commands a vast empire from the confines of his motorized chair and has literally become a deus ex machina, but he is really only a perfunctory imitation of a god in the materialistic world, just as the other male figures who pretend to govern the forces of history and society with their strange antics. Yet he carries far less significance for Oskar than the Great Earth Mother and her feminine counterparts who ultimately dominate all of life and nature in this novel. Therefore the fear and trembling which Oskar expresses here before Bebra (again with tongue in cheek) hardly compare in degree to the fear which will seize him at the approach of the Black Cook.

The fact that Bebra plays the simultaneous roles of judge, earth-shaker, and purveyor of Oskar's fate should not disturb us if we recall that most ancient gods, and Zeus in particular, were worshiped in accordance with circumstance under a multitude of titles.[7] Depending on his function at the moment, Zeus was named the god of justice, of order, and of retribution, and so forth; but perhaps his most impressive epithet for mankind was "leader of the fates." It was Zeus (or Poseidon in the case of Odysseus) who as judge and jury weighed men's lives and informed the fates of his decision, and they, in turn, were obliged to carry out his decisions.

Oskar, like countless heroes of classical mythology, carries responsibility for the death of his parents; but punishment is temporarily averted to allow time to restore the balance of justice. Oskar is therefore compelled to sign this contract and oblige himself to go out into the world and use his gifts for the benefit of men and in part for his own redemption. By placing his signature on the contract, Oskar officially becomes a culture hero (again we follow Susanne Langer), a fresh embellishment to his previous heroic image.

> This widely represented fictional character [culture-hero] is a hybrid of subjective and objective thinking; he is derived from the hero of folktale, representing an individual psyche, and consequently retains many of that personage's traits. But the symbolic character of the other beings in the fairytale has infected him, too, with a certain supernaturalism; he is more than an individual wrestling with powers of society. Just what else he is, must be gathered from his personality as it reveals itself in the legendary mode.

> He is half god, half giant-killer. . . . His deeds only begin with his escape from thraldom; they go on to benefit mankind.[8]

To travel this road, Oskar reminds us with a disavowal that he has to reenact the ritual bond with the "devil" as a wager for his soul and a requirement "to commit some monstrous crime." But a major transgression is in fact perpetrated when Oskar agrees to place his sacred gifts at the disposal of a commercial enterprise (with, for the second time, Bebra at its head). The implication arises, of course, that the materialistic society of the West is in its own way as profane and desacrilized as was Bebra's former dehumanizing order of the Third Reich. Of course Oskar must face the consequences of this decision along with others as his story approaches an end, but for the moment the agency West makes good its part of the contract and prepares the way for Oskar to become the cosmic drummer of his time.

Publicity posters soon identify him as a magician, a faith healer, a Messiah; and he appears to live up to his title in every respect. In his performances before huge audiences Oskar succeeds in rejuvenating the old, the tired, and the weary. He transports the suffering, the decrepit, the disheartened and wealthy adults back to the dawn of their own particular mythogenesis, each to his own particular Danzig, to his own forgotten nursery rhymes and black cook, to the wellsprings of his life and spirit. Oskar had in fact "become a healer of the body and the soul" (p. 671), an achievement which returns us to Joseph Campbell's central conception of the heroic deed.

> The hero-deed to be wrought is not today what it was in the century of Galileo. . . . The Modern Hero-deed must be that of questing to bring to light again the lost Atlantis of the co-ordinated soul. . . .
>
> The problem of mankind today, therefore, is precisely the opposite to that of men in the comparatively stable periods of those great coordinating mythologies which now are known as lies. Then all meaning was in the group, in the great anonymous forms, none in the self-expressive individual; today no meaning is in the group—none in the world; all is in the individual. But there the meaning is absolutely unconscious. One does not know toward what one moves. One does not know by what one is propelled. The lines of communication

> between the conscious and the unconscious zones of the human psyche have all been cut, and we have been split in two.[9]

This is precisely the division which Oskar helps men overcome in themselves. His drumming succeeds in tying together the profane man with his sacred past so that the two may become one significant totality. If Santayana is correct in saying that the man who rejects his past is doomed to relive it, then Oskar's ability to reify the total experience of childhood in the present makes it possible for his listeners to liberate themselves from the eternally recurring needs and patterns of infantilism which dominate their lives in restrictive patterns.

Oskar's success is staggering. He achieves everything anticipated and more. "Oskarism" soon appears as a popular concept, and a cult is founded in his name. Then, having proven himself a master drummer even in a social context, Oskar returns for a second time to visit Bebra. This time, considering Oskar's new status, the conversation evolves quite amiably as the two reminisce about days past and people they had known. Oskar is even given a motorized wheelchair to ride around in identical to the one that Bebra has. The image of Oskar buzzing around in an electric wheelchair appears absurd but is not really inappropriate at this point in the action. The message is apparently that Oskar has found atonement ("at-one-ment") with Bebra, that in the light of his tremendous success as a universal drummer Oskar now has claim on equal power and position ex machina. But even if Oskar has received acceptance and forgiveness in Bebra's eyes, Grass lets the reader know through the bizarre scene of racing wheelchairs that this is little more than a parody on equality. This machine designed for a senile cripple is for Oskar merely a mechanical toy that reflects the hollow achievements of the commercial and technological world over which Bebra reigns. Enjoyable as the engineered toys and the promise of mechanical power may be, Oskar has no difficulty leaving it all behind to embark upon another major drumming tour.

Oskar's next few rounds of drumming concerts confirm his status as a culture hero. Great acclaim follows him everywhere. Like Orpheus, the gifted musician of Greek mythology, Oskar soon turns out to be "more priest than musician."[10] His drumming sessions induce trancelike states that allow his followers to depart with him upon an ecstatic journey of spiritual discovery. The drumming séance, not unlike the musical rites of the Orphics, summons up the spirits of the past and travels with them into the forgotten recesses of the soul and down to the very center of Hades.

Oskar is quite obviously a priestly psychopompos and mystagogue in the present context, performing chthonic rites of travel to the world below and to the realm of the ancestral past. Thus he seems to have reached the apogee of his career and the completion of his destiny; having united his knowledge of elusive mysteries with social purpose, he now abounds in success and wealth and is worshiped by the masses as a divinity. But then, unfortunately for Oskar, Bebra dies and along with him goes Oskar's desire to continue his work as the universal drummer. Bebra's death, the death of a man that Oskar has come to think of as a timeless being, triggers in Oskar excessive feelings of loneliness, of transiency, and of the hopeless dissolution that is also awaiting him. After completing another tour or two, he breaks his contract and refuses to continue his career as a professional drummer.

For Oskar the death of Bebra apparently signifies an end to his own losing battle against meaninglessness and solitude. Bebra is really the last of Oskar's mythic or spiritual parents for whom he could have proven himself. Outwitting his parents, opposing the monsters and institutions of their society, and finally having even put them to death in a manner of speaking, Oskar has won a great pyrrhic victory that leaves him alone on the empty field of an existential battle. Now with his ambitions partially fulfilled and partially dissolved, Oskar is left to deal with the pursuing forces of his own immediate destiny rather than the projected monsters of an opposing nature and society. Oskar therefore gives up his financial goals and social acclaim and becomes for the most part a dangling man to the very end of the novel. He does engage in a few additional adventures, and occasionally the earth spirits come to his aid again when Oskar manifests a need for help; but viewed in relationship to his mighty and miraculous early adventures, the conclusion of the novel is a record of Oskar, like Orpheus, playing his music and descending.

In a state of complete loneliness and melancholy, Oskar decides to rent a dog for company, an action that turns out to be another call to adventure. Oskar's dog, just as Faust's Mephistophelian poodle (with whom he is literally compared), becomes the herald that "rings up the curtain, always, on a mystery of transfiguration—a rite, or moment, of spiritual passage, which, when complete, amounts to a dying and a birth."[11] So what appears to be an incidental anecdote of loneliness turns into another oracular omen for Oskar. The name of the dog that he rents for company, a shiny pitch-black Rottweiler, happens to be Lux (or light in Latin), the root of the name for the archangel "Lucifer" before his fall, and, of course, the masculine equivalent to the name of Oskar's old nemesis, Luzie. Just as Mephistopheles made his way into Faust's life as a poodle in order to set off a chain of events that led Faust to death and final judgment, this black dog becomes the precipitant for a series of incidents that puts Oskar irrevocably onto a path leading to the final encounter with the Black Cook.

As Lux and Oskar take their daily walks, it is the dog that leads the way, first to the waters of the Rhine where he barks at the ships, then on to the woods where he barks at lovers. On the third day Lux takes Oskar to the town of Gerresheim (literally meaning the home of fermentation) and along a path that winds carefully between small gardens and large grainfields. There Oskar lets the dog run free while he sits down on an old cable drum and begins beating out the rhythm of his past life. In contrast now to his practice as a performing drummer, Oskar turns his vision completely inward: "Now we want to see once and for all what you are, and where you come from" (p. 675). Straddling the drum and beating it first with his knuckles and then with some sticks which he finds on the ground, Oskar begins another of his ecstatic journeys into the past.

This flurry of drumming promises to be especially revealing for the reader since Oskar announces in advance that he is intent on finding out what he is and where he really comes from, but before he can finish his investigation he is interrupted from his séance by his dog who has brought from the field "a feminine finger. A ring finger. A feminine ring finger. A feminine finger ringed in good taste." Oskar does not notice it at first and tries to kick his dog away, but Lux insists that Oskar receive this special object of death and dismemberment as a response to his drumming. Finally, amid the thriving growth and greenery of nature, Oskar takes the ring finger, puts it into his pocket, and makes his way home again.

Oskar embalms the ring finger in a preserving jar, in *spiritus*, and places it in Dorothea's room on the cosmetic table in front of a mirror. Since her departure Oskar has taken over the nurse's room and turned it into a mausoleum of sorts at the center of which he now places the most holy of reliques, the ring finger. The finger episode can best be understood in a double perspective: first, in its concrete significance of bones, dismemberment, and taboo; and, second, as Oskar's vision of its former saintly possessor, the nurse Dorothea. Beginning, in several soliloquies, with the scars on Herbert Truczinski's back (an implied tableau of the emasculated mythic gods and heroes–Kronos, Osiris, Adonis, etc.) Oskar follows fond memories of sexual parts and phallic symbols from early life to the present, associating them all in a teleological fashion with the dismembered ring finger and his own sexual impotence.

> In the same category [with Herbert Truczinski's scars] I would put parts of a few young girls and women, my own pecker, the plaster watering can of the young Jesus, and the ring finger. . . . whose joints I can count and feel when I grab my drumsticks. . . . Even before Herbert's scars made promises, it was my drumsticks, from my third birthday on, which promised scars, reproductive organs, and finally the ring finger . . . [and, retrogressing in time while expanding the scope of associations] also playing with my umbilical cord promised me successively drumsticks, Herbert's scars [etc. including all items from his special birth to the ring finger] and . . . it promised me my own sex as a fickle monument to the limited powers and possibilities which I carry about with me–
>
> Today I have come back to my drumsticks. As for scars, tender parts, my own equipment which only occasionally shows strength nowadays, I recall them only indirectly by means of my drum. (pp. 205-6)

Like the priest at Delphi, deep in a trance and half in frenzy, speaking, reciting fundamental truths which are not only true but also kerygmatic, Oskar unravels in this speech one strand of a cryptic mystery that extends from birth to death. The umbilical cord gives promise before birth of masculinity and drumsticks, the object cathexis between the sacred artist (the mystagogue-psychopompos) and the *homo sexualis*. Oskar in turn receives his drumsticks, his sacred music as a substitute force with which he can, like Orpheus, bring lost souls back from the underworld. His sexuality, therefore, is transmuted into a cultural purpose, although this is hardly the uplifting message he now receives in the depths of confusion before the symbolic ring finger.

The subjective message which confirms that Oskar is indeed the chosen one also imparts the requirement that he too must now descend to the lowest depths of the underworld, beyond Trophonios, and be embraced by the Black Cook herself. In his contemplation of the ring finger, he begins to anticipate the terror of dissolution without yet sensing that the envisioned "reduction to the skeleton indicates a passing beyond the profane human condition and, hence, a deliverance from it. . . . To reduce oneself to the skeleton condition is equivalent to re-entering the womb of this primordial life, that is, to complete renewal, a mystical rebirth."[12] From birth to rebirth is the precise aim of Oskar's endeavors: "Oskar's goal is to return to the umbilical cord; and that is the sole purpose and the reason for dwelling on Herbert Truczinski's back. . . . I shall have to be thirty before I am able to celebrate my third birthday again" (p. 206). On Oskar's thirtieth birthday he will be released from the asylum and there waiting for him, as we shall see, ready to embrace him will be his personal Hecate herself, the queen of the underworld, the Black Cook. She is the one Oskar has always feared and avoided, and the message of the ring finger has forced on him the knowledge that there is no way of eluding her.

The specter of the Black Cook "has been following me for a long while now, coming closer and closer" and she even "kissed my hump," but now she will be approaching Oskar face to face, the Black Cook who "borrowed Luzie Rennwand's triangular fox face" (p. 711), and this time she is not to be avoided. And if that is to be Oskar's greatest and most threatening challenge, then one might well regard the current imposition of abstinence as one of the preparatory requirements in anticipation of that frightful act which apparently lies just one page beyond the conclusion of this novel. But if that is where the present series of adventures is to end, the whole idea of it is too horrible at the moment for Oskar to countenance. It is no wonder therefore that he tries to reject the funerary and morbid implications of meaning that this severed finger has to offer, and that he attempts to conjure up instead an antithetical image of a divine goddess of salvation. The resultant image is, of course, Dorothea, who emerges of necessity as the opposing image to the forces of dissolution. The reaction is not unique with Oskar, for one may go back as far as the writings of Pausanias on mythology, who in a similar context declares: "They say that when the goddesses would drive Orestes mad they appeared to him black, but after he had bitten off his finger they seemed to him white."[13]

In the present situation, then, it is no wonder that Oskar prays and drums "in extreme devotion" to the white goddess, the drum wedged between his knees, reciting in the fashion of an occultist priest a litany that turns out to be a perplexing terra incognita of his own fragmented state of mind. The loosely organized, broken statements of his prayers appear to resolve themselves into three areas: the question of identity, the principle of feminine dominance of life, and the immanence of illness and death.

The prayer to the preserving glass begins with the question of who is praying, "I" or "Oskar," the corporeal and protean ego, soul, spirit; or "Oskar," the restless "romantic" hero and socially projected self. Oskar plays here for a few minutes with a relationship that has probably been a source of perplexity for the reader throughout the book, namely the relationship of the sentient center oscillating between "I" the narrator and "Oskar" the agent of involvement. The prayer asserts that "I" am full of insight because I have no recollections while Oskar is full of insight because he is full of memories. The "I" has no recollections because it operates in the timeless sphere of subjectivity and inspired creation, where all that is thought, regardless when, becomes immediate reality. It is the dominant a priori self that accepts elected greatness by the gods before individual identity is established under the epithet of a name that becomes a function of the social world.

The relationship between these two aspects of self which often blend in varying proportions is elusive to say the least, regardless of the nomenclature one uses: I and Oskar, ego and image, or sacred (mythic) and profane (objective) consciousness. While "Oskar" appears more or less projected into the world of social engagement, "I" responds to situations from a greater depth, from a point removed from the immediate contingencies of time and challenge. In the very last chapter, for example, after Oskar undergoes a dramatic transformation and embarks on his highly personal magic flight, he uses "I" exclusively. Only on the second last page of the book, when overwhelmed by the approaching image of the Black Cook, does he return to the third-person self to say: "Don't ask Oskar who she is!" Of course Oskar wouldn't know because the objective self can never explain the underlying emotional significance of a mythological phantasmagoria.

Expressing his most confused state of mind in the novel, Oskar says that he is praying to a preserving glass with a ring finger in it. Whose finger? He begins with some particulars of Dorothea, whom he has never really seen: "Blond, who is blond, of medium height? Five feet four or five? With a mole inside of the arm? The right one or the left one? Religion? Reformed! Born when? Where? in Hanover," and so on and on for a half page, recalling, mixing, arranging and rearranging characteristics belonging to Dorothea, Maria, Mrs. Greff, Agnes; or, in short, Oskar is praying to an impressionistic pattern of elements characterizing all of the women who have ever contributed some maternal significance to his life. Then the prayer concludes on a blacker note: "Illness not itself, death not itself, yet, no, don't know, don't want to, I picked cornflowers,[14] there came, no, accompanied already beforehand, I can't any longer . . . amen, amen" (p. 688).

What Oskar has covered in his prayer here is a huge arc of experience ascending through the many relationships he has had with women into a basically idealized conception of Dorothea as the vision of the Saving Grace. But by praying to the good and helpful "mothers" in the single composite image of Dorothea, Oskar is attempting to do what he once realized could not be done. He is attempting to assert the presence and efficacy of a great white goddess who can save him, but of course the exact opposite occurs. The psychic law of contiguous differentiation forces one closer to damnation the more one insists on salvation; and by singling out the pure and ethereal image of the nurse Dorothea, Oskar unknowingly succeeds in conjuring up an even more horrendous image of the Black Cook. The white nurse and the dark goddess cannot be separated into independent categories as long as "Oskar" and the "I" live in intimate confusion with one another. The projected monster (the aboriginal self) that derives its force from a primeval formless state of existence is as common a figure in mythology as the epic hero himself, for the monsters with which the hero must do battle are as much a part of him as are his conscious moral qualities. Indeed the final heroic dimension of the mythic demigod himself is in large measure defined by the nature of the specters he vanquishes. And more often than not, there is a resolved unity after the fierce battle as the hero perhaps bathes in the blood of the dragon or acquires its fabulous treasures or supernatural power as an indication of new *mana* or integration of self. A similar and equally terrifying battle appears to be taking place now within Oskar and as the tide of battle swerves and changes here at the end of this novel, so do the images of his projected goddesses.

From the very beginning when Oskar first perceived the picture of his mother in a nurse's uniform, the theme of the uniformed nurse as the solicitous and spiritual (rather than craving sexual) woman has been established. For two pages Oskar gives a detailed résumé of his associations with nurses in sickness and in health, leaving it up to the reader to surmise that these nurses who formerly quieted pain and affliction should now be able to remove the torment of his emotional anguish (pp. 580-81). In Oskar's eyes Dorothea, the idealized nurse, has become a vision of the divine redeeming mother. It is no wonder then that when the evils of loneliness, dismemberment, and death begin to plague him that he should turn to the deified image of the saving nurse mother as an only hope of escape or regeneration. But Oskar's efforts soon prove themselves to be as useless as the dead objects which he venerates. Later on, and only after his confinement in the hospital, does Oskar realize and admit that "the mystery of nurses tempts, possesses, and dominates me," to which Bruno, Oskar's male nurse, adds. "The mania of patients to have themselves taken care of by female nurses is an additional symptom of illness . . . she plays the woman and entices the patient into health or death, the latter of which she makes palatable with eroticism" (pp. 579-80).

Oskar, in his worship of Dorothea, wishes her to remain superior, pure and as unblemished as her uniform. But the uniform, we recall, is merely a thin disguise behind which the earth mother in another one of her incarnations is hiding, so it seems that Oskar's supreme effort of will to create the celestial goddess as an ideal in a uniform must end in failure.[15] Certainly, the pure goddess soon proves to be ineffective, as Eliade recognizes in *Shamanism,* and Oskar is forced to abandon her. "Benevolent as the gods and spirits 'above' may be, they are unfortunately passive and hence of almost no help in the drama of human existence. They inhabit 'the upper spheres of the sky, scarcely mingle in human affairs, and have relatively less influence on the course of life than the spirits of the "*bis* below," who are vindictive, closer to the earth, allied to men by ties of blood.' "[16] It seems that Oskar has deluded himself by trying to separate blackness from light so that he may avoid one by being saved by the other. As other mythological heroes before him have learned, the two worlds are tightly interwoven; and Oskar must therefore, like Dante, first make his way deep underground to the very seat of horror and fear beyond which escape lies. Oskar even recognizes the inevitability of such a journey in his prayer as it ends with the paradoxical allusion to the Black Cook who is illness but "illness not itself" and death that is "death not itself," the knowledge of which has "accompanied [him] already beforehand." His destiny is to submit himself to the darkest of mysteries in the amorous embrace of the Black Cook and experience the ultimate "illness not itself" as a cure for the confusing illness that now haunts him; and he must suffer "death not itself" in which something dies and yet results in new life.

The ring finger episode logically concludes a series of episodes built around Oskar's great success as a magic drummer and epitomizes the great spiritual depression into which he, like so many other mythic heroes, falls following the greatest of deeds. He plays another concert tour or two, visits acquaintances, and spends a bit of time with a newly-found friend of dubious quality; but all in all his energy, determination, and purpose seem to have vanished. He drifts through a last few formal episodes and even performs an impressive miracle once again, which, although beautiful in a pathetic way, contributes little toward redeeming the hero from his profound despair.

Contrary to Oskar's wish in Dorothea's closet that everything white could be collected in one category and everything black in another so that one could balance the Black Cook off against the whiteness of the nurses, a paradoxical mixture of forces dominates his actions with the result that as one critic points out, the closer to the light the moth (Oskar) flies the larger and more disproportionate is the shadow he throws;[17] or whereas Oskar is exploring and discovering life on the one hand he is, on the other, learning how to die.[18] The shattering effect of this perplexity is openly reflected in the broken language of Oskar's prayer, in his futile devotion to a dead object, in his indifference toward his profession, in his spiritual despair, and, finally, in his subsequent desire to subject himself to trial, public condemnation, and incarceration.

# TEN *A Streetcar Ride to Folly & Misfortune*

All the while that Oskar is in the field drumming out his story and receiving the gift of the ringed finger from his rented dog, he is being carefully observed by a man lying in the crook of an apple tree, a reptilian-looking gentleman by the name of Gottfried von Vittlar, who says of himself, "I am the last of our line." Vittlar suggests that Oskar might be inclined to take him for a snake and this tree for the apple tree of Eden, but Oskar passes the whole idea off, perhaps a bit too quickly, as "allegorical rubbish," for soon he (and the reader also) is caught in the contradiction of rational disavowal and an obvious allegorical development. Vittlar not only takes on the physical appearance of the serpent stretching his upper body, shooting his tongue out (*züngeln*) like a snake, hissing and whining in a strange voice; but he also acts out the biblical role of the serpent as provocateur for the sake of recognition. By special appointment Vittlar also gets Oskar into trouble with the supreme authorities, who remove him from his appointed rounds and subject him to the outside world of measurable time, practical justice, and mortal concerns.

The initial meeting between Oskar and Vittlar, like several other crises in Oskar's life, has its two versions. Oskar's rendition implies that it is Vittlar who is acting out allegorical rubbish as the serpent of Eden. He insists that he hasn't "the slightest desire to discuss the fruit situation in Paradise" with Vittlar, but as the conversation drifts to the ring finger which Lux has brought him, Oskar's perception of Vittlar begins to focus on him as the divine duality of an angel and a reptilian Proteus. "If angels exist, they must certainly look like Vittlar. . . . You don't see Vittlar at first. Showing a certain aspect, he can make himself in accordance with surroundings look like a thread, a scarecrow, a clothestree, or the forked limb of a tree. That is why I failed to notice him as I sat on the cable drum and he lay in the apple tree. The dog didn't even bark, for dogs can neither smell, see nor bark at an angel" (p. 680). In Vittlar's opinion, however, it is Oskar who forces the image of the Edenic serpent on him: "I cannot understand why, just because I was lying in a tree, he should have taken me for a symbolic snake and even suspected my mother's cooking apples of being the Paradise variety. It may well be a favorite habit with the Tempter to lie in the crook of trees" (p. 683).

Regardless of perspective the obvious metaphorical analogies are designed to direct the reader's attention to the impending mythological motifs of choice, temptation, banishment, and perhaps redemption. The name of Gottfried von Vittlar also reveals something of the paradoxical role which he is to play. "Gott-fried" (meaning God's peace) refers to the angelic quality which Oskar recognizes in Vittlar, while the stem of his family name is a compound of the Latin word *vita* (life) and the German suffix *-lar* (signifying a dwelling place or residence). Vittlar, who does in fact dwell as much as possible in this tree of life, becomes the expositor of life for Oskar by forcing him to break with his sacred and subjective garden, his mythology, and be cast into the profane world of struggling men.

Before that moment of truth is reached, Oskar and Vittlar become better acquainted, feast, chat, roam around, and finally experience one last great mythic adventure together. The episode begins when Oskar and Vittlar steal a streetcar late one night and then stop along the route to pick up three men. One of the men, apparently half-blind and oblivious of where he is, turns out to be Viktor Weluhn, the helpless postal clerk who had lost his glasses years before during the defense of the Polish post office. His two companions, we discover, are former members of the SS who are still trying to carry out an order to execute Viktor. Oskar immediately decides that Viktor must be saved. In keeping with the locale or place magic of myths, the streetcar takes them all back to Gerresheim, the place where Oskar and Lux found the ringed finger of the nurse Dorothea and where Oskar first met Vittlar wound around the branch of an apple tree. This garden of Vittlar's mother—the allegorical garden of Eden and the first sacred residence of man—has been chosen for the place of execution.[1] Viktor is tied to the apple tree, the two men pull out their machine guns and advise Oskar to leave; but instead of leaving, Oskar pulls out his drum and begins to beat out the rhythm of the Polish nation, "lost but not yet lost, Poland is not yet lost!" Then Viktor, who knows the text of the song, joins Oskar's melodic beat: "Poland is not lost as long as we live." Then, as the drumming gets louder and louder, and the executioners pause, the Polish cavalry suddenly rides onto the scene. Oskar beats his drum; short-sighted Viktor, like Teiresias robbed of his sight but bestowed with the gift of prophecy, sings in wavering tones that Poland will live, live again. The "ground trembles under the beat of horses: hoofs thunder, nostrils snort, spurs ring, steeds whinny, hooray and hooray. . . . There was no doubt that it was a squadron of Polish Uhlans, for the red and white pennants clung to their lances like the red and white did to Mr. Matzerath's lacquered drum. . . . . They floated like toys out of a box, phantoms, . . . Polish cavalry of knotted string, soundless yet thundering, fleshless without blood, and yet Polish, down upon us they thundered, and we threw ourselves upon the ground while the moon and Poland's horsemen passed over us. . . . But they did not harm the gardens. They merely took along poor Viktor and the two executioners and were lost in the open fields under the moon–lost yet not lost, they galloped off towards the East, towards Poland beyond the moon" (p. 695).

This scene distinguishes itself as an indisputable tour de force from among Oskar's impressive list of achievements. More convincing even than his successes as a redeeming cultural drummer, this miraculous and majestic apparition of the former Polish cavalry becomes dramatic confirmation of Oskar's supernatural ability. The exact status of Oskar's demidivinity and role as a hero will be discussed in the last chapter, but for the moment it suffices to recognize that Oskar may conjure up or communicate at will with powerful forces from the sacred center of his creation; and although life for Oskar may degenerate at times into lesser experiences of a profane or mundane nature, it is never completely divorced from the divine realm of the gods. The monsters of society, the Nazis in this case, may defeat gallant men again and again, but the real heroes of old continue to reside in "sacred space" and may be recalled in a ritual of summoning up deceased ancestors or spirits of the dead for divine aid. By drumming up the Polish cavalry to take this last victory, to rescue this "Viktor" who survived the destruction of the post office, Oskar gives form to the vital memory of a holy land and confirms in grand style the eternal transhuman quality of existence.

The final victory is precipitated by the person of Viktor Weluhn, whose name literally means victory [to the] Uhlanen, his surname perhaps being a phonological anagram for Uhlan. Now, as long as Viktor lives in the timeless realm of spirits, the possibility remains that the sacred ideal may someday again emerge from this Garden of Eden through which Viktor is removed from the world of recorded history and returned to the sphere of sanctified spirits for preservation during the hard times ahead. "The threshold that separates the two spaces also indicates the distance between two modes of being, the profane and the religious. The threshold is the limit, the boundary, the frontier that distinguishes and opposes two worlds—and at the same time the paradoxical place where those worlds communicate, where passage from the profane to the sacred becomes possible."[2] Thus, with Viktor's survival, the ideal of the sacred land, the romanticized and holy image of the place of creation and eternal order, the lost Garden of Eden for Oskar and Weluhn is lost but "is not lost as long as we live."

Oskar's adventures are only beginning in this sacred center that manifests itself wherever man engages his gods or witnesses the wonder of hierophany. Even Vittlar, who is a cynic, is duly impressed by the fantastic drama that has played out before his eyes, and he compliments Oskar lavishly on his new success; but instead of feeling elated, Oskar suddenly appears to be drained of his energy, his magic, his purpose. He expresses weariness, apathy, and indifference—possibly in the face of this genuinely miraculous achievement which outstrips in magnitude all of Oskar's previous successes. When Vittlar reminds him of his great fame and fortune, Oskar merely "lay on his back," twisted his hump into the soft earth, pulled out grass with both hands and threw the clumps high into the air and laughed like an inhuman god who can do everything" (p. 696). As a ploy, then, Oskar arranges to have Vittlar give his briefcase (which holds Dorothea's ring finger) to the police so that they may indict Oskar for the murder. By that means Vittlar will achieve the measure of fame which he desires, if only as an informer. Vittlar's name will be published in all the newspapers, and Oskar will have found retribution for his transgressions.

While Vittlar, in search of fame and notoriety, goes off to inform on Oskar, Oskar "lay laughing in the night black grass behind Gerresheim, rolled laughing under several visible deathly earnest stars, twisted his hump into the warm earth, and thought: Sleep, Oskar, sleep another hour before the police wake up. You shall never lie so free as this under the moon" (p. 697). This quotation reflects a dramatically abrupt change of mood for Oskar and an equally abrupt reversion to his chthonic bond with the realm of earth. Like any earth spirit, especially Antaeus, the son of the earth mother who gains his strength in contact with her, Oskar lies in the "night black grass" and literally buries his hump in the earth to become at one with it. He laughs, half-planted in the earth, evidently liberated in part from a burden of guilt; but more in keeping with the symbolic context of the moment, we apprehend in Oskar's exhilaration another ecstatic adventure of death and renewal. His complex of experiences in the West–for Oskar a profane land of walking dead–has become a constricting shell that suddenly begins to shatter. Sensing the return of freedom and yet terrified by the phenomenon, Oskar returns to the source of his inspiration and literally plants himself in the earth, sleeps a sleep of strengthening, vitalizing restoration in preparation for his magic flight. Never again, he says, will he "lie so free as under this moon," which along with the "deathly earnest stars" watches over him while he draws fresh strength from the "warm earth."

Both mothers–of the earth and of the sky–are present in the scene if we are to believe at all the observation that Erich Neumann makes in his book *The Great Mother.* "The symbol of the all-knowing, all-seeing, many-eyed God belongs to the archetypal image in which the stars of the night sky appear as the eyes of the godhead. The link between the upper and lower regions is characteristic for diverse phases of the Great Mother's rule. As goddess of the tomb, she rules over the world of the dead, but at the same time she governs the celestial world, whose luminaries are her eyes."[3] Neumann then refers to the Great Goddess as a kind of celestial cow, nourishing the earth and looking after her creation. Oddly enough, Grass creates the identical image for Oskar: "The next morning amid bright light and warm sunshine Oskar was awakened by a cow licking him." The cow also happens to be black and white, punctuating the dichotomy of colors for Oskar: day and night, celestial light and chthonic darkness, Black Cook and White Nurse, or, to carry the symbolism back into the older realms of mythology, we find the Yin and Yang cosmic combination of the Orient and the white

Olympians or astral gods and the black chthonians in the Occident. All in all there can be little doubt that this cow is another of the mother figures as Oskar announces "he has been licked, washed, and his hair has been combed by a cow so that he may now begin his flight." Oskar would like to linger there and await the police but decides instead that he must flee: "You can't have a bona fide denunciation without a bona fide flight." The day is bright and Oskar warns himself that he must not spend too much time with this cow, even though she looks at him in such a heavenly way (*himmlisch*), soothing him. Thus Oskar embarks upon a parodistic chase that takes him in a fury of activity as far as Paris.

The cow and the moon are intricately related in mythology—first for their feminine qualities—their symbolic fertility—and then the horns in the form of the lunar crescent. The comparisons to be made are numerous, but most interesting in the immediate arrangement of the passage is that Oskar looks longingly at the moon during the last moment before falling asleep and is awakened briefly thereafter by the cow licking his face. The generalized abstraction becomes for him during the course of his sleep a concerned corporeal spirit that prepares Oskar for his flight by cleansing him. Oskar has now evidently won "the blessing of the goddess or the god and is then explicitly commissioned to return to the world with some elixir for the restoration of society. . . . [But on the other hand, because] the hero's wish to return to the world has been resented by the gods or demons, [that is, the Black Cook,] then the last stage of the mythological round becomes a lively, often comical pursuit."[4] Comical and lively are perhaps two of the very best words to characterize Oskar's magic flight westward, as he is simultaneously pursued like the heroes of old.

Although at times the nature of Oskar's flight becomes as frantic as Perseus's pursuit by the Gorgons after he has slain Medusa, the quality of lightness prevails in this escapade as a result of a change that has taken place in Oskar's disposition. Vittlar, true to his name and tradition, has succeeded in forcing Oskar out of his mythic garden (his fixed mythology) and into a state of mind in which he can see immediate reality more clearly than ever before. Oskar's statements, such as "it was broad daylight" and "the flies were buzzing," are lucid perceptions of a newly unveiled world that enters his consciousness through the loosening ferric bonds of a dominating myth. "Leave the cow to her mooing and make your getaway," Oskar admonishes himself, and he abandons the past again by "leaving my drum with the cow," who, metaphorically speaking, gave it to him in the first place. A transition has taken place, and Oskar experiences an exhilarating feeling of liberation as he ' burst into a gale of fresh, early-morning laughter." Oskar then goes on to associate the advent of his flight with the celebration of his birthday. "He was born [in September] under the sign of Virgo," Oskar reminds us on his thirtieth birthday, the month in which astrologists find "reference to the Immaculate Conception of a Messiah," or "the birth of a god or a demigod."[5]

In a certain sense Oskar's flight is more genuinely buoyant and light-hearted here than in any of the other epic adventures that have previously engaged him. Oskar himself does not fail to see its comic overtones, and at first he even regards the flight as a kind of fiction, as a good hide-and-seek scenario for a detective film with Chaplin or perhaps Picasso as leading man playing himself. Then the pursuing demon begins to catch up with him and terror alternates with earlier playful fantasies in a pattern of fair and foul. Although narrative, adventure, and suspense dominate in epic myths, they are seldom found without the humor necessary to offset the suspense and horror. From beginning to end of this novel even the most intense of fears and concerns are seldom more than a finger's distance from humor in diversified forms of satire, irony, parody, or just plain wit. But humor in this current episode also lies at the structural basis of narration in the form of *parabasis,* playful incongruity or deviation between performance and oblique explanation. Oskar's insistence that his flight is an imitation of popular suspense drama posits an obvious attempt to precede the dreadful outcome of the novel with a kind of satyr play of chase and capture in an illusory fashion, but the illusion soon turns to reality as first the memory and then the actuality of the Black Cook begins to close in on him.

Although all this time Oskar has been traveling safely in a train and then underground in the subway of Paris, his dreams of escape are astrodreams. He plans to arrive at the Orly airport and take a plane that will ascend with him into the heavens. Then, at the last moment, Oskar chooses instead of the last station to leave the underground at the *Maison Blanche* station, the "white house." Riding up the long escalator that will carry him out of the bowels of the earth to the surface once again, he first imagines that he is the poet Dante who is returning from hell, and then that he is Goethe returning from the "realm of the mothers." A bizarre association also presents him with the vision of Goethe as the Black Cook standing at the foot of his bed, terrifying him in yet another mask. Goethe's Olympian tranquility, so uncomfortable to Oskar in his earlier years, suddenly looms up as a frightening silence that outstrips even the excesses of Rasputin. What hope does Oskar have if the Apollo of form, the prince of poetry himself, must one day join the camp of darkness!

Still riding upward, ruminating and recollecting his past, recombining past memories and present anxieties into loose symbolic configurations, Oskar abruptly returns to the present moment to observe "the lovers above me and the woman with the hat below me" on the escalator. Oskar makes a point of stating that these two lovers are not one, but two steps above him on the escalator. Thus he is able to put his suitcase between them and himself, reconfirming the barrier that exists between Oskar and healthy young lovers such as these. As they kiss and fondle each other Oskar surmises that this has all been done before and will soon again be repeated. Exactly two steps behind Oskar, but with her head on the same level as his, is a woman wearing a huge hat decorated with fruit. At first Oskar suspects her of being the Black Cook in disguise–which may not be far amiss. In the mythic view this could well be the dual mother of all seasons, Persephone, the Queen of Hades, ascending as the vegetation goddess, Demeter, to the earth's surface again, bringing with her the yearly gift of copious vegetation, preceded by young lovers, fertility gods, and little Iacchus (Oskar himself) who leads part of the procession of emergence in the Eleusinian mysteries. But then, to round out this rich, mythopoetic spectrum of images, Oskar mentions as he ascends out of the underworld that he would most "like to see the exact opposite of the Black Cook: my grandmother Anna Koljaiczek should be standing there like a mountain and take me and my retinue after a successful ascendancy under her skirts, into the center of the mountain" (p. 709). The image of Anna Koljaiczek's skirts as a symbol of the cosmic mountain and the *axis mundi* of creation changes slightly here into a vision of refuge or escape from the Black Cook, "The function of protection . . . is particularly evident in the mountain, which in German (*Berg*) is symbolically related to *sich bergen,* 'taking refuge'; *sich verbergen,* 'hiding'; *Geborgenheit,* 'safety'; and *Burg,* 'castle.' "[6] As always Oskar's most profound wish is to enter the cosmic mother-mountain "after a successful ascendancy" and pass from one mode of existence to another. As far as he is concerned, below Anna Koljaiczek's four skirts must be another of those places "exactly where the cosmos came into existence and began to spread out toward the four horizons, and where, too, there is the possibility of communication with the gods. . . . at the Center of the World and by the same token at the very sources of absolute reality. . . . In short, this religious nostalgia expresses *the desire to live in a pure and holy cosmos, as it was in the beginning, when it came fresh from the Creator's hands.*"[7]

Whenever Oskar expresses the desire in Book 3 to return to the womb, or to its cosmic equivalent (his grandmother's skirts), he finds himself all the more threatened by the Black Cook. We conclude, therefore, that Oskar's relationship to the dual Earth Mother Koljaiczek - Black Cook polarity is contingent on his own changing position in the cycle of life. Whereas he once experienced the pleasure, safety, protection, and tranquillity of his grandmother's skirts early in life, he now lives in terror of the suffering, death, and dissolution which the approaching Black Cook has to offer. As he approaches the end of his escalator ride, Oskar's fears have also mounted so that one feels he will literally be catapulted into the arms of the Black Cook.

As Oskar steps off the escalator, thrown up again from underground and onto the surface of the everyday world, he is taken from the realm of the supernatural and summarily arrested as Oskar Matzerath. Disguises, mysterious claims, and strange antics are regarded on the earth's surface only as a sign of madness. From the point of view of society he has been rescued from his mythological cycle here (from the escalator) as he once was taken from the madly whirling carrousel by the benevolent wizard Herr Fajngold. Like the never-ending turning of that mad carrousel in Danzig, this escalator has begun to take on the proportion of a cosmic wheel that has "no first step" and no "journey's end." And Oskar's lengthy escalator ride has also reflected those threefold images, as we have seen, that are common to the circular religious concepts that "have as their imagistic vehicles not only the Upward, with its numerous mythologies of a sky god or gods in an upstairs world, but also the Downward, with its mythically powerful underworld sources of life and death, and the Inward, as the ideal center of the moving wheel of life."[8] Campbell, as well as Wheelwright, moves beyond the geometry of the image to conjecture on the final crisis and purpose of the heroic circle: "This brings us to the final crisis of the round, to which the whole miraculous excursion has been but a prelude—that, namely, of the paradoxical, supremely difficult threshold-crossing of the hero's return from the mystic realm into the land of common day. Whether rescued from without, driven from within, or gently carried along by the guiding divinities, he has yet to re-enter with his boon the long-forgotten atmosphere where men who are fractions imagine themselves to be complete. He has yet to confront society with his ego-shattering, life-redeeming elixir, and take the return blow of reasonable queries, hard resentment, and good people at a loss to comprehend."[9] For the moment Oskar wins a reprieve by claiming, when taken into custody, "I am Jesus." And on that note Oskar leaves the story he is relating and returns to the present time, to himself as author of his story, and to his thirtieth birthday two years later in the mental institution.

The last two pages of the novel take us into the midst of Oskar's immediate concerns regarding his reentrance into society. What should he do, he asks himself, upon leaving this mental hospital: "Get married? Stay single? Emigrate? Be a model? Get a stone quarry? Gather disciples? Found a sect?" Actually, however, these are academic questions whose formulations and answers he has already examined closely or experienced in the past. To return to them would be commensurate with reversing the direction of his life and violating his basic principle of development and expansion. He said that all of those possibilities are open to a man of thirty nowadays and must be examined, but they have been examined, and the result of that examination has become a novel embodying Oskar's life—this very book we are reading—*The Tin Drum.* Oskar's whole period of time in a sanatorium has been dedicated to the creation of a careful and intimate record of his existence. He has stated time and again that he wanted to find out who he is, so starting in a logical manner, he "proceeded from the past to the present," assuming that past history might at one point become the source of present definition. After all, if the past of one's life does not define the nature of one's existence at a given moment, then what would? The inquiry takes us back to a point where history fails as clarification, and only the ultimate confrontation with the blackest and most horrendous of demons can resolve the question of self and yield up the greatest (but never the final) victory of redemption.

Oskar realizes perhaps that there is no further development possible in the context of old concepts, no real decisions to be made through the evasion of life in the hospital, no future liberation possible from his psychic and physical guardians without a direct and final confrontation with the Black Cook. "And so I will drum up that little ditty which has become more and more real and terrifying to me: I shall call up the Black Cook and consult her" (p. 710). The Black Cook has been the sine qua non of Oskar's adversaries from the very beginning, having come to him even at birth in the double form of the night moth and his spiritual mother of darkness. Throughout the novel she sends in her stead the representatives of the night world to Oskar–Susi Kater (even the brats in the retinue of Harry Schlager, Axel Mischke, Nuchi Eyke, Hänschen Kollin),[10] Luzie Rennwand, Niobe, and Lux. Oskar names them all now in the last drumming ditty to conjure up the Cook; and along with her other figures of negative aspect, he points to her presence at all past catastrophes and the manifestation of her powers in the eerie sounds of night in the darker corners of all existence. She assumes now a threatening, grotesque dimension, like the "maternal *ouroboros* [sic] . . . a devouring monster who would rather kill her children than let them go free. This primal urge can be felt in consciousness as fear of a giantess or as a drag back to unconsciousness, which is its reciprocal opposite."[11] It is this devouring monster then in its ultimate and unveiled form with which Oskar must finally struggle before his mythic journey will be complete.

Until now he has only been wrestling with the shadow figures of the Black Cook, with her bizarre surrogates. In initiatory combat he has passed only through the *shadow* of the Valley of Death, he has been only to the "door of hell," and has descended only into the upper limbo of the underworld; but he has avoided direct encounter with the figure of death itself, with the satanic figure that Dante had to penetrate *in corpore* to escape the Inferno. Oskar's journeys have been dark and threatening, but they have merely been initiatory conflicts in preparation for the ultimate encounter which Oskar must experience before fulfilling his quest as a hero. However, the novel closes at this point, just one page short of a meeting between Oskar and the supreme mother of darkness, a meeting which, because it is in the realm of ineffable horrors and ultimate mysteries, remains somewhere beyond the descriptive powers of an author even so gifted in the creation of powerful images as Günter Grass. But to take us at least to the threshold of the encounter, Grass has Oskar drum up a last great review of his past experiences, direct and indirect, with the chilling excrescences of the Black Cook.

Determined now to ferret out the source of his most profound fears, Oskar resolutely begins drumming and narrating with nervous laughter, controlled fear, broken syntax, darting associations. He makes his way back to the cellar steps, to the eels that clamored for his mother, to the amber eye and consuming green body of Niobe who casts her shadow of death first upon Herbert Truczinski, then upon Sigismund Markus and his toys, and later upon Danzig and all of Poland. Then Oskar drums up the diabolical children of his apartment house and, above all, Suzi Kater, who forced Oskar to drink that vile brick soup in the name of the Black Cook, who all sang together, Oskar recalls: "Is the Black Cook here? Yes, yes, yes!" Oskar through his drum traces the Black Cook's presence from Suzi Kater to Luzie Rennwand, who comes to throw the dark shadow of the Black Cook's cloak across him. It is her shadow now, Oskar tells us, that multiplies and continues to follow "his sweetness," consuming whatever it touches. Then Oskar's drum, on its mythological journey into the past, begins to juxtapose a bevy of Catholic and subterranean symbols, mostly stones, foods, and memories of death and dissolution: "basalt, tufa dorit, nests in shell lime, alabaster so soft . . . all shattered glass, glass transparent, glass blown to hair thinness . . . and all the groceries, all the flour and sugar in blue pound and a half bags . . . tomcats . . . potatoes tumbling down from scales . . . boxes tapered at the footend, cemeteries I stood in" and on and on, until the focus comes to rest on the immediate approach of the Black Cook who "was following before, then kissed my hump, but now and from now on is coming closer in front of me."

The novel is then concluded with a children's rhyme, which is Oskar's theme song to the universal fear that follows one throughout life.

> The Cook has always been behind me black
> Now let her come towards me black facing me.
> Words, coat turned over black.
> Black payment with black currency
> While the children, if singing, sing no more:
> Is the Black Cook here? Yes, yes, yes![12]

Oskar tells us that the Black Cook has always been behind him, from the first day of creation down to the present moment in which the fable and reality of Oskar Matzerath become one. Suddenly, at the edge of darkness, with life and death stretched out before him, he grasps about in vain for past stratagems, resolutions, beliefs that might prepare him for his next and most terrible of adventures. Now, having reached midpoint in his life adventures, thirty years of age, the age (he points out) "when Jesus began to gather disciples," Oskar Matzerath begins his descent on his drum while the underworld queen rises up to meet him: transformed into an even blacker black than one might have imagined—coat, words, and currency of repayment for prior transgressions appear black, black, black. Indeed the word *black* appears as the prevalent image on every line of the poem except one, the second to last in which the singing children become so paralyzed with fear of the Black Cook that they freeze in silence. And what remains is only the final affirmation of her immediate presence: "Yes, yes, yes!"

In the American translation of *The Tin Drum* the name *Cook* was unfortunately translated as *witch*, a word that may appear more dramatic at first glance but proves to be rather misleading for the critical reader. Although a witch may also cook her magic brew, her final product is apt to be only a magic potion rather than dissolution of the victim and the ritual reenactment of cosmic chaos. Oskar's maternal demon is both *cook* and *black* in the alchemic sense of organic fermentation or putrefaction. In that context she takes on even larger significance as the chthonic cook herself who is ever-present in life and death, ready to gather more human ingredients for her huge, simmering cauldron somewhere at the bottom of the life cycle. Into that cauldron go the occasionally shattered egos as well as the deceased hulks of life to dissolve in a vast amorphous chaos. Yet the term *cook* is largely a creative one, for the substance she decomposes initially becomes with time the nutrients for the regeneration of new life and another round of creation.

As far as the immediate evidence of the novel is concerned, the Black Cook is viewed only in her initial destructive aspect as a chthonic goddess that must be dealt with at this, Oskar's next consciously willed stage of development. She is the dark and terrible mother who now draws near to Oskar from the "dark hole of the depths, the devouring womb of the grave and of death, of darkness without light, of nothingness," as the opposite aspect of creation. Thus, for Eric Neumann, this is the figure "who generates life and all living things on earth [and] is the same who takes them back into herself, who pursues her victims and captures them with snare and net. Disease, hunger, hardship, war above all, are her helpers, and among all peoples the goddesses of war and the hunt express man's experience of life as a female extracting blood. This Terrible Mother is the hungry earth, which devours its own children and fattens under corpses; it is the tiger and the vulture, the vulture and the coffin, the flesh-eating sarcophagos voraciously licking up the blood seed of men and beasts and, once fecundated and sated, casting it out again in new birth, hurling it to death, and over and over again to death."[13] In the face of such an apocalyptic vision, it is no wonder that Oskar gropes for words, searches the past, and posits vague hopes for knowledge of the future. Then one last time he beats out the ditty of the Black Cook on his drum, and the rest is silence. His determination to pursue his destiny to its very end has compelled him to drum up the depths of his mythic world, sensing intuitively that perhaps his "myth is but the penultimate; the ultimate is openess–that void, or being, beyond the categories–into which the mind must plunge alone and be dissolved."[14]

# ELEVEN *Epilegomena to a Drumming Dwarf*

Having now completed a study of mythic allusions, images, archetypal events, and the epic structure of *The Tin Drum,* one may justifiably protest that the larger questions about Oskar's status as a god or hierophant, his glass-shattering voice, his size, or even the tin drum as a central symbol of the novel have not been answered. Definite answers—even at this point—and ipso facto conclusions that attempt to roll the endless strings of Oskar's adventures into wieldy packages of explanation would certainly run the risk of distortion by oversimplification; and yet, having come this far, one feels compelled to extend observation into speculation and gamble with chances of misunderstanding for the sake of added clarity and perspective. On several points, however, where fixed conclusions fail to crystallize and traditional concepts fail to come to our aid, then a cursory examination of ambiguities must satisfy us, such as those surrounding our first and most important questions relating to Oskar's status. Is he a mad mortal? A human hero? A demigod?

Without reintroducing the details of past evidence, let us simply begin by reaffirming our prior assumption that Oskar is related in spirit and body to the *chthonioi* and to borrow a definition from W. K. C. Guthrie, "apply the name chthonian to all gods or spirits of the earth, whether their functions are concerned with agriculture or with the grave and the world beyond, or (as often) with both."[1] Anna Bronski in the East and Korneff in the West clearly position themselves among the life and death gods of agriculture. One should keep in mind that "the earth does two services for men. By its fertility it provides them with the means of life, and it takes them into its bosom when they die. The *chthonioi* accordingly have two primary functions: they ensure the fertility of the land, and they preside over, or have some function or other connection with, the realm of the souls of the dead" (Guthrie, p. 218). But this novel chooses primarily to emphasize and explore the funerary aspect the *chthon* or "tomb" parameter of the total cycle, the darker half which Northrop Frye designates as "The Mythos of Autumn" and "The Mythos of Winter." In his words (with no reference to *The Tin Drum*) he asserts of the former that "At the end of this phase we reach a point of demonic epiphany, where we see or glimpse the undisplaced demonic vision, the vision of the *Inferno*. Its chief symbols, besides the prison and the madhouse, are the instruments of a torturing death."[2] The Mythos of Winter also tends to end at the point of a demonic epiphany: "Sinister parental figures naturally abound, for this is the world of the ogre and the witch, of Baudelaire's black giantess, . . . of the siren with the imprisoning image of shrouding hair, and, of course, of the *femme fatale* or malignant grinning female, 'older than the rocks among which she sits.' . . . Tragedy and tragic irony take us into a hell of narrowing circles and culminate in some such vision of the source of all evil in a personal form."[3]

From the night moth to the approach of the Black Cook this chthonic mythos of Oskar's with its pantheon of dark gods continues to reveal the immediate presence of a demonic and apocalyptic world that persists throughout this novel as a single unchanging reality, as the omnipresent source of Oskar's powers and the determiner of his destiny. The cycles of submersion into cellars, closets, grandstands, pillboxes, under tables, etc. establish beyond a doubt a necessary pattern of action for Oskar to return in a repeated ritual to his subterranean source of strength and energy. The symbolic implications of such a pattern center on a death-and-rebirth cycle that subjects the hero to the experiences of death metaphorically for himself or definitively for others, and then allows him to reemerge from the shadows into life once again. The immortality of primitive gods was not generally based on a constant condition but rather on a process of death and rebirth as a reflection of nature, a ritual of spirit, and a theology of regeneration. In Greek classical mythology hardly a hero of any repute failed to make at least one major descent to the underworld which Oskar, to a major or a minor degree, visits on every possible occasion. In this respect he perpetuates the principle of the early double god Zeus-Chthonios and other upper and yet underworld entities such as Amphiaraos of Thebes and the Boeotian Trophonios who since the incident of the Onion Cellar is familiar to us. Oskar apparently fits in somewhere along the line with the person who evolved into an earth deity, Trophonios; but knowing Oskar is greater detail than we do any of the classical gods, we shall not be able to place him in his many stages of development quite so easily into a fixed category.

On questions of status and placements even the classicists are not overly confident of their conclusions. Discussing chthonians, such as Oskar might be designated, the classical scholar also asks: "What should we call these beings: gods, heroes or what? . . . The *chthonioi* undoubtedly included both gods and heroes, and it is sometimes difficult to know which name is most appropriate to a particular individual" (Guthrie, p. 220). At this point Guthrie begins to draw heavily on the observations and theories of Lewis R. Farnell, who, in "Heroes and Heroines of Divine or Daimoniac Origin," suggests a series of classifications intended to lend discriminating clarity to the question of the status and function of hybrid gods and heroes. "We can reduce the facts to some order by distinguishing seven types or classes of heroes and heroines: (a) the hieratic type of hero-gods and heroine-goddesses whose name or legend suggests a cult-origin; (b) sacral heroes or heroines associated with a particular divinity, as apostles, priests, or companions; (c) heroes who are also gods, but with secular legend, such as Herakles, the Dioskouroi, Asklepios; (d) culture–and functional heroes, the 'Sondergötter' of Usener's theory, usually styled ηρωες by the Greeks themselves; (e) epic heroes of entirely human legend; (f) geographical, genealogical, and eponymous heroes and heroines, transparent fictions for the most part, such as Messene and Lakedaimon; (g) historic and real personages."[4] For our part it must be concluded that Oskar fits to a greater or lesser degree each of these categories at one time or another. Unlike the followers of a primitive cult who view the history of the divine hero in a theological context ranging from early afflictions to later deification, we experience as readers the whole spate of Oskar's history with its tightly interwoven threads of myth, psychology, society, theology, and so forth. Farnell, sensing the presence of ambiguities in the legends of mythic personages, asks the questions: "Are we to consider their humanity or their divinity the aboriginal fact? Did they begin their career as human personalities real or imaginary, who were afterwards exalted to the rank of deities, or as deities who gradually degenerated into merely glorious men and women?" (p. 20) If classical scholars must settle for something less than clarity in the thoroughly raked soil of Greek mythology, then we should settle for the broader concept of chthonic hero and demigod in Oskar's case.

Oskar begins his dual life as a mortal, but never is he more purely divine or sacred than at the moment in which he tears himself from the womb at birth fully conscious of his strengths and ready for his mission. He is the providential heir apparent, the *deus humanus* of that divine cosmogenesis that took place as creation on the Kashubian potato fields years ago and now perpetuates itself in human form. As an epic hero Oskar travels from the holy realm of the four skirts to the gates of hell without ever becoming denizen of either. He confronts numerous figures of Hades, monsters from the limbo of society, sexual goddesses and goddesses of destruction, bizarre teachers and guides, all of whom contribute to his supernal strength and knowledge until he reaches the point where he may use his skills to help redeem men or even grant salvation to someone like Viktor Weluhn. Oskar therefore fulfills Farnell's standards for classification as a divinity or demigod. He does redeem people: he saves them from panic and chaos in the Onion Cellar, and (on his great drumming tours) he succeeds in helping men overcome the spiritual divisions within themselves, just as the priests of the Elusinian mysteries once did by leading suppliants down to the depths of the earth and into themselves for a visit to Trophonios and returning them with greater wholesomeness to the world above. As with Greek gods there is a cult formed around Oskar (Farnell's ultimate measure of imputed divinity); and if there is still doubt about Oskar's mythic divinity, one needs only to recall his ability to drum up the whole Polish cavalry or to converse on occasions with Jesus and with Satan. For all that Oskar is no less human at times, plagued by loneliness and frustration, beset by confusion and fear. Thus human and divine, we must accept Oskar, depending on the situation, as a mortal and a minor deity, hierophant and psychopompos, an epic culture hero and a popular legend, and a shaman or a mad "seer" whose pronouncements, like those of the Cumaean Sibyl in the *Aeneid* (Book 6) or the mad oracles at Delphi, ring a note of greater truth than logic can grasp.

Farnell further suggests that for greater illumination and understanding of the hero-deity one should examine "the quality and character of the myth or saga" that characterizes the practices of a given cult (p. 20); and if that can in fact contribute a new measure of understanding, then we must retrace our steps and carefully examine Oskar's primary symbol and emblem—the tin drum. The tin drum, even where it is conspicuously absent, makes itself felt in every episode and adventure throughout the book. As a visual symbol, its colors[5] and its shape[6] are of some importance but certainly less significant for this novel than the fact that the drum is an instrument of rhythms forceful enough to penetrate the furthest corners of existence and yet remain a central point of focus and communication. Positioned as it is between Oskar and the external world, it serves as a barrier or armor of sorts which effectively removes Oskar from the immediate grasp of the external world and gives him a degree of distance or isolation which others lack. As Oskar points out when describing the Goethe-Rasputinesque polarity of the external world: "That polarity was to define and influence my life, at least *that life* which I presumed to lead *on the other side of my drum*" (italics mine, p. 101). Implied is that Oskar's adventures of an external order take place in a polarized sphere beyond the drum which one might refer to as objective reality, while the self, the "I" or sentient center of Oskar's narration, remains as the vital and vague entity hidden behind the instrument. As such he carries his drum around much as one might its equivalence in form—the Delphic omphalos. The meaning of the word in Greek is of course "navel," and as a religious artifact the omphalos designated the point of connection *and* division between the two great cosmic bodies of spiritual realms. Oskar's use of the drums as the medium of union and division with both the sacred and social worlds, as we have seen, is highly complex.

On examination we find that the tin drum, along with Oskar, undergoes historical development, and its significance cannot be fixed at any one point without doing violence to its meaning:

1) On the first few pages, for example, the drum is introduced as the invocative tympanum of the muses, an instrument that induces an ecstatic state of creation and conjures up Mnemosyne to help Oskar recall and record his story. As such, the tin drum becomes the creative sine qua non instrument of this novel itself, for only with the aid of the drum is he able to regain contact with the spiritual world through which he is preparing to travel.

2) The early history of the drum begins with a flashback to the

day of Oskar's birth and his mother's statement that he will receive a drum when he is three. The night moth introduces Oskar to the universal principle of rhythm and therefore of time itself, the first principle of creation. As Oskar learns to play the drum, he can produce only noise, cacophonous banging, auditory irritation, distance and dissension between the adult world and himself. At that time the drum becomes his megaphone of protest, supplanting the perhaps less abrasive crying and screaming of normal children. And when the adults attempt to take his drum away, the chthonian bestower of dark gifts provides him with a supernatural skill to protect his supernatural instrument.

Oskar receives a glass-shattering voice so that he, unlike the moth, may demolish glass as an expression of his hostility. With only a few minor exceptions[7] Oskar uses his voice to extinguish light and order. Either he shatters light bulbs and plunges the world into darkness, breaks (or as he says "blackens") windows that reflect light; or he breaks glass containers (as in the doctor's office) to release the vile stench and dead organisms from their imprisonment. The voice therefore arrives with the drum and augments its initial powers by allowing Oskar to dispel light (a symbol of solar and spiritual illumination), to plunge the world temporarily into primeval blackness, and subsequently to permit the reentry of darker forces of licentiousness, crime, and dissolution. Once the drum is buried at Alfred Matzerath's funeral, Oskar's voice goes along with it, never to return. The sublimated, spiritualized drum that is resurrected in Book 3 has no need of that voice.

3) The drum becomes a vocal echo and organizing principle of Oskar's newly acquired knowledge and experience. With it he is better able to grasp and redirect philosophical concepts, political ideologies, and even simple human emotions. Once a central rhythm is mastered by him, he can in a homeopathic manner reach out and visibly control people and events. His purpose as a drummer needs no detailed interpretation in this instance for he tells us precisely that his present function is as "a small, displaced, half-god to harmonize chaos and intoxicate reason" (p. 386).

4) Drumming also becomes an extended metaphor for sexuality. It is Oskar himself who associates drumming and sexual intercourse when he speaks of his penis as a drumming stick during the seduction of Maria. The double meaning of drumming and sexual

intercourse is reiterated by Oskar as he later recalls "drumming on Maria's moss." On Oskar's trip west with Bebra's Miracle Theater he acquires as his one and only mistress of any duration, Roswitha, whose name literally means "red-white," the color of his drum.

5) On the trip west Oskar also begins to use his drum merely as a musical instrument for the entertainment of the troops, a commercial venture which is repeated on a vaster plane in Book 3 when Oskar becomes the drummer in a jazz band.

6) Last and most important, in Book 3 Oskar begins to utilize his drum for purposes of salvation of lost souls: first in the Onion Cellar, then for the redemption of the lost child in man on his drumming tours, for drumming up the whole Polish cavalry, and, finally, for conjuring up the Black Cook as the terminal specter of this whole narrative.[8]

In the last quarter or so of the novel, Oskar uses his drum in the religious fashion of the high priest or shaman, as Mircea Eliade generically refers to such mystagogues in *Shamanism:* "The shamanic drum is distinguished from all other instruments of the 'magic of noise' precisely by the fact that it makes possible an ecstatic experience. . . . magical music, like the symbolism of the shamanic drum and costume and the shaman's own dance, is one of many ways of undertaking the ecstatic journey or ensuring its success."[9] Certainly Oskar's drumming experiences approach that of *ecstasis,* a state of trance, such as in a séance, where one is lifted outside of one's immediate surroundings and transported to another realm which is inhabited by the spirits or memories of his dead ancestors, images of heroic past events, and the demons of darkness. Oskar always returns in his musical excursions to familiar themes of the sacred world of the past, but yet each trip contains its own uniqueness and variety, for Oskar, as virtuoso of the drum, can exploit its vast potential as a musical instrument at one end of the scale as well as a supernatural aid at the other. Eliade observes that "many shamans also drum and sing for their own pleasure; yet the implications of these actions remain the same: that is, ascending to the sky or descending to the underworld to visit the dead. This 'autonomy' to which instruments of magico-religious music finally attain has led to the constitution of a music that . . . [may] narrate ecstatic journeys to the sky and dangerous descents to the underworld."[10]

Oskar's drumming therefore, often even as entertainment, becomes the vehicle for a ritualistic journey (trance or reverie) to the land of the dead and his deceased ancestors. The capacity literally to "drum together" another world rests on a premise that one can capture primary and universal rhythms that lie within the nature of things. The mechanics of this ability run parallel to Frazer's theories of sympathetic magic in assuming that there is a particular or nuclear rhythm inherent in all things. Oskar mentions time and again that he must practice to capture the rhythm of a certain experience, thing, or concept which, when mastered, may be rearranged in new associative patterns on different planes of existence. These rhythmic correspondences then, in the fashion of free association, may be "drummed together" into unifying medleys that integrate landscapes, people, and objects as diverse as potato fields, Grandmother Koljaiczek, birth, death, Danzig, and the East. Whereas in more technological and "civilized" societies visual logic becomes the dominating principle for categorizing the endless number of things that occupy this world, in a primitive society and in the mythological scheme of things common rhythmic feelings lead to the correlation of such diverse elements as heavenly bodies, the birth of kings, national crises, historical conflicts, creation, dissolution, seasonal cycles, and the whole ebb and flow of life. Once this all becomes part of one's personal and cultural heritage, it must be revived from time to time in sacred ritual, probably with the aid of music and dance, in a form of *participation mystique*.

The shaman, medicine man, and cosmic drummer have in common the singular ability to beat out those rhythms to which spirits, visions, forces of nature, and members of the community must respond. With that, and in spite of the apparent multiplicity of beings in this world or the elusive inaccessibility of spirits in the other, the shamanic drummer may, as Eliade insists, succeed in uniting them all with the aid of his drum: "By drumming. . . . the shaman is able to share in the nature of the theriomorphic ancestor; in other words, he can abolish time and re-establish the primordial condition of which the myths tell. In either case we are in the presence of a mystical experience that allows the shaman to transcend time and space."[11] Objectively stated then, drumming becomes the essential form of communication between the present profane world and that sacred one beyond measured time, that past world of lost and dead ancestors that are ritualistically revived and reified in the ecstatic drumming ritual. In a sense this is the crux of Oskar's final redemptive or miraculous powers. In his drumming séances he conjured up the full panoply of ancestors and memories from the past. Even the Black Cook that lies ahead in Oskar's future is drummed up out of the past as a dark theme that has interlaced his whole history.

At this point a juncture of themes–ancestor worship and the divine hero–appear to coincide in a long-standing classical tradition. "Hero-worship, that is, the elevation of ancestors or other dead men to a semi-divine status with all the apparatus of prayer and cult, was widespread in Greece, and what other name could be given to them but *chthonioi,* since their habitation is beneath the earth? The dead kings, says Pindar, hear of the achievements of their descendants with 'chthonian mind,' or 'soul beneath the earth' " (Guthrie, p. 220). Drumming and dialogue with the dead therefore blend into one overall pattern of ancestor worship that embraces the disparate adventures to reaffirm in rites of initiation and communion Oskar's ties to a lost world: consider his regular visits to an *adyton* or subterranean cave, pit, hollow, dark room, closet, as a metaphor of the tomb; the sacrifice of ancestors as well as animals; the frequent visits to cemeteries or Oskar's engagement in mortuary tasks (caskets, caves, burials, gravestones) to maintain proximity and spiritual contact with the dead; prevalence of the chthonian color black; night and evening narrations rather than day or morning; madness, music, and a dwarfish distorted shape.[12]

Oskar's childlike stature, his elfin antics and mocking mischievous ways have led a good number of critics to classify him as a kind of later-day Eulenspiegel or picaro, as though the contrived and satirical characteristics of those uncommitted figures of literature could illuminate by comparison the full significance of Oskar's existence. The comparison is defensible only at minor points, such as at the conclusion of the Polish post office episode or at the trial of the Dusters after which Oskar claims childhood innocence by virtue of his size and is consequently absolved of all guilt; yet such deceits are used not only by picaros, whose activity usually begins and ends with trickery, but also by cunning epic heroes or captured dwarfs in fairytales, legends, and sagas of a mythic and mystic nature. Like Oskar they too are closely related to the earth and live in holes and caves. The dwarf, we recall, is derived traditionally from the mythological race of Cabiri or Dactyls, the industrious earth spirits, the untiring subterranean beings that thrive on their abundance of energy and primordial instincts but never accept or develop the full spiritual capacities of man. Also, as a nature sprite, the dwarf is generally indifferent to the aims or purposes of civilization and is therefore especially impatient with pomposity or pretension and willingly opposes by violence or ridicule whatever he finds as flat, pompous, or smug. But, as Eliade reminds us, "We must not forget that many of the divinities and powers of the earth and the underworld are not necessarily 'evil' or 'demonic.' They generally represent autochthonous and even local hierophanies that have fallen in rank as a result of changes within the pantheon."[13] Such figures come with time often to represent the challenges of active existence, of suffering, desires, and struggle. Perhaps in that respect, as history and presumed rationality shifted focus from mythologies to a more "logical mystification" of man and his institutions, the dwarf was reinterpreted as an inversion of a royal figure whose size confirmed his closeness to the earth and guaranteed continuance of favorable powers of a disturbing chthonic order within the limits of society.

Dwarfdom, ancestor worship, magico-religious drumming, ritual combat and clandestine love-making, a plethora of mortuary images and symbols, rejection of the sky god Jesus and loss of the angelic Dorothea, madness, great revivals, miraculous conjury of ghostly horsemen, and finally the impending embrace with the Black Cook add up to a fictive world of *chthonioi*, spirits of the earth, past and present, in a shadowy dialogue on the nature of religious and profane existence spoken in the language of mythopoesis. Still one is ultimately justified in asking: what is the purpose of such an exercise? In response, and in concert with Farnell and Guthrie, one may simply answer—the desire for immortality, divine election, and/or apotheosis![14] "A buried man could easily be transformed into a god!" (Guthrie, p. 223), and then his progeny, Oskar for example, could inherit the divine lineage as indication of his special destiny as a Messiah. It is no secret that Oskar, from the very outset of this book, is in search of immortality *on his own terms.* Drumming would be his mark, as the lyre was with Orpheus or the club with Heracles; and with his tin drum he soon learns to banish demons, vanquish monsters, charm people, and acquire the power of healing with a flourish of music that makes people more "human, that is, childlike, curious, complex, and immoral."

The miracle worker, the deified hero of a cult, the heir to a divine creation, and, most important, a Messiah (another kind of cult hero) all lay serious claim to immortality, if not in heaven then at least in the memory of men. Up to the very end Oskar continues to ruminate on the possibility of going out when he is thirty and gathering disciples. Dreams of immortality dominate him therefore from beginning to end; but what can be the fate of such dreams for any mortal or demigod who must face the inevitability of death? Beyond the pale of hopes and illusions with which men construct their existence in a more or less archaic mythological fashion stands that towering form, the ontological reality of the Great Mother who cast life upon her earth and then, when the time comes, calls it back once again to the realm of primeval darkness. Admittedly dozens of motifs and themes play a dynamic part in this existential drama of Oskar Matzerath, but in the last analysis the central significance of this work resides in the primordial states, ritual adventures, and mythological prototypes which Günter Grass so masterfully develops.

# Genealogy

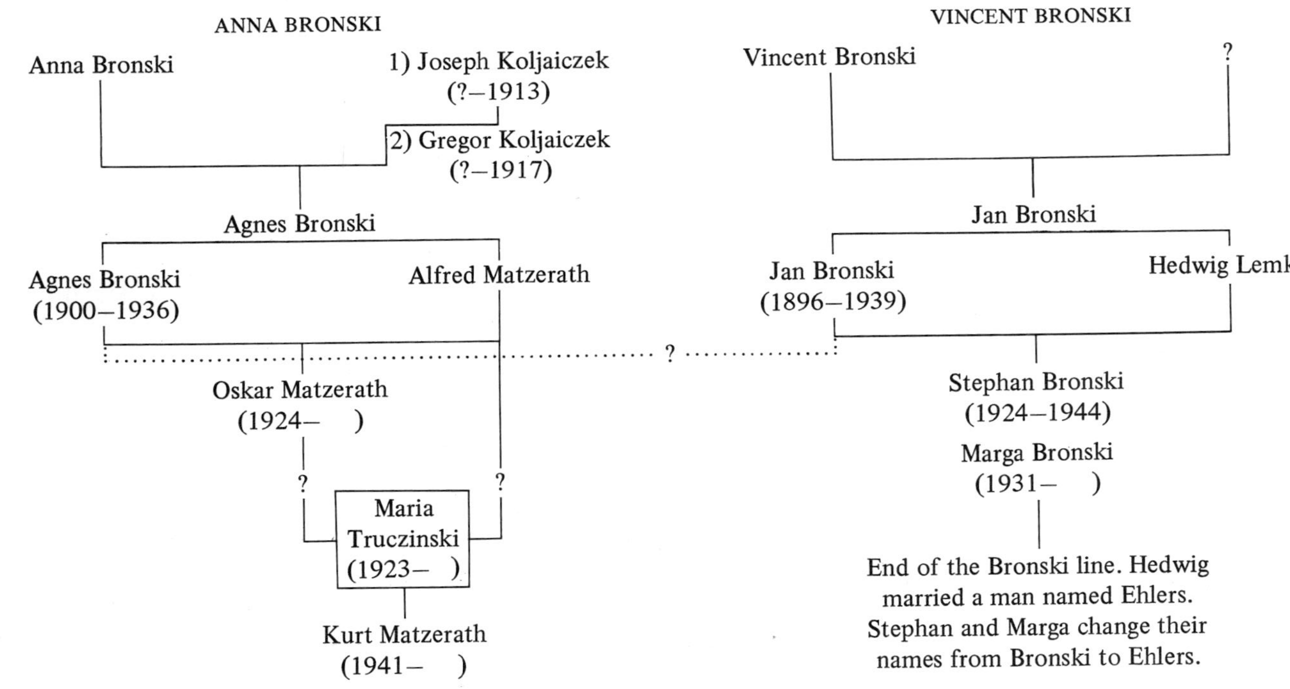

ANNA BRONSKI
Anna Bronski
1) Joseph Koljaiczek
(?–1913)
2) Gregor Koljaiczek
(?–1917)
Agnes Bronski
Agnes Bronski
(1900–1936)
Alfred Matzerath
Oskar Matzerath
(1924– )
?
?
Maria
Truczinski
(1923– )
Kurt Matzerath
(1941– )
?
VINCENT BRONSKI
Vincent Bronski
?
Jan Bronski
Jan Bronski
(1896–1939)
Hedwig Lemke
Stephan Bronski
(1924–1944)
Marga Bronski
(1931– )
End of the Bronski line. Hedwig
married a man named Ehlers.
Stephan and Marga change their
names from Bronski to Ehlers.

# Chronology

1899 Anna Bronski and Joseph Koljaiczek in Kashubian potato field.
1900 Agnes Koljaiczek is born.
1913 Joseph Koljaiczek (alias Wranka) drowns.
Anna marries Joseph's brother, Gregor.
1917 Gregor Koljaiczek dies.
1918 Agnes, as nurse, meets Alfred Matzerath in Silberhammer Hospital.
1920 Jan Bronski and Hedwig Lemke marry.
1923 Agnes and Alfred marry.
1924 Oskar born in September (Danzig).
Call to adventure by night-moth.
1927 Oskar is three years old (gets his first drum).
Falls into cellar (first threshold).
1928 Oskar gets second drum.
1929 Oskar meets Sister Inge.
1930 Attends kindergarten (Auntie Kauer).
Attends the Pestalozzi School (Spollenhauer).
Begins own education. Meets Gretchen Scheffler.
Studies Goethe and Rasputin.
1932 Oskar is eight. Susi Kater and gang brew up the potion which Oskar is forced to drink. Gains added vocal powers as a result and breaks windows in Stadt-Theater from a long distance.
Gets third drum.
1933 Visits the theater with his mother.
1934 Meets Bebra and given advice on being a dwarf.
Attends the rallies of the Nazis.
Plays "Jimmy-the-Tiger" and breaks up the meeting of Brown Shirts.
1936 Plays the tempter by breaking glass in store windows.
Causes Jan to steal a necklace.
Visits the Church of the Sacred Heart. Asks Jesus to play the drum.
Visit to Neufahrwasser-Brösen (horse's head incident).
Agnes dies and is buried. Oskar meets Leo Schugger.

1937 Oskar meets Herbert Truczinski, who dies same year.
1939 Oskar and Jan at Polish post office.
Jan is killed.
Meets Maria–Oskar's first love.
1940 First seduces Maria (subsequent claim to Kurt as his son).
Alfred Matzerath seduces and marries Maria.
1941 Oskar makes love to Lina Greff.
1942 Greff kills himself.
Kurt is born.
1943 Oskar joins Bebra and goes to Atlantic Wall.
Falls in love with Roswitha.
1944 Roswitha killed (June 6, 1944).
Oskar returns home.
Kurt rejects him and his drum.
Oskar attends church with Maria.
Oskar asks Jesus to play drum and He does.
Joins the "Dusters." Becomes leader.
Meets Luzie Rennwand.
Arrested at Christmas play in church.
1945 Oskar and Dusters are put on trial.
Danzig in ruins. Russians invade.
Matzerath's death caused indirectly by Oskar.
Oskar attends funeral of Matzerath and starts growing.
Oskar leaves Danzig and travels west (June 12, 1945) with Maria and Kurt.
Meets Luzie again in freight car.
Recuperates in hospital from August 1945 to May 1946.
Meets Gertrud and other nurses.
Lives in Düsseldorf.
1946 Goes to night school.
1947 Works for Korneff the stonecutter.
Sees Sabber Willem. Thinks he's Leo Schugger.
Luzie again.
Has date with Gertrud.
1948 Maria refuses to marry Oskar.
Takes job as a model and meets Ulla.
1949 "Madonna 49."
Moves in at Mr. Zeidler's.
Goes back to work at Korneff's.
Talks of Black Cook.
Meets Klepp and forms jazz band.
Meets Sister Dorothea and cannot seduce her (she leaves).
Plays in band in Onion Cellar.

1950 Goes back to Normandy with Lankes for a visit.
Goes to work for Dösch (Agency West) and meets Bebra.
Bebra dies.

1951 Gets the dog Lux.
Finds Dorothea's finger.
Meets Vittlar.

1954 Learns that Sister Beata killed Dorothea.
Oskar spends thirtieth birthday in a mental hospital.
Black Cook closing in on him.

# *German-English Concordance*

The reader may approximate the location of quoted passages in the English edition of *The Tin Drum* by using the German page numbering cited in the text of this study and finding its English equivalent in the right hand column below. The left column lists the chapter titles and pagination of the German edition of *Die Blechtrommel* published by Luchterhand Verlag. The English pagination given in the right column is taken from the paperback version of *The Tin Drum,* Pantheon Books, because of its current predominant use in college classes and its ready availability.

| *Erstes Buch* | | *Book One* | |
|---|---|---|---|
| Der weite Rock | 9 | The Wide Skirt | 9 |
| Unterm Floß | 21 | Under the Raft | 19 |
| Falter und Glühbirne | 36 | Moth and Light Bulb | 31 |
| Das Fotoalbum | 50 | The Photograph Album | 43 |
| Glas, Glas, Gläschen | 65 | Smash a Little Windowpane | 55 |
| Der Stundenplan | 79 | The Schedule | 66 |
| Rasputin und das ABC | 93 | Rasputin and the Alphabet | 77 |
| Fernwirkender Gesang von Stockturm aus gesungen | 107 | The Stockturm. Long-Distance Song Effects | 89 |
| Die Tribüne | 123 | The Rostrum | 101 |
| Schaufenster | 142 | Shopwindows | 116 |
| Kein Wunder | 154 | No Wonder | 126 |
| Karfreitagskost | 168 | Good Friday Fare | 138 |
| Die Verjüngung zum Fußende | 184 | Tapered at the Foot End | 151 |
| Herbert Truckzinskis Rücken | 195 | Herbert Truczinski's Back | 161 |
| Niobe | 212 | Niobe | 175 |
| Glaube Hoffnung Liebe | 229 | Faith, Hope, Love | 188 |
| *Zweites Buch* | | *Book Two* | |
| Schrott | 243 | Scrap Metal | 197 |
| Die polnische Post | 259 | The Polish Post Office | 210 |
| Das Kartenhaus | 277 | The Card House | 224 |

# *Notes*

*Chapter 1*

[1] Cf. Gilbert Murray, *The Rise of the Greek Epic;* W. P. Ker, *Epic and Romance;* and Gero von Wilpert, *Sachwörterbuch der Literatur.*

[2] The most convincing proponents of this interpretation are Willy Schumann, "Wiederkehr der Schelme," pp. 467-74; Horace Gregory, "The Ancient Follies are Still in the Ascendency"; Wilfried Van der Will, *Pikaro heute;* Mable Blanch, "Variations on a Picaresque Theme"; Henri Plard, "Verteidigung der Blechtrommeln." Convincingly opposing this interpretation is the article by Hans Mayer, "Felix Krull und Oskar Matzerath–Aspekte des Romans," pp. 35-67.

[3] Alan McGlashan, "Daily Paper Pantheon," *Lancet,* p. 238.

[4] Notable exceptions are Henry Hatfield, "Günter Grass: The Artist as Satirist"; Erhard M. Friedrichsmeyer, "Aspects of Myth, Parody, and Obscenity in Grass' *Die Blechtrommel* and *Katz und Maus";* Karl August Horst, "Günter Grass" in *Kleines Handbuch der deutschen Gegenwartsliteratur,* pp. 181-87; and Kurt Lothar Tank, *Günter Grass,* who, without analysis or further elaboration however, makes frequent reference to the mythos in *The Tin Drum.* John Simon, in "The Drummer of Danzig," declares the actual presence of a Günter Grass mythology but gives only the brief example of nuns and nurses in testimony of the fluid interrelation of forms and the mythopoesis of Grass's literary creation (pp. 151-52).

[5] "Today I know that everything watches, that nothing goes unseen, and that even wallpaper has a better memory than ours. It isn't God in His heaven that sees all. A kitchen chair, a coat-hanger, a half-filled ash tray, or the wooden replica of a woman named Niobe, can perfectly well serve as an unforgetting witness to every one of our acts" (Grass, *Die Blechtrommel,* p. 223). Cf. Alexander Gelley's accurate description of the resultant style of the mythopoeic phenomenon: Objects "become alive with an inexplicable potency, giving rise to feelings all the more insistent because they are freed of any subjective sentiment. . . . An illogical network is established amongst the inanimate objects and we sense an operative power on the physical plane which we know to be linked in some mysterious kinship with the animate world and the life of the psyche" ("Art and Reality in *Die Blechtrommel,*" p. 118). Cf. also Ernst Cassirer, *Philosophie der symbolischen Formen,* part 2: "Der Mythos als Anschauungsform," pp. 95-107.

[6] Although one of the first writers to praise *The Tin Drum* as a great novel, Hans Magnus Enzensberger (in "Wilhelm Meister auf Blech getrommelt") fails to identify any underlying coherence in the work and concludes in fact that

"it is a tale told by an idiot, full of sound and fury, signifying nothing." Cf. also Karl August Horst, "Wut ohne Pathos"; Walter Jens, "Das Pandemonium des Günter Grass"; A. F. Bance, "The Enigma of Oskar in Grass' *Blechtrommel";* Günter Blöcker, "Günter Grass: *Die Blechtrommel";* Karl Migner, "Der getrommelte Protest gegen unsere Welt"; Larry P. Vonalt, "Barbaric, Mystical, Bored"; Richard Plant, "Rhythms of Pandemonium"; and, of major importance, W. Gordon Cunliffe, *Günter Grass.* Strangely enough, however, history and politics are only the *mise en scène* in this novel, merely of secondary significance as a formal backdrop. In only one incident does Oskar drum against Nazidom. Otherwise he is involved only twice in a situation that vaguely resembles political engagement.

[7] Walter Jens complains in no uncertain terms about the length of the novel and prescribes the number of pages it should be cut. Malcolm Bradbury, Neal Ascherson, R. C. Andrews, and others criticize also, in vaguer fashion, the unnecessary digressions and effusive formlessness of the work.

[8] Philip Rahv, *The Myth and the Powerhouse,* p. 6.

[9] René Wellek and Austin Warren, *Theory of Literature,* p. 180.

[10] Campbell divides these general stages into subcategories, most of which we shall allude to at some point in our study. In the first major stage, *departure,* he includes "The Call to Adventure," "Refusal of the Call," "Supernatural Aid," "The Crossing of the First Threshold," and "The Belly of the Whale." The second stage, *initiation,* includes "The Road of Trials," "The Meeting with the Goddess," "Woman as the Temptress," "Atonement with the Father," "Apotheosis," and "The Ultimate Boon." The categories of the third stage, *return,* are "Refusal of the Return," "The Magic Flight," "Rescue from Without," "The Crossing of the Return Threshold," "Master of the Two Worlds," and "The Freedom to Live." For a more detailed, but still general, outline, see Joseph Campbell, *The Hero with a Thousand Faces,* pp. 36-37. Oskar Matzerath, as we shall see, experiences this whole spectrum of adventures with only few exceptions.

[11] We shall have recourse to both applications of the concept of archetypes in this study—as abstracted archetypes in the Jungian sense and/or by virtue of their frequent recurrences in historical myths. The two are not necessarily identical: whereas myths may be archetypal, archetypes are not myths. However, and with some reluctance, let me point out some impressive parallelism of themes of *The Tin Drum* and C. G. Jung's *Symbole der Wandlung* (translated as *Symbols of Transformation,* New York, 1956). Both works emphasize the motifs of cosmogonic creation, artistic fantasy and creativity, the symbol of the moth and its central relationship to the light, the diverse adventures and transformations of the mythic hero, the dominance of the Mother Earth and the Black Goddess figure (the Dual Mothers), and the final descent and sacrifice. One may speculate that Günter Grass had this lengthy study by Jung in hand as he searched for ideas and their development for *The Tin Drum,* considering alone the chapter headings of Jung's book ("Two Kinds of Thinking," "The Hymn of Creation," "The Song of the Moth," "The Origin of the Hero," "Symbols of Mother and Rebirth," "The Dual Mother," etc.) This study of *The Tin Drum* that follows is, however, *not based* on Jungian

psychology, although it does occasionally draw support from its vast wealth of material in the area of myth and psychology. Insofar as *Symbole der Wandlung* is concerned, it remains the secret of the author as to whether the similarities between it and *The Tin Drum* are coincidental or not.

[12]These and additional manifestations of mythic elements in literature (with the exception of etymologies) are fully discussed by E. W. Herd, "Myth Criticism: Limitations and Possibilities," pp. 69-77.

[13]"Wie sind Sie auf den Blechtrommler gekommen?" *Frankfurter Neue Presse,* 14 Nov. 1959. Also in K. L. Tank, *Günter Grass,* p. 57.

[14]Ernst Cassirer, *Philosophie der symbolischen Formen,* 2:12, and cf. Ch. 1 regarding mythic consciousness of objects ("*mythisches* Gegenstandsbewusstsein").

[15]Ernst Cassirer, *Language and Myth,* p. 97.

[16]Cf. esp. René Breugelmans, "Alienation, the Destiny of Modern Literature." See also Northrop Frye, *Anatomy of Criticism,* pp. 121-22, and Philip Wheelwright, "Notes on Mythopeia," in *Myth and Literature,* ed. John B. Vickery, pp. 59-67.

*Chapter 2*

[1]Ernst Cassirer, *Philosophie der symbolischen Formen,* p. 16.

[2]Joseph Campbell, *The Hero with a Thousand Faces,* p. 71.

[3]"The road leading to the center is a 'difficult road' . . . arduous, fraught with perils, because it is, in fact, a rite of the passage from the profane to the sacred, from the ephemeral and illusory to reality and eternity, from death to life, from man to the divinity" (Mircea Eliade, *Cosmos and History,* p. 18).

[4]Erich Neumann, *The Great Mother: An Analysis of the Archetype,* p. 98.

[5]Helton Godwin Baynes, *Mythology of the Soul,* pp. 625-26.

[6]"Marriage rites too have a divine model, and human marriage reproduces the hierogamy, more especially the union of heaven and earth. . . . Even in Vedic times, husband and bride are assimilated to heaven and earth. . . . In the procreation ritual transmitted by the *Brhadāranyaka Upanisad,* the generative act becomes a hierogamy of cosmic proportions. . . . Dido celebrates her marriage with Aeneas in the midst of a violent storm (Virgil, *Aeneid,* VI, 160); their union coincides with that of the elements; heaven embraces its bride, dispensing fertilizing rain" (Mircea Eliade, *Cosmos and History,* pp. 23-24). Also, during the sacred marriage or *hierosgamos* of the Eleusinian mysteries, "a short and simple prayer, consisting of two words, 'rain' and 'conceive,' was addressed to, presumably, the sky and the earth" (Herbert Jennings Rose, *Religion in Greece and Rome*, p. 73).

[7]Jacob and Wilhelm Grimm, *Deutsches Wörterbuch,* p. 397.

[8]C. D. Jerde, "A Corridor of Pathos," p. 560.

[9]Campbell, *The Hero with a Thousand Faces,* pp. 196-97.

[10]James G. Frazer, *The Golden Bough,* pp. 105, 413. Frazer's translation of "Demeter" here is unusual. It is usually taken to mean Mother Earth, *De* being a variant of *Ge;* but certainly meanings may shift where the name is applied to foreign counterparts of a deity.

[11] C. G. Jung, *Psychology of the Unconscious,* p. 375.

[12] Frazer, *The Golden Bough,* p. 12.

[13] Neumann, *The Great Mother,* p. 307.

[14] Cf. "The sun sinks down in the west, where it dies and enters into the womb of the underworld that devours it. For this reason the west is the place of death, and the hostile and rending 'Old Woman in the West' is the image of the Terrible Mother" (ibid., p. 158).

[15] Charles Williams, *Witchcraft,* p. 164.

[16] Campbell, *The Hero*, pp. 302-3.

[17] Frazer, *The Golden Bough,* p. 471.

[18] Neumann, *The Great Mother,* pp. 71-72.

[19] Ibid., p. 72.

[20] Cf. Franz J. Dölger, *Ichthys,* p. 20.

[21] The Finnish ship serves to reinforce both the funerary and sexual imagery of this scene. As a death ship it makes entry into the harbors and finally comes to rest there like the eels in the sack. The possibility that it too has come for Agnes is implicit later on in Oskar's surmises at her funeral when he sees her sailing away in her "fish-belly coffin."

[22] This eel is taken from the horse's ear, the place where Tom Thumb (previously identified with Oskar) sits; and Oskar also identifies himself with it while in Dorothea's closet, where it becomes a key image in the configuration of the nurse's black belt, her ring finger, and Oskar's penis.

[23] Grant, *Myths of the Greeks and Romans,* p. 116.

[24] The close interrelation of pagan religions and Christianity as expressed in *The Tin Drum* may be followed thematically in Hugo Rahner, *Greek Myths and Christian Mystery* (London, 1957); James George Frazer, *Folklore in the Old Testament,* (New York, 1927); Carl Krümm, *Der Christliche Glaube und die Alt-heidnische Welt* (Leipzig, 1935); *Das Christentum als Neuheitserlebnis: Durchblick durch die Christlich-Antike Begegnung* (Freiburg, 1939); and, in an older but no less interesting work, Georg Anrich, *Das antike Mysterienwesen in seinem Einfluss auf das Christentum,* (Göttingen, 1894).

[25] Campbell, *The Hero,* p. 111.

[26] Neumann, *The Great Mother,* pp. 189, 176.

[27] Ibid., pp. 152-53.

[28] William Rose Benet, ed., *The Reader's Encyclopedia,* p. 489.

*Chapter 3*

[1] Oskar tells us that Bruno is watching him and never lets him out of his sight. As Oskar tells him his stories, Bruno makes knotted figures out of pieces of string which he picks up in the patients's rooms after visiting hours; when he has finished with his knot sculptures, he dips them in plaster and lets them harden, before mounting them on knitting needles that he fastens to little wooden pedestals. Bruno is incapable of listening to Oskar's stories without creating a knot sculpture to go along with each story. Bruno says,

> In order to rest his overtired fingers, he asked me to write for him today and not to make any knotted figures. Nevertheless, I have put some

> string in my pocket and as he tells his story, I shall start the lower limbs of a figure which, in accordance with Mr. Matzerath's story, I shall call "The Refugee from the East!" This will not be the first figure I have taken from my patient's stories. So far, I have made knots of his grandmother, whom I named "The Potato in Four Skirts" . . . and with knot after knot I have made the Vistula and the Seine rivers flow and dash the waves of the Baltic and Atlantic against the string-knotted coasts. I have shaped pieces of string into Kashubian potato fields and Norman pastures. (p. 505)

Later Bruno tells us:

> It often happens that I no sooner apply some plaster to firm up my knot sculptures than as likely as not I smash them with my fist. I am thinking especially of the commission my patient gave to me some months back. He told me that I should combine Rasputin, the Russian faith healer, and Goethe, the German poet prince, into a single figure with plain, ordinary string and they should have a striking resemblance to himself. I don't know how many miles of string I have tied in knots trying to create a valid configuration of these two extremes. But like the partisan whom Mr. Matzerath considers an ideal, I remain restless and dissatisfied; what I knot up with my right hand, I undo with my left; what my left hand creates, my right fist shatters. (p. 510)

The allusion to fate here should be easy to recognize. With miles of string Bruno makes the Vistula flow and forms Kashubian potato fields and other people and events from Oskar's life. Fate weaves the strings of human experience into knots with one hand and unties the knots with the other hand in the fashion of the Greek fates who are also said to have worked with threads or strings as a metaphor of life. Whereas Clotho spun the thread of life on her spindle, Lachesis measured it, and finally Atropos snipped it (see Graves, *The Greek Myths,* 1:48). Bruno seems more occupied with the complex events and the flow of experiences (as represented by knots) than by the birth or death of Oskar. His string figures parallel the complexities of Oskar's story, but of greater importance is the question of the connection between the two. If Bruno is in fact one of the parthenogenous determiners of fate, then even the gods cannot contend against him; but if he merely produces in visible form what Oskar drums and narrates, then his function is posited ex post facto, and he becomes something of a shadowy analogue and echo of Oskar's machinations. Another possibility is that in spite of proximity the two of them really operate and create in unison but on different levels of expression, an alternative which seems less satisfying but which, as we shall see later on, most accurately reflects the conditions of their strange relationship.

[2] This purpose for drumming holds true also for numerous rituals, mythologems, and folk tales. "The shamanic drum is distinguished from all other instruments of the 'magic of noise' precisely by the fact that it makes possible an ecstatic experience," and "by drumming . . . the shaman is able to share in the nature of the theriomorphic ancestor; in other words, he can abolish time and reestablish the primordial condition of which the myths tell.

In either case we are in the presence of a mystical experience that allows the shaman to transcend time and space" (Mircea Eliade, *Shamanism,* pp. 174, 171).

[3]For a short, instructive analysis of Grass's style in *The Tin Drum* and in other works, see Klaus Wagenbach's essay, "Günter Grass," in Klaus Nonnenmann, *Schriftsteller der Gegenwart,* pp. 122-26; also Hennig Brinkmann, "Der komplexe Satz in deutschen Schrifttum der Gegenwart," and Heinz Fischer, "Sprachliche Tendendenzen bei Heinrich Böll und Günter Grass."

[4]Campbell, *The Hero with a Thousand Faces,* p. 58.

[5]Guthrie, *The Greeks and Their Gods,* p. 220.

*Chapter 4*

[1]Frye, *Anatomy of Criticism,* p. 190.

[2]Ibid.

[3]H. J. Rose, *A Handbook of Greek Mythology,* p. 145.

[4]Later on Oskar again claims special protection from Mercury, Hermes' counterpart in Roman mythology: "And Mercury, god of thieves and commerce, would bless us because I, born in the sign of Virgo, possessed his seal, which I occasionally imprinted on hard objects" (ibid., p. 213).

[5]J. E. Cirlot, *A Dictionary of Symbols,* p. 25.

[6]L. A. Holland, *Janus and the Bridge,* pp. 275-76. Also see O. Schrader, *Sprachvergleichung und Urgeschichte,* II, 297.

[7]Robert Graves, *The Greek Myths,* I: 260.

[8]Cf. "We have already seen a classical example–woman assimilated to the soil and to Mother Earth, the sexual act assimilated to the hierogamy Heaven-Earth and the sowing of the seed. But the number of such homologies established between man and the universe is very large. Some of them seem to force themselves on the mind spontaneously, as, for example, *the homology between the eye and the sun*" (italics mine). Mircea Eliade, *The Sacred and the Profane,* p. 168.

[9]Oskar also comments in no uncertain terms on this animated, conscious quality of all things: "Today I know that everything watches, that nothing goes unseen, and that even wallpaper has a better memory than people do. It isn't God who sees all! A kitchen chair, a coat-hanger, a half-filled ash tray, or the wooden replica of woman named Niobe, can perfectly suffice as unforgetting witnesses to our every act" (p. 223).

[10]A. C. Vaughan, *The House of the Double Axe,* pp. 172-73.

[11]"*Labyrinthos* meant to the Cretan, 'The House of the Double Axe' " (H. E. L. Mellersh, *Minoan Crete,* p. 37).

[12]Frye, *Anatomy of Criticism,* p. 209.

[13]Cf. the German saying: *sie findet keine Petersilie,* "she can't find a man," or even the implications of the children's counting poem:

Petersilie, Suppenkraut
Wächst in unserm Garten.
Unsre Anna ist die Braut,
Soll nicht länger warten.

[14] Frye, *Anatomy of Criticism,* p. 209.

[15] Although these two victims of nemesis are at best mere snapshots of divine heroes, something of the following statement on "hanging men" (perhaps their location of isolation between two worlds) applies to both: "The tragic hero is typically on top of the wheel of fortune, halfway between human society on the ground and the something greater in the sky. Prometheus, Adam, and Christ hang between heaven and earth, between a world of paradisal freedom and a world of bondage" (ibid., p. 207).

[16] The polar nature of these two deaths, based on some conjecture and speaking broadly, carries overtones of the Rasputin-Goethe (Scylla-Carybdis, black-white, chaos-reason, harmony-chaos, etc.) dichotomy that threads its way through the novel. Herbert Truczinski, peaceful though he might be in his mother's apartment, is a powerful, passionate, and battle-scarred warrior who ends his life by flinging himself in uncontrollable desire on the forbidden symbol of destructive sexuality, all in contrast to Greengrocer Greff who quietly tends his cabbages, worries about balance in nature, lives in classic austerity, remote from everyone except his beloved boy scouts. These concerns, by a slight stretch of the imagination, all resemble stereotyped images which one has of Rasputin and of Goethe. Therefore the Rasputin and the Goethe that Oskar read earlier as literature now become, in mutated form, corporealized as Truczinski whose Rasputinesque sexuality and violence is expressed by his scars (which Oskar compares to male organs) and Greengrocer Greff, an austere nature-lover like Goethe himself who was obsessed by a need of balance, a select group of friends, a sense of tradition, and a desire for light. In fact Greff floods the basement with light at the time of his death, recalling the last words of Goethe, which supposedly were "Light! More light!"

*Chapter 5*

[1] Cf. Mircea Eliade, *Sacred and Profane,* pp. 68-72.

[2] W. Gordon Cunliffe, "Aspects of the Absurd in Günter Grass," p. 318.

[3] Eliade, *Sacred and Profane,* p. 95.

[4] Richard Hinton Thomas and Wilfred van der Will, *Der deutsche Roman und die Wohlstandsgesellschaft,* p. 91.

[5] Eliade, *Eternal Return,* p. 29.

[6] Ibid., p. 28.

[7] Frye, *Anatomy of Criticism,* p. 150.

[8] Ibid.

[9] Ibid., p. 217

[10] Eliade, *Sacred and Profane,* p. 53.

[11] Susanne K. Langer, *Philosophy in a New Key,* p. 157.

[12] Paul Radin, *The Trickster,* p. ix.

[13] Joseph Campbell, *The Hero,* p. 98.

[14] H. R. Ellis Davidson, *Gods and Myths of Northern Europe,* pp. 146-47.

[15] Eliade, *Sacred and Profane,* p. 185.

[16] Juan E. Cirlot, *Dictionary of Symbols,* p. 334.

[17] Cf. Martin P. Nilsson, *Geschichte der griechischen Religion,* 1:724.

[18] Erich Neumann, *Great Mother,* p. 149.

[19] Eliade, *Sacred and Profane,* p. 49.

*Chapter 6*

[1] This claim of sacredness can be substantiated for the reader of German who will note that although the promise of a drum is loosely attributed to Oskar's mother Agnes, the statement "Wenn der kleine Oskar drei Jahre alt ist, soll er eine Blechtrommel bekommen," (p. 47) is something of an anomaly. First of all the statement is made in *High German* and *not* in the Danzig German dialect which Agnes consistently speaks. Secondly Oskar is referred to by that "heathen name" (p. 156) which he does not yet possess and which he will receive only after some debate and confusion. Thirdly the speaker of this statement is not precisely identified, although it *is* Agnes who gives him his drum on his third birthday. Finally it is significant that the voice uses the word *soll* (meaning "is to") so that the effect of the statement resembles a biblical commandment in style and echoes a sacred annunciation from some distant providential realm.

[2] Cf. the trapdoor "verlangte ein Opfer und trieb mir schon damals, wie immer, wenn mir ein Opfer abverlangt wird, den Schwei*ß* auf den Kopf" (p. 66).

[3] Reinhold Niebuhr describes this same condition in Christian terminology by saying that "the sin of man consists in the vanity and pride by which he imagines himself, his cultures, his civilizations, to be divine. . . . He overestimates the completeness of his knowledge and even more the self-sufficiency of his existence. . . . One aspect of this human cry is man's refusal to acknowledge the dependent character of his life. . . . The sin of man is that he seeks to make himself God" (*The Nature and Destiny of Man,* 1:137-40).

[4] Williams, *Witchcraft,* p. 86.

[5] C. G. Jung, *Psychologie und Alchemie,* pp. 595-96.

[6] Dorothea Forstner, *Die Welt der Symbole,* pp. 272-74.

[7] "The womb [of the Dark and Terrible Mother] becomes the deadly devouring maw of the underworld, . . . the dark hole of the depths, the devouring womb of the grave and of death, of darkness without light, of nothingness" (Erich Neumann, *The Great Mother,* p. 149).

[8] We have and will continue to refer to Schugger as one of the *manes* or shades, but in view of the fact that all the dead were viewed by the ancients as shades, one should discriminate and identify this bizarre but generally benevolent spirit as a *Lar,* or one of those "good men who, after death, loved to hover about their old homes and to preserve the welfare of their family and possessions." We point out that two machine-gunners cannot kill Schugger as he flees, and, also, if the *Lares* are as offended as Schugger is by Oskar's growth, "they had the power of causing disease, especially neuroses and psychic disorder." (Consider Oskar's ensuing illness.) Walter A. Jayne, *The Healing God of Ancient Civilizations,* p. 460.

[9] Joseph Campbell, *The Masks of God: Occidental Mythology,* p. 505.

[10] An impressive similarity exists between Oskar's supernatural chaotic

merry-go-round and the ritualistic orphic "bronze wheel known by a name that translates as 'a thing for purifying.' . . . The one salvation offered by the creator is that the spirit free itself from the wheel of birth. This is what those who are initiated by Orpheus to Dionysos and Kore pray that they may attain, to 'Cease from the Wheel and breathe again from ill.' The notion of escape whether from the tomb of the body, or from the restless Wheel or from the troubled sea, haunts the Orphic." The punishment, cures, and passage out of the circle and the subsequent transformation for the orphic closely parallel the illness, suffering, madness, transformation, recuperation, and trip west for Oskar. See Jane Ellen Harrison, *Prolegomena to the Study of Greek Religion,* p. 592.

[11] Consider Grass also "In a conversation with Horst Bienek Günter Grass explained that his home city Danzig and suburb Langfuhr were for him the metropolis, the middle point of the world; all other German cities, even Dusseldorf, Hamburg, Cologne and Berlin were only environs of this center around which even today everything revolves that touches him, Günter Grass and his world. In truth the literary works of Günter Grass are unthinkable without Danzig and the delta of the Weichsel river" (Kurt Lothar Tank, *Gunter Grass,* p. 12).

[12] Juan E. Cirlot, *A Dictionary of Symbols,* p. 34.

[13] W. K. C. Guthrie, *The Greeks and their Gods,* p. 43.

[14] Suzanne K. Langer, *Philosophy in a New Key,* p. 155.

[15] Cf. the amazing similarity between the mythic aspects of the night sea journey described by Leo Frobenius, *Das Zeitalter des Sonnengottes,* vol. 1 (Berlin, 1904), and Oskar's experiences on his journey west in *The Tin Drum.* Oskar's journey really begins at his father's grave at the point of departure, implying that the two of them, each in his own way, is about to embark upon an underground journey. The difference is that Oskar "begins to grow: the first symptom being a violent nosebleed" (p. 487) that resembles a "blood-red sunrise connected with the idea that a birth is taking place" (Frobenius, p. 30). The hero is enveloped in darkness (madness or illness) and snatched from the jaws of death by a patronizing spirit (Fajngold) or frees himself by expanding in size to burst the bondage of his enclosure—swelling from "the size of a thumb" to a "gigantic size" (Frobenius, p. 173). Oskar hardly swells to a gigantic size, merely to four feet and one inch; but he does grow, and his back does swell into a hump. The hero's journey also takes place in a container, animal, or fish (Oskar's boxcar). The hero also travels in the company of a woman (Frobenius, p. xxii), just as Oskar travels in the care of Maria and also notices that the Black Cook, Luzie Rennwand is along on the trip. Oskar admits that it was really only another girl with "a nameless triangular fox face" and "slits for eyes." The hero may also lose a knife, or some other weapon or tool (Oskar's drum and voice), but finally the container, monster, or fish lands somewhere on solid firmament and the hero, as well as all of those who were previously devoured, are freed (Frobenius, p. 421). Even a touch of the "fire-lighting" element is present in the person of Kurt, Oskar's claimed and perverse son, who thrives in the West as the purveyor of "firestones"—in opposition to Oskar, whose attention will be

focused on "gravestones." All the elements of a mythic rebirth are present, but at the outset Oskar does not blossom (as Kurt does) in the Land of the West, even though he is discharged on the western shore with a modicum of optimism and "the hope that I might embark on a new and adult life" (p. 516).

*Chapter 7*

[1] J. G. Frazer, *The Golden Bough,* p. 429. Frazer allocates a subchapter of his book to the killing of the corn spirit and the rituals of its demise and burial. He touches on too many similarities with Korneff to be mentioned here, but the following quotations should suffice to establish the fact that Korneff and his furuncles have more than a superficial similarity with primitive vegetation rituals. "The corn-spirit is conceived in human or animal form, and the last standing corn is seen as part of its body—its neck, its head, or its tail" (p. 447). "The corn-spirit is represented by a man, who lies down under the last corn; it is threshed upon his body" (p. 429); and the kernels are literally removed (as in this Oskar-Korneff incident): "In the Tyrol, husks of corn are stuck behind the neck of the man who gives the last stroke of the threshing" (ibid.), the purpose of which is to act out in a homeopathic fashion one aspect of the mysterious death-to-life continuum.

[2] Johnson, "Loss of Innocence," p. 49.

[3] Erich Neumann, "Art and Time," *Art and the Unconscious,* p. 97.

*Chapter 8*

[1] What interests us at this point, the beginning of Oskar's descent, is that he encounters Zeidler, the "beekeeper." Besides recalling that Oskar's grandmother sold honey and that Maria dealt in artificial or "black" honey in the West, the theme anticipates the next stage of Oskar's descent into the Onion Cellar with its *tholos* or subterranean ovenlike shape. Residence in Zeidler's house ultimately leads Oskar, by means of his subsequent association there with Klepp, into the adventure in an Onion Cellar that (as we shall see) resembles the descent to Trophonios in form and content. "To enter the sanctuary of Trophonios was then to visit the infernal regions. It was a 'descent into Hades' as much as the legendary 'descents' of Herakles, Theseus, Orpheus and other bold heroes. It was therefore no wonder that it was a terrifying exploit." In Greek ritual one would enter "the 'ovenlike shape of the sunken entrance to the *adyton* by the supposition that it was the *tholos* or beehive-tomb of an old Boetian king" (W. K. C. Guthrie, *The Greeks and Their Gods,* p. 231).

[2] Campbell, *The Hero with a Thousand Faces,* p. 43.

[3] This quotation is part of the only one in the novel that deals with the *meaning* of the Finnish ship. The ship and eels together here serve to block out the image of the white (or pure) aspect of the nurse. The ship that is viewed as coming into harbor adds to the sexual imagery of the scene, but it also casts a second meaning as a death ship "rusty like the fence of the cemetery" (p.

597). The double significance therefore underscores the contiguity of sexuality and death in Agnes's fateful experience at the Newfahrwasser pier.

[4]Campbell, *The Hero with a Thousand Faces,* pp. 255-68.

[5]The Great Earth Mother, *Ge,* is the earth itself, and subsequent personifications are based on some limited aspect of her nature. For a precise analysis see Wilamonwitz, *Der Glaube der Hellenen,* 1:210-11.

[6]Even at the risk of oversimplifying I would like to point out the following similarities: 1) the Onion Cellar is "a chasm in the earth, not natural, but artificially constructed after the most accurate masonry." 2) The "bread-oven" shape and baker or "feeder" allusions occur in both, as do 3) the precarious descents to the bottom. 4) The barley cakes seem a far cry from an onion, but both are respected in rituals as "Demeter's grain," and while barley cake is provided to sustain life ("feed the serpents"), the onion (in Germany) is regarded as a fruit of fertility. 5) The honey image appears again elsewhere as we recall, with Maria in the West, who dealt in artificial honey on the black market. 6) "The body swiftly drawn in" as a river metaphor implies nothing less than being torn along or being drowned by one's own powerful emotions. It is at this low point of descending that Oskar must take over and draw the people out of their self-made chaos and 1) renew them for the future by integrating them with the past. 2) He teaches them "through hearing," "also some learn by sight," i.e., seeing the Black Cook, and 3) he returns the people to the surface where 4) they are called to the Chair of Memory by policemen who ask who they are and what they have done. Each person is 5) then sent home, entrusted to his relatives who take them 6) "paralyzed with terror and unconscious both of himself and his surroundings." 7) Afterward, we discover, that these travelers to Trophonios (and to Oskar) do in fact recover all their faculties.

[7]Frazer, *The Golden Bough,* p. 320-22.

*Chapter 9*

[1]Langer, *Philosophy in a New Key,* p. 157.

[2]Cunliffe, *Günter Grass,* p. 83.

[3]Jane E. Harrison, *Prolegomena to the Study of Greek Religion,* p. 564.

[4]Walter A. Jayne, *The Healing Gods,* p. 222; cf. Farnell, *The Cults of the Greek States,* pp. ix, 113-16.

[5]Harrison, *Prolegomena,* p. 60.

[6]Michael Grant, *Myths of the Greeks and Romans,* pp. 340-41.

[7]"The possibility must be considered that Poseidon as Zeus was from the very beginning a single god to all Greeks" (M. P. Nilsson, *Geschichte der griechischen Religion,* 1:447).

[8]Langer, *Philosophy in a New Key,* pp. 156-57.

[9]Joseph Campbell, *Hero with a Thousand Faces,* p. 388.

[10]See Harrison, *Prolegomena,* p. 460.

[11]". . . the call rings up the curtain, always, on a mystery of transfiguration–a rite, or moment, or spiritual passage, which, when complete, amounts to a dying and a birth. The familiar life horizon has been outgrown; the old

concepts, ideals, and emotional patterns no longer fit; the time for the passing of a threshold is at hand" (Campbell, *Hero,* p. 51).

[12]Mircea Eliade, *Shamanism,* p. 63.

[13]Pausanias, *Pausanias' Description of Greece*, 8. 34. 3.

[14]This allusion to the picking of cornflowers opens the door to uncertainty, possessing no contextual referents in this novel. The statement appears to contribute little to the total meaning of the present incident; but it does draw attention, apparently by virtue of its incongruence. Oskar evidently envisions Dorothea picking cornflowers before she is murdered, but even that image is couched in an ambiguous syntactical construct. Mythologies and folklore may contribute an illuminating image, as for example in the picking of a forbidden flower or in the breaking of a sacred branch or limb. The best known study of the subject is of course Sir James Frazer's *The Golden Bough,* the title of which is taken from the *Aeneid* (Book 6), where a leaf or bough of mistletoe (a "cornflower" for Oskar) is picked by Aeneas to allow him passage down to the queen of darkness and the realm of death.

> In a dark tree there hides
> A bough, all golden leaf and pliant stem
> Sacred to Proserpine. This all the grove
> Protects, and shadows cover it with darkness.
> Until this bough, this bloom of light, is found,
> No one receives his passport to the darkness,
> Whose queen requires this tribute.

It is Frazer's opinion that Virgil's golden bough is the seat of the deity's life and that, when broken, presages death. Mythogems of this order begin to appear entirely natural for Frazer as he investigates primitive modes of homeopathic thought and discovers that once "a person's life [Dorothea's in this case] is conceived as embodied in a particular object, with the existence of which his own existence is inseparably bound up, and the destruction of which involves his own, the object in question may be regarded and spoken of indifferently as his life or his death" (p. 701).

[15]The nurses, like most of Oskar's deifications, possess a dual aspect, a mixture of the angelic and the satanic visages of the transforming goddesses. Agnes, for example, as a nurse in the photograph album seemed pure and white enough, but she transforms in time into a terrible, devouring mother. The nurses of the East are played off against their black counterparts, the nuns, of the West (N.B. The ambiguity of duality is linguistically developed with "nurse" and "nun," commonly rendered by the same word in German, *Schwester* [sister], and exploited fully by the author). Or elsewhere, the nurse Gertrud, whom Oskar invited out in Düsseldorf, exposes herself as unsophisticated when she dons mufti. And Dorothea also, as we have seen, had her shoddy and earthy aspect, judging by the sloppiness of the room in which she lived and by her sensual performance on the fiber rug with a would-be Satan. Only in her closet where her uniforms were kept was she able to preserve her sacred aura in Oskar's eyes (although even there, to him her black leather belt was transformed into a phallic eel).

[16] Eliade, *Shamanism,* p. 186.

[17] C. D. Jerde, "Corridors of Pathos: Notes on the Fiction of Günter Grass," p. 560.

[18] Robert Maurer, "The End of Innocence: Günter Grass's *The Tin Drum,*" p. 60.

*Chapter 10*

[1] The question of the geographic location of the point of creation, the omphalos, the *axis mundi,* the spiritual center, be it the Kashubian potato fields or the edenic garden of Vittlar's mother, may bother the casual reader more than the mythologists or theologians who seem to agree that "the center of the universe, . . . the Immovable Spot, . . . the omphalos . . . the tree of life, . . . the World Navel, then, is ubiquitous" (Joseph Campbell, *The Hero with a Thousand Faces,* pp. 40-44). Northrop Frye believes that such centers "may be analogous forms of the point of epiphany. . . . [Spenser's] Gardens of Adonis, like Eden in Dante, are a place of seed, into which everything subject of the cyclical order of nature enters at death and proceeds from at birth" (*Anatomy of Criticism,* p. 205). Mircea Eliade briefly discusses this "Symbolism of the Center" in his book *Cosmos and History* (esp. pp. 12-17) and again in detail in *Images and Symbols,* chap. 1, "Symbolism of the Centre," pp. 27-51.

[2] Mircea Eliade, *The Sacred and the Profane,* p. 25. Eliade also explains in *Shamanism* the necessary proximity of this sacred center for the performance of a miracle such as Oskar's: "Only they know how to make an ascent through the 'central opening'; only they transform a cosmo-theological concept into a *concrete mystical experience. . . .* In other words, what for the rest of the community remains a cosmological ideogram, for the shamans (and the heroes, etc.) becomes a mystical itinerary" (p. 265).

[3] Neumann, *The Great Mother,* p. 127.

[4] Campbell, *The Hero with a Thousand Faces,* pp. 196-97.

[5] J. E. Cirlot, *Dictionary of Symbols,* p. 341.

[6] Neumann, *The Great Mother,* pp. 45-46.

[7] Eliade, *The Sacred and the Profane,* pp. 64-65.

[8] Philip Wheelwright, *The Burning Fountain,* p. 27.

[9] Campbell, *The Hero with a Thousand Faces,* p. 216.

[10] Not all character names in *The Tin Drum* are readily comprehensible. Of the youngsters in Oskar's neighborhood who play in the courtyard, for example, Nuchi Eyke and Hänschen Kollin combine bizarre associations lexically and onomatopoeically, but these results remain vague and unconfirmable. However, Harry Schlager (English cognate, "slugger") clearly means "the hitter or beater," while Harry ("Heinrich") means sovereign or ruler (Charlotte Yonge, *History of Christian Names,* p. 41). Axel Mischke mixes two ingredients, urine and pulverized brick, in the repulsive soup which the gang forces on Oskar; and *mischen,* the root of Axel's name, means literally "to mix."

[11] Mary E. Harding, *Journey into Self,* p. 224.

[12] My translation here makes every effort to render the meaning and

images accurately rather than to capture the emotional overtones of the original German rhyme.

[13] Neumann, *The Great Mother,* pp. 149-50. Cf. also "The Pathos in Guenter Grass is played off between gloom–made eternal and inevitable by the changeless cycle of existence–and death, its only release. We can make any choice available pertaining to life and how we will live it, but though we would be gnashers of teeth like Matern in *Hundejahre* or a master of the tin drum like Oskar, our most important task is to learn how to die." (C. D. Jerde, "A Corridor of Pathos," p. 560).

[14] Campbell, *The Hero with a Thousand Faces,* p. 258.

*Chapter 11*

[1] Guthrie, *The Greeks and Their Gods,* p. 219. Subsequent citations from this work appear parenthetically in the text.

[2] Frye, *Anatomy of Criticism,* p. 223.

[3] Ibid., pp. 238-39.

[4] Lewis R. Farnell, *Greek Hero Cults and the Ideas of Immortality,* p. 19. Subsequent citations from this work appear parenthetically in the text.

[5] The question of color symbolism in *The Tin Drum* has numerous implications, a number of which are quite ably examined by A. L. Willson, "The Grotesque Everyman in Günter Grass' *Die Blechtrommel,*" pp. 131-38, and touched on by Wilhelm Emrich, "Oskar Matzerath und die deutsche Politik," pp. 89-93. For the sake of mythological argument I submit that the colors also have a sacred context beginning with the red fires (set by Koljaiczek) at which the Virgin Mary presumably appeared. The fire, therefore, as the red on Oskar's drum, is symbolic of passion, first in patriotism and then in love. Oskar notices that "some of the red on my drum diminished when my mother died," an appropriate comment if we recall that she was also cast in the role of the "Queen of Hearts," a goddess of love. Red as passionate longing is also developed further in the color of the nurse's insignia, the red cross pin. Oskar is pained and pursued by that red cross image in a number of drumming journeys, the most notable of which are the fish sacrifice on the west coast where the setting sun takes on the form of a burning red cross, a reminder of the unattainable love which is the source of Oskar's frustrations, and the "flaming-sword-in-the-sky" concept, a reminder of the destiny which pulls him onwards as a distant force of "the eternally feminine." But his primary colors thus are chthonic black and idealized white, an indication again of the extreme duality that preoccupies him. (For a short examination of opposites in *The Tin Drum,* see John Simon, "The Drummer of Danzig," pp. 451-52, and Alexander Gelley, "Art and Reality in *Die Blechtrommel,*" pp. 124-25.)

[6] A detailed discussion of the form and construction of the shamanic drum can be found in Mircea Eliade, *Shamanism,* pp. 168-80, and also in J. E. Cirlot, *A Dictionary of Symbols,* p. 85.

[7] When Oskar first discovers his power, he breaks the glass on the clock, leaving the mechanism (time) unaffected; and then he also breaks bottles for entertainment with Bebra's Miracle Theater.

[8]Cf. Alexander Gelley's examination of this issue in "Art and Reality in *Die Blechtrommel,*" pp. 121ff. For a supportive but nonmythic list of usages of Oskar's drum, see Heinz Ide, "Dialektisches Denken im Werk von Günter Grass," pp. 608-9.

[9]Eliade, *Shamanism,* pp. 174-75.

[10]Ibid., p. 180.

[11]Ibid., p. 171.

[12]Cf. Guthrie, p. 221; Farnell, pp. 110-206; and esp. Philip Wheelwright, *The Burning Fountain,* pp. 173-80.

[13]Eliade, *Shamanism,* p. 187.

[14]Cf. Gunthrie, p. 223; Farnell, p. 402, and Arthur B. Cook, *Zeus,* 1:1070.

# *Bibliography*

I. *About Grass and his Works**

Ahl, Herbert. "Ohne Scham, ohne Tendenz, ohne Devise." *Literarische Portraits,* pp. 28-35. Munich and Vienna: Langen / Müller, 1962.

Arnold, Heinz Ludwig. "Die unpädigogische Provinz des Günter Grass." *Text und Kritik* 1, No. 1 (1963-64):13-15.

_____. "Grass-Kritiker." *Text und Kritik* 1, no. 1 (1963-64):32-36.

Baumgart, Reinhard. "Kleinbürgertum und Realismus: Überlegungen zu Romanen von Böll, Grass und Johnson." *Neue Rundschau* 75 (1964):650-64.

Bentley, Eric. "Im Bahnhof Friedrichstrasse." *Partisan Review* 33 (Winter 1966):97-109.

Böhm, Anton. "Ärger mit Günter Grass." *Wort und Wahrheit* 16 (1961):407-8.

Bondy, Francois. "Avec Günter Grass." *Preuves,* no. 194 (April 1967):30-34.

_____. "Le 'scandale' Günter Grass." *Preuves,* no. 115 (September 1960):23.

Botsford, Keith. "Günter Grass Is a Different Drummer." *New York Times Magazine Section* (May 8, 1966), p. 28.

Boveri, Margret. "Variationen des Selbstverständlichen." *Merkur* 22 (1968):765-71.

Brinkmann, Hennig. "Der komplexe Satz im deutschen Schrifttum der Gegenwart." In *Sprachkunst als Weltgestaltung: Festschrift für Herbert Seidler,* edited by Adolf Haslinger, pp. 13-26. Salzburg and Munich: Anton Pustet, 1966.

Büscher, Heiko. "Günter Grass." In *Deutsche Literatur seit 1945,* edited by Dietrich Weber, pp. 455-83. Stuttgart: Kröner, 1968.

Cunliffe, William G. "Aspects of the Absurd in Günter Grass." *Wisconsin Studies in Contemporary Literature* 7 (Autumn 1966):311-27.

*For a complete bibliography of Günter Grass see Jean M. Woods, "Günter Grass Biography," *West Coast Review* 5, no. 3, and 6, no. 1. (1917).

Cunliffe, William G. *Günter Grass.* New York: Twayne, 1969.

Durzak, Manfred. *Der deutsche Roman der Gegenwart.* Stuttgart: Kohlhammer, 1971.

Edschmid, K. "Rede auf den Preisträger des Georg-Büchner-Preises Günter Grass." *Jahrbuch der deutschen Akademie für Sprache und Dichtung in Darmstadt* (Berlin: Akademie Verlag 1965-66), pp. 82-91.

Enright, D. J. "Three New Germans." *Conspirators and Poets,* pp. 190-200. London: Chatto and Windus, 1966.

Esslin, Martin. *Four Plays,* Introduction to Günter Grass, pp. vii-xiii. New York: Harcourt, Brace and World, 1967.

_____. *The Theatre of the Absurd,* pp. 195-96. Garden City, N.Y.: Anchor, 1961.

Fehse, Wilhelm. "Günter Grass," *Von Goethe bis Grass,* pp. 227-31. Bielefeld: Gieseking, 1963.

Fischer, Heinz. "Sprachliche Tendenzen bei Heinrich Böll und Günter Grass." *German Quarterly* 40 (1967):372-83.

Forster, Leonard. "Günter Grass." *University of Toronto Quarterly* 38 (1968-69):1-16.

Friedrichsmeyer, Erhard M. "Aspects of Myth, Parody, and Obscenity in Grass' *Die Blechtrommel* and *Katz und Maus." Germanic Review* 40 (1965):240-50.

Gittlemann, Sol. "Guenter Grass: Notes on the Theology of the Absurd." *Crane Review* 8 (Fall 1965):32-35.

Grau, Werner. "Günter Grass." *Der Jungbuchhandel* 15 (1961): 466-67.

Günter Grass Biography. *Current Biography Yearbook,* edited by Charles Moritz, pp. 161-63. New York: H. W. Wilson, 1964.

Hamburger, Michael. "An Embattled Playground: The German Literary Scene." *Encounter* 26 (April 1966):55-64.

Harrington, Michael. "The Politics of Günter Grass." *Atlantic* 223 (April 1969):129-31.

Hatfield, Henry. "The Artist as Satirist." In *The Contemporary Novel in German,* edited by Robert R. Heitner, pp. 117-34. Austin: University of Texas Press, 1967.

Hoffmann, Jens. "Laudatio aus ein Ärgernis: Günter Grass und der Georg-Büchner-Preis." *Christ und Welt* 18 (1965):25.

Höllerer, Walter. "Die Bedeutung des Augenblicks in modernen Romanfang," In *Romanenanfänge: Versuch zu einer Poetik des Romans,* edited by Norbert Miller, pp. 370-77. Berlin: Literarisches Colloquium, 1965.

_____. "Letter from Germany." *Evergreen Review* 4 (November-December 1960):135-38.

Holthusen, Hans Egon. *Avantgardismus und die Zukunft der modernen Kunst,* pp. 51-58. Munich: Piper, 1964.

———. "Günter Grass als politischer Autor," *Pläydoy für Einzelnen,* pp. 48-68. Munich: Piper, 1967. Also in *Monat* 16 (September 1966):66-81.

Honsza, Norbert. "Günter Grass und kein Ende?" *Annali Instituto Universitario Orientale, Napoli, Sezione Germanica* 9 (1966):177-87.

Horst, Karl August. "Günter Grass." In *Handbuch der deutschen Gegenwartsliteratur,* edited by Hermann Kunisch, pp. 216-17. Munich: Nymphenburger, 1965.

———. *Kritischer Führer durch die deutsche Literatur der Gegenwart,* pp. 148-50. Munich: Nymphenburger, 1962.

Hyman, Stanley E. "An Inept Symbolist," *Standards: A Chronicle of Books for Our Time,* pp. 168-72. New York: Horizon, 1966.

Ide, Heinz. "Dialektisches Denken im Werk von Günter Grass." *Studium Generale* 21 (1968):608-22.

Ihlenfeld, Kurt. "Rarität und Realität." *Eckart Jahrbuch* 30 (1961):278-80.

Jerde, C. D. "A Corridor of Pathos: Notes on the Fiction of Guenter Grass." *Minnesota Review* 4 (1964):558-60.

Kasten, Kurt. "Autoren, die im Gespräch sind." *Magnum* (February 1960):51-52.

"Keeping off the Grass." *London Times Literary Supplement* 64 (30 September 1965):859-60.

Kellen, Konrad. "Grass and Johnson in New York." *American German Review* 31 (June-July 1965):35-37.

Klunker, Heinz. "Günter Grass und seine Kritiker." *Europäische Begegnung* 4 (1964):466-69.

Kurz, Paul K. "Von und über Günter Grass: Über neue literarische Erscheinungen." *Stimmen der Zeit* 94 (1969):321-29.

Lennartz, Franz. *Dichter und Schriftsteller unserer Zeit,* pp. 231-33. Stuttgart: Kröner, 1963.

Levitt, Morton Paul. "From a New Point of View: Studies in the Contemporary Novel." Ph.D. dissertation, Pennsylvania State University, 1965.

Loetscher, Hugo. "Günter Grass." *Du* 20 (June 1960):15-20.

Loschütz, Gert, ed. *Von Buch zu Buch: Günter Grass in der Kritik.* Neuwied and Berlin: Luchterhand, 1968.

Mandel, Siegfried. "The German Novel in the Wake of Organized Madness." In *Contemporary European Novelists,* edited by Siegfried Mandel, pp. 109-24. Carbondale: Southern Illinois University Press, 1968.

Mayer-Amery, Christian. "Gruppe 47 at Princeton." *Nation* 202 (16 May 1966):588-90.

Mlechina, T. "Grass's Wrong Turn." *Atlas* 12 (December 1966):48-50.

Moore, Harry T. "Three Group 47 Novelists: Böll, Johnson, Grass," *Twentieth-Century German Literature,* pp. 193-206. New York: Basic Books, 1967.

Morlock, Martin. "Die schmutzigen Finger." *Der Spiegel* 19 (31 March 1965):145.

Nechuschtan, Abner. "Bekenntnis und Kritik: Günter Grass in Israel." *Europäische Begegnung* 7 (1967):269-70.

Neubert, Werner. "Die Groteske in unserer Zeit." *Neue deutsche Literatur* 13 (January 1965):102-16.

"Not des Bürgers." *Der Spiegel* 21 (2 October 1967):186-88.

"Ost Kongress." *Der Spiegel* 15 (7 June 1961):68.

Parry, Idris. "Aspects of Günter Grass's Narrative Technique." *Forum for Modern Language Studies* 3 (April 1967):100-114.

Pongs, Hermann. *Dichtung im gespaltenen Deutschland,* pp. 36-40, 423-26, and 481-82. Stuttgart: Union Verlag, 1966.

Reich-Ranicki, Marcel. "Günter Grass, unser grimmiger Idylliker," *Deutsche Literatur in West und Ost,* pp. 216-30. Munich: Piper, 1963.

Ritter, Jesse Paul, Jr. "Fearful Comedy: The Fiction of Joseph Heller, Günter Grass, and the Social Surrealist Genre." Ph.D. dissertation, University of Arkansas, 1967.

Rühmkorf, Peter. "Erkenne die Marktlage." *Sprache im technischen Zeitalter* 9 (1964):781-84.

Scherman, David E. "Günter Grass: His World of Worms, Eels and a Mad Dwarf." *Life* 58 (4 June 1965):56.

Schröer, Henning. "Theologische Momente moderner deutscher Literatur." *Kerygma and Dogma* 12 (April 1966):83-106.

Schwarz, W. J. *Der Erzaehler Guenter Grass.* Bern and Munich: Francke, 1969.

"Sowas durchmachen." *Der Spiegel* 23 (11 August 1969):86-100.

Stone, Michael. "The Author." *Saturday Review* 48 (29 May 1965):26-27.

Subiotto, Arrigo. "Günter Grass." In *German Men of Letters,* Vol. 4, edited by Brian Keith-Smith, pp. 215-35. London: Wolff, 1966.

Tank, Kurt Lothar. *Günter Grass.* Köpfe des XX. Jahrhunderts, Vol. 38. Berlin: Colloquium, 1965.

_____. *Günter Grass.* Translated by John Conway, with a bibliography by W. V. Blomster, pp. 117-27. New York: Ungar, 1969.

Thomas, Richard Hinton and Wilfried van der Will. "Günter Grass,"

*The German Novel and the Affluent Society*, pp. 68-85. Manchester: Manchester University Press, 1968.

Vormweg, Heinrich. "Keine Antwort für Günter Grass." *Civis* 13, no. 1 (1967):29-30.

Wagenbach, Klaus. "Günter Grass." In *Schriftsteller der Gegenwart*, edited by Klaus Nonnemann, pp. 118-26. Olten und Freiburg im Breisgau: Walter, 1963.

Wallerand, Theodor. "Günter Grass. Ein Danziger Schriftsteller" *Unser Danzig* 14, no. 3 (1962):8.

Wegener, Adolph. "Günter Grass, der realistische Zauberlehrling." In *Helen Adolf Festschrift*, edited by Sheema Z. Buehne, James L. Hodge, and Lucille B. Pinto, pp. 285-98. New York: Ungar, 1968.

Yates, Norris W. *Günter Grass: A Critical Essay*. Grand Rapids, Mich.: Eerdmans, 1967.

Zimmermann, Werner. "Von Ernst Wiechert zu Günter Grass." *Wirkendes Wort* 15 (1965): 316-26.

II. *On* The Tin Drum

Andrews, R. C. "The Tin Drum." *Modern Languages* 45 (1964):28-31.

Ascherson, Neal. "Poison Dwarf." *New Statesman* 64 (28 September 1962):418.

Bance, A. F. "The Enigma of Oskar in Grass' *Blechtrommel*." *Seminar* 3 (Fall 1967):147-56.

Barrett, William. "Reader's Choice." *Atlantic* 211 (May 1963):132, 134.

Baumgart, Reinhard. "Der große Bänkelsang." *Neue deutsche Hefte*, no. 65 (December 1959):861-63.

Blanch, Mable. "Variations on a Picaresque Theme: A Study of Two Twentieth-Century Treatments of Picaresque Form." Ph.D. dissertation, University of Colorado, 1966.

Blöcker, Günter. "Günter Grass: *Die Blechtrommel*," *Kritisches Lesebuch*, pp. 208-15. Hamburg: Leibniz, 1962.

Blomster, Wesley V. "Oskar at the Zappoter Waldoper." *Modern Language Notes* 84 (1969):467-72.

Boa, Elizabeth. "Günter Grass and the German Gremlin." *German Life and Letters*, n.s. 23 (January 1970):144-51.

Bradbury, Malcolm. "Two German Novels." *Punch* 244 (23 January 1963):140.

Calisher, Hortense. "Fiction: Some Forms Offshore." *Nation* 196 (16 March 1963):229-32.

Damian, Hermann Siegfried. "Die Blechtrommel von Günter Grass:

Versuch einer Analyse." Master's thesis, University of Tasmania, 1967.

Davenport, Guy. "Novels with Masks." *National Review* 14 (9 April 1963):287-88.

Delez, Bernard. "Les Lettres Allemandes: Un admirateur de Rabelais." *La Revue Nouvelle* 35 (1962):285-87.

Droste, Dietrich. "Gruppenarbeit als Mittel der Erschließung umfangreicher Romane: Grimmelshausens *Abenteuerlicher Simplicissimus* und Grass' *Die Blechtrommel." Deutschunterricht* 21 (December 1969):101-15.

"Drum of Neutrality." London *Times Literary Supplement* 61 (5 October 1962):776.

Elliott, John R., Jr. "The Cankered Muse of Günter Grass." *Dimension* 1 (1968):516-23.

Emmel, Hildegarde. "Das Selbstgericht," *Das Gericht in der deutschen Literatur des 20. Jahrhunderts,* pp. 82-119. Bern and Munich: Francke, 1963.

Emrich, Wilhelm. "Oskar Matzerath und die deutsche Politik," *Polemik,* pp. 89-93. Frankfurt am Main: Athenäum, 1968.

Enzensberger, Hans Magnus. "Wilhelm Meister auf Blech getrommelt," *Einzelheiten,* pp. 221-33. Frankfurt am Main: Suhrkamp, 1962. Also in *Frankfurter Hefte* 14 (1959):833-36.

Ferguson, Lore Schefter. *"Die Blechtrommel* von Günter Grass: Versuch einer Interpretation." Ph.D. dissertation, Ohio State University, 1967.

Field, G. W. Review of *The Tin Drum. Queen's Quarterly* 70 (1963):461-62.

Gelley, Alexander. "Art and Reality in *Die Blechtrommel." Forum for Modern Language Studies* 3 (April 1967):115-25.

"Grass: Der Trommelbube." *Der Spiegel* 13 (18 November 1959):80-82.

Gregory, Horace. "The Ancient Follies Are Still in the Ascendency." *Commonweal* 78 (26 April 1963):146-48.

Grumbach, Doris. Review of *The Tin Drum. Critic* 21 (June 1963):81.

Grundy, Priscilla. "Well-Made Nightmare." *Christian Century* 80 (20 March 1963):370-71.

Grunfeld, Fred. "Drums along the Vistula." *Christian Century* 80 (20 March 1963):370-71.

"The Guilt of the Lambs." *Time* 81 (4 January 1963):69-71.

Hamm, Peter. "Verrückte Lehr- und Wanderjahre." *Du* 19 (December 1959):132-36.

Hanson, William P. "Oskar, Rasputin and Goethe." *Canadian Modern Language Review* 20 (Fall 1963):29-32.

Hartung, Rudolf. "Schläge auf die Blechtrommel." *Neue deutsche Hefte,* no. 67 (1960):1053-56.

Horst, Karl August. "Günter Grass: Heimsuch." *Merkur* 13 (1959):1191-95.

_____. "Wut ohne Pathos." *Merkur* 17 (1963):1209-14.

Ivey, Frederick M. *The Tin Drum; or Retreat to the Word.* Wichita State University Studies, no. 66. Wichita, Kan.: Wichita State University, 1966.

Johnson, Lucy. "Loss of Innocence." *Progressive* 27 (May 1963):48-50.

Klinge, Reinhold. "Die Blechtrommel im Unterricht." *Deutschunterricht* 18, no. 2 (1966):91-103.

Klöckner, Klaus. "Zuchtvoll entfesselt: Günter Grass. *Die Blechtrommel.*" *Pädagogische Provinz* 19 (1965):537-46.

Lerner, Laurence. "New Novels." *Listener* 68 (4 October 1962):533.

Lewald, H. E. Review of *Die Blechtrommel. Books Abroad* 35 (Autumn 1961):339.

Lodge, David. "Reverberations." *Spectator,* 28 September 1962, p. 446.

Maier, Wolfgang. Review of *Die Blechtrommel. Sprache im technischen Zeitalter* 1 (1961):68-71.

Mander, John. "Variations on a Tin Drum." *Encounter* 19 (November 1962):77-84.

Matsuda, Nobuo. "Die Komik in Günter Grass' Roman *Die Blechtrommel.*" *Doitsu Bungaka* 35 (1965):1-11.

Maurer, Robert. "The End of Innocence: Günter Grass's *The Tin Drum.*" *Bucknell Review* 16 (May 1968):45-65.

Mayer, Hans. "Felix Krull und Oskar Matzerath." *Das Geschehen und das Schwrigen.* Frankfurt am Main: Kohlhammer, 1971.

McGovern, Hugh. Review of *The Tin Drum. America* 108 (9 March 1963):344.

Migner, Karl. "Der getrommelte Protest gegen unsere Welt: Anmerkungen zu Günter Grass' Roman *Die Blechtrommel.*" *Welt und Wort* 15 (1960):205-7.

Morton, Friedrich. "Growing up with Oscar." *New York Times Book Review,* 7 April 1963, p. 5.

Oppen, Beate Ruhm von. "Two German Writers of the Sixties." *Massachusetts Review* 5 (Summer 1964):769-78.

Pisco, Ernest S. "Satire from West Germany." *Christian Science Monitor,* 7 March 1963, p. 10.

Plant, Richard. "Rhythms of Pandemonium." *Saturday Review* 46 (9 March 1963):35-36.

Plard, Henri. "Verteidigung der Blechtrommeln: Über Günter Grass." *Text Und Kritik* 1, no. 1 (1963-64):1-8.

Quinn, John J. Review of *The Tin Drum. Best Seller* 23 (1 April 1963):12-13.

Renek, Morris. "Ballyhoo." *Midstream* 9 (June 1963):109-11.

Review of *The Tin Drum. Virginia Quarterly Review* 39 (Spring 1963):xlix.

Scharfman, William L. "The Organization of Experience in *The Tin Drum.*" *Minnesota Review* 6 (1966):59-65.

Schneider, Marcel. Review of *Le tambour. La Table Ronde,* no. 170 (March 1962): 117-18.

Schumann, Willy. "Wiederkehr der Schelme." *PMLA* 81 (December 1966):467-74.

Simon, John. "The Drummer of Danzig." *Partisan Review* 30 (Fall 1963):446-53.

"The Sound of Madness." *Newsweek* 61 (25 March 1963):111.

Valerius, E. "Giftzwerg Oskar rührt die blasphemische Blechtrommel." *Das neue Journal* 8, no. 5 (1960):33-35.

Van Abbé, Derek. "Metamorphoses of 'Unbewältigte Vergangenheit' in *Die Blechtrommel.*" *German Life and Letters,* n.s. 23, no. 2 (January 1970):152-60.

Van der Will, Wilfried, *Pikaro heute: Metamorphosen des Schelms bei Thomas Mann, Döblin, Brecht, Grass.* Stuttgart: Kohlhammer, 1967.

Vonalt, Larry P. "Barbaric, Mystical, Bored." *Sewanee Review* 71 (Summer 1963):522-24.

West, Anthony. "Ordeal by Fire." *New Yorker* 39 (27 April 1963):169-70.

West, Paul. "Turning New Leaves." *Canadian Forum* 43 (July 1963):85-86.

Widmer, Walter. "Geniale Verrücktheit." *Basler Nachrichten,* 18 December 1959.

"Wie sind Sie auf den Blechtrommeler gekommen?" *Frankfurter Neue Presse,* 14 November 1959, p. 17.

Wieser, Theodor. "Die Blechtrommel: Fabulierer und Moralist." *Merkur* 13 (1959):1188-91.

Willson, A. Leslie. "The Grotesque Everyman in Günter Grass's *Die Blechtrommel.*" *Monatshefte* 58 (Summer 1966):131-38.

Woodtli, Susanna. Review of *Die Blechtrommel. Reformatio* 11 (1962):365-69.

III. *Literary and Mythological References*

Auerbach, Erich. *Mimesis.* New York: Doubleday, 1957.

Aymar, Brandt, ed. *Treasury of Snake Lore.* New York: Greenberg, 1956.

Baynes, H. G. *Mythology of the Soul.* New York: Humanities Press, 1955.

Bowra, C. M. *Landmarks in Greek Literature.* London: Weidenfeld & Nicolson, 1966.

Breugelmans, René. "Alienation, the Destiny of Modern Literature?" *Mosaic* 2, no. 1 (Fall 1968):18-28.

Briffault, Robert. *The Mothers.* New York: Macmillan, 1931.

Brown, Norman O. *Hermes the Thief.* New York: Random House, 1947.

Campbell, Joseph. *The Hero with a Thousand Faces.* New York: Meridian Books, 1956.

_____. *The Masks of God: Occidental Mythology.* New York: Viking, 1964.

_____. *The Masks of God: Creative Mythology.* New York: Viking, 1968.

Cassirer, Ernst. *Philosophie der symbolischen Formen (Das mythische Denken,* II). Berlin: Cassirer, 1925.

_____. *Language and Myth.* New York: Dover, 1946.

Cirlot, J. E. *A Dictionary of Symbols.* New York: Philosophical Library, 1962.

Cook, Arthur B. *Zeus: A Study in Ancient Religion.* 3 vols. Cambridge: University Press. Vol. I, 1914; Vol. II, 1924; and Vol. III, 1940.

Cornford, F. M. *From Religion to Philosophy.* London: Arnold, 1912.

Cox, G. W. *An Introduction to the Science of Comparative Mythology and Folklore.* London: Kegan, 1883.

Curtius, Ernst Robert. *Europäische Literatur und lateinisches Mittelalter.* Bern: Francke, 1958.

Davidson, H. R. Ellis. *Gods and Myths of Northern Europe.* Baltimore: Penguin, 1969.

_____. *Pagan Scandinavia.* New York: Praeger, 1967.

Dölger, Franz J. *Ichthys.* Münster in Westpalia: Aschendorff, 1928.

Eliade, Mircea. *Cosmos and History: The Myth of the Eternal Return.* New York: Harper, 1959.

_____. *Images and Symbols: Studies in Religious Symbolism.* New York: Search, 1969.

Eliade, Mircea. *The Sacred and the Profane.* New York: Harcourt, Brace, 1959.

——. *Shamanism: Archaic Techniques of Ecstasy.* New York: Pantheon, 1964.

Farnell, Lewis Richard. *Greek Hero Cults and Ideas of Immortality.* Oxford: Clarendon, 1921.

Fiske, John. *Myths and Myth-Makers.* Boston: Houghton, Mifflin & Co., 1887.

Forster, H. A. *Die Literatur des klassischen Altertums.* Munich: Goldmann, n.d.

Forstner, Dorothea. *Die Welt der Symbole.* Innsbruck: Tyrolia-Verlag, Tyrolia, 1967.

Frazer, James G. *Adonis, Attis, Osiris.* London: Macmillan, 1906.

——. *The Golden Bough.* New York: Macmillan, 1945.

Frye, Northrop. *Anatomy of Criticism.* New York: Atheneum, 1965.

Grant, Michael. *Myths of the Greeks and Romans.* Cleveland: World, 1962.

Graves, Robert. *The Greek Myths.* 2 vols. 2d ed. Baltimore: Penguin, 1955.

Grimm, Jacob. *Teutonic Mythology.* Translated by J. S. Stallybrass. 4 vols. New York: Dover, 1966.

—— and Grimm, Wilhelm. *Deutsches Wörterbuch,* II. Leipzig, 1893.

Guthrie, W. K. C. *The Greeks and Their Gods.* Boston: Beacon, 1955.

Harding, Mary Ester. *Journey into Self.* New York: McKay, 1963.

Harrison, Jane Ellen. *Prolegomena to the Study of Greek Religion.* Cambridge: University Press, 1903.

Herd, E. W. "Myth Criticism: Limitations and Possibilities." *Mosaic* 2, no. 3 (Spring 1969):69-77.

Holland, Louise A. *Janus and the Bridge.* Rome: American Academy, 1961.

Hubert, Henri and Mauss, Marcel. *Sacrifice: Its Nature and Function.* Translated by W. D. Hall. Chicago: University of Chicago Press, 1964.

Jayne, Walter Addison. *The Healing Gods of Ancient Civilizations.* New Haven: Yale University Press, 1925.

Jung, Carl G. *Psychologie und Alchemie.* Zurich: Rascher, 1954.

——. *Symbols of Transformation.* New York: Pantheon, 1956.

——. and Kerényi, Karl. *Essays on a Science of Mythology.* Translated by R. F. C. Hull. New York: Pantheon, 1949 and Princeton: Princeton University Press, 1969.

Ker, William P. *Epic and Romance.* London: Macmillan & Company, 1897.

Kerényi, Karl. "The Mysteries of the Kabeiroi," *The Mysteries.* Translated by R. Manheim and R. F. C. Hull. In *Papers from the Eranos Yearbook,* 2. New York: Pantheon, 1955.

_____. "The Trickster in Relation to Greek Mythology." In Paul Radin, *The Trickster,* pp. 173-91. New York: Philosophical Library, 1956.

Kluckholn, Clyde. "Recurrent Themes in Myths and Myth-Making." *Daedalus* 88 (Spring 1959):268-79.

Kluge, Friedrich. *Etymologisches Wörterbuch der deutschen Sprache.* Berlin: de Gruyter, 1963.

Kunisch, Hermann. *Kleines Handbuch der deutschen Gegenwartsliteratur.* Munich: Nymphenburger, 1967.

Langer, Susanne K. *Philosophy in a New Key.* 2d ed. New York: Mentor, 1948.

*Larousse Encyclopedia of Mythology.* New York: Prometheus, 1959.

Latte, Kurt. "Römische Religionsgeschichte." In *Handbuch der Altertumswissenschaft.* Vol. 4. Munich: C. H. Beck'sche Verlagsbuchhandlung, 1960.

McGlashan, Alan. "Daily Paper Pantheon." *Lancet* 264, no. 6753, (Jan. 31, 1953):238-39.

Mellersh, Harold Edward Leslie. *Minoan Crete.* London: Evans Bros., 1967.

Murray, George Gilbert. *Five Stages of Greek Religion.* New York: Columbia University Press, 1925.

_____. *The Rise of the Greek Epic.* London: Oxford University Press, 1924.

Mylonas, George E. *Eleusis and the Eleusinian Mysteries.* Princeton: Princeton University Press, 1961.

Neumann, Erich. *The Great Mother.* Translated by Ralph Manheim. New York: Pantheon, 1955.

_____. *The Origins and History of Consciousness.* New York: Pantheon, 1954.

Niebuhr, Reinhold. *The Nature and Destiny of Man.* Vol. 1. New York: Scribner's, 1964.

Nilsson, Martin P. "Geschichte der griechischen Religion." In *Handbuch der Altertumswissenschaft.* Vol. 2, no. 1. Munich: C. H. Beck'sche Verlagsbuchhandlung, 1955.

_____. *Greek Folk Religion.* New York: Harper, 1961.

_____. *Greek Popular Religion.* New York: Columbia University Press, 1940.

Nilsson, Martin P. *A History of Greek Religion.* 2d ed. Oxford: Clarendon Press, 1949.

Nonnenmann, Klaus. *Schriftsteller der Gegenwart.* Olten and Freiburg: Walter, 1963.

Norman, Dorothy. *The Hero: Myth / Image / Symbol.* New York and Cleveland: World, 1969.

Pausanias. *Description of Greece.* Vol. 1. Translated by James G. Frazer. London: Macmillan, 1898.

Pollard, John. *Seer, Shrines and Sirens.* London:Allen and Unwin, 1965.

Radin, Paul. *The Trickster.* New York: Philosophical Library, 1956.

Raglan, Lord. *The Hero: A Study in Tradition, Myth, and Drama.* New York: Vintage, 1956.

Rahv, Philip. *The Myth and the Powerhouse.* New York: Farrar, Straus and Giroux, 1965.

Rank, Otto. *The Myth of the Birth of the Hero.* New York: Knopf, 1964.

Robertson, J. M. *Christianity and Mythology.* London: Watts, 1910.

Rose, Herbert J. *A Handbook of Greek Mythology.* 6th ed. London: Methuen & Co., 1958.

_____. *Religion in Greece and Rome.* New York: Harper & Row, 1959.

Schmidt-Henkel, Gerhard. *Mythos und Dichtung.* Berlin and Zurich: Gehlen, 1967.

Seyffert, Oskar. *A Dictionary of Classical Antiquities.* Edited by H. Nettleship and J. E. Sandys. London: Sonnenschein, 1885.

Slater, Philip E. *The Glory of Hera.* Boston: Beacon Press, 1968.

Smith, Homer W. *Man and His Gods.* New York: Grosset & Dunlap, 1957.

Vaughan, Agnes Carr. *The House of the Double Axe.* New York: Doubleday, 1959.

Vickery, John B., ed. *Myth and Literature.* Lincoln: University of Nebraska Press, 1966.

Wellek, René, and Warren, Austin. *Theory of Literature.* 2d ed. New York: Harcourt, Brace, 1956.

Wheelwright, Philip. *The Burning Fountain.* Bloomington: Indiana University Press, 1968.

White, John J. *Mythology in the Modern Novel.* Princeton: Princeton University Press, 1971.

Williams, Charles. *Witchcraft.* New York: Meridian, 1959.

Wilpert, Gero von. *Sachwörterbuch der Literature.* Stuttgart: A. Kröner, 1961.

Yerkes, Royden Keith. *Sacrifice in Greek and Roman Religions and Early Judaism.* New York: Scribner's, 1952.

Yonge, Charlotte M. *History of Christian Names.* London, 1884.

Ziolkowski, Theodore. *Fictional Transfigurations of Jesus.* Princeton: Princeton University Press, 1972.

# Index

Since this book deals essentially with progressions of change and symbols of transformation, it is often impossible to identify the point where one concept ends and another begins. A character may appear in one guise on one page and in another on the next; a symbol may change in implication from paragraph to paragraph; a hero of one incident may become the sacrificial victim of the next. This index of sources, characters, and concepts therefore is not exhaustive and at times indicates only points of development. No one entry by itself will provide complete coverage of a typical category. There are four basic kinds of entries: 1) authors used as sources; 2) mythological figures used literally or as models for characters in *The Tin Drum,* 3) characters in the novel (see also the separate listing elsewhere), 4) selected topics, images, and motifs that recur in significant patterns.